Artificial Intelligence: An Introduction

Artificial Intelligence: An Introduction

Lambert Jones

WILLFORD **P**RESS

www.willfordpress.com

Published by Willford Press,
118-35 Queens Blvd., Suite 400,
Forest Hills, NY 11375, USA

ISBN: 978-1-64728-019-2

Cataloging-in-Publication Data

Artificial intelligence : an introduction / Lambert Jones.
p. cm.
Includes bibliographical references and index.
ISBN 978-1-64728-019-2
1. Artificial intelligence. 2. Neural computers. 3. Fifth generation computers. I. Jones, Lambert.
Q335 .A78 2022
006.3--dc23

For information on all Willford Press publications
visit our website at www.willfordpress.com

Contents

Preface

The intelligence displayed by machines is known as artificial intelligence. Autonomously operating cars, intelligent routing in content delivery networks, natural-language understanding, etc. are some of the modern machine capabilities which are generally classified as AI. There are three types of artificial intelligence systems- humanized, human-inspired, and analytical artificial intelligence. The long-term goal of artificial intelligence is to develop general intelligence. A few of the other goals are planning, learning, reasoning and perception. Artificial intelligence finds its applications in many fields such as software engineering, operations research and computer science along with healthcare, economics and video games. This book unfolds the innovative aspects of artificial intelligence which will be crucial for the progress of this field in the future. Some of the diverse topics covered in this book address the varied branches that fall under this category. It will serve as a valuable source of reference for graduate and postgraduate students.

To facilitate a deeper understanding of the contents of this book a short introduction of every chapter is written below:

Chapter 1- The intelligence that is exhibited by machines is known as artificial intelligence. It plays a crucial role in software engineering and operations research. This chapter aims to discuss the diverse aspects of artificial intelligence along with its types, pros and cons.

Chapter 2- Knowledge, reasoning and intelligent agents are three primary areas of study within artificial intelligence. This chapter will discuss in detail the varied types of knowledge representation, reasoning and intelligent agents along with their role in artificial intelligence.

Chapter 3- There are many algorithms which are used in artificial intelligence in order to solve complex problems such as search algorithm. An algorithm which helps in solving search problems is referred to as a search algorithm. All the diverse principles of problem solving and search algorithms have been carefully analyzed in this chapter.

Chapter 4- The algorithms and statistical models used by computer systems to perform tasks are studied under machine learning. Computer vision aims to advance the level of understanding of computers through digital images. This chapter discusses in detail the theories and methodologies related to machine learning and computer vision.

Chapter 5- The form of logic in which the truth values vary between the real numbers of 0 and 1 is known as fuzzy logic. It is primarily applied in artificial intelligence. This chapter discusses the use of fuzzy logic in this field.

Chapter 6- Artificial intelligence has applications in diverse sectors such as agriculture, robotics, marketing, video games, etc. All these significant applications of artificial intelligence have been carefully analyzed in this chapter.

I would like to share the credit of this book with my editorial team who worked tirelessly on this book. I owe the completion of this book to the never-ending support of my family, who supported me throughout the project.

Lambert Jones

Introduction to Artificial Intelligence

The intelligence that is exhibited by machines is known as artificial intelligence. It plays a crucial role in software engineering and operations research. This chapter aims to discuss the diverse aspects of artificial intelligence along with its types, pros and cons.

Artificial intelligence (AI) is the ability of a digital computer or computer-controlled robot to perform tasks commonly associated with intelligent beings. The term is frequently applied to the project of developing systems endowed with the intellectual processes characteristic of humans, such as the ability to reason, discover meaning, generalize, or learn from past experience. Since the development of the digital computer in the 1940s, it has been demonstrated that computers can be programmed to carry out very complex tasks—as, for example, discovering proofs for mathematical theorems or playing chess—with great proficiency. Still, despite continuing advances in computer processing speed and memory capacity, there are as yet no programs that can match human flexibility over wider domains or in tasks requiring much everyday knowledge. On the other hand, some programs have attained the performance levels of human experts and professionals in performing certain specific tasks, so that artificial intelligence in this limited sense is found in applications as diverse as medical diagnosis, computer search engines, and voice or handwriting recognition.

What is Intelligence?

All but the simplest human behaviour is ascribed to intelligence, while even the most complicated insect behaviour is never taken as an indication of intelligence. What is the difference? Consider the behaviour of the digger wasp, Sphex ichneumoneus. When the female wasp returns to her burrow with food, she first deposits it on the threshold, checks for intruders inside her burrow, and only then, if the coast is clear, carries her food inside. The real nature of the wasp's instinctual behaviour is revealed if the food is moved a few inches away from the entrance to her burrow while she is inside: on emerging, she will repeat the whole procedure as often as the food is displaced. Intelligence—conspicuously absent in the case of Sphex—must include the ability to adapt to new circumstances.

Psychologists generally do not characterize human intelligence by just one trait but by the combination of many diverse abilities. Research in AI has focused chiefly on the following components of intelligence: learning, reasoning, problem solving, perception, and using language.

Learning

There are a number of different forms of learning as applied to artificial intelligence. The simplest is learning by trial and error. For example, a simple computer program for solving mate-in-one chess problems might try moves at random until mate is found. The program might then store the solution with the position so that the next time the computer encountered the same position it would recall the solution. This simple memorizing of individual items and procedures—known as rote learning—is relatively easy to implement on a computer. More challenging is the problem of implementing what is called generalization. Generalization involves applying past experience to analogous new situations. For example, a program that learns the past tense of regular English verbs by rote will not be able to produce the past tense of a word such as jump unless it previously had been presented with jumped, whereas a program that is able to generalize can learn the "added" rule and so form the past tense of jump based on experience with similar verbs.

Reasoning

To reason is to draw inferences appropriate to the situation. Inferences are classified as either deductive or inductive. An example of the former is, "Fred must be in either the museum or the café. He is not in the café; therefore he is in the museum," and of the latter, "Previous accidents of this sort were caused by instrument failure; therefore this accident was caused by instrument failure." The most significant difference between these forms of reasoning is that in the deductive case the truth of the premises guarantees the truth of the conclusion, whereas in the inductive case the truth of the premise lends support to the conclusion without giving absolute assurance. Inductive reasoning is common in science, where data are collected and tentative models are developed to describe and predict future behaviour—until the appearance of anomalous data forces the model to be revised. Deductive reasoning is common in mathematics and logic, where elaborate structures of irrefutable theorems are built up from a small set of basic axioms and rules.

There has been considerable success in programming computers to draw inferences, especially deductive inferences. However, true reasoning involves more than just drawing inferences; it involves drawing inferences relevant to the solution of the particular task or situation. This is one of the hardest problems confronting AI.

Problem Solving

Problem solving, particularly in artificial intelligence, may be characterized as a systematic search through a range of possible actions in order to reach some predefined goal or solution. Problem-solving methods divide into special purpose and general purpose. A special-purpose method is tailor-made for a particular problem and often exploits very specific features of the situation in which the problem is embedded. In contrast, a general-purpose method is applicable to a wide variety of problems. One general-purpose technique used in AI is means-end analysis—a step-by-step, or incremental, reduction of the difference between the current state and the final goal. The program selects actions from a list of means—in the case of a simple robot this might consist of Pickup, Putdown, Moveforward, Moveback, Moveleft and Moveright—until the goal is reached.

Many diverse problems have been solved by artificial intelligence programs. Some examples are finding the winning move (or sequence of moves) in a board game, devising mathematical proofs, and manipulating "virtual objects" in a computer-generated world.

Perception

In perception the environment is scanned by means of various sensory organs, real or artificial, and the scene is decomposed into separate objects in various spatial relationships. Analysis is complicated by the fact that an object may appear different depending on the angle from which it is viewed, the direction and intensity of illumination in the scene, and how much the object contrasts with the surrounding field.

At present, artificial perception is sufficiently well advanced to enable optical sensors to identify individuals, autonomous vehicles to drive at moderate speeds on the open road, and robots to roam through buildings collecting empty soda cans. One of the earliest systems to integrate perception and action was FREDDY, a stationary robot with a moving television eye and a pincer hand, constructed at the University of Edinburgh, Scotland, under the direction of Donald Michie. FREDDY was able to recognize a variety of objects and could be instructed to assemble simple artifacts, such as a toy car, from a random heap of components.

Language

A language is a system of signs having meaning by convention. In this sense, language need not be confined to the spoken word. Traffic signs, for example, form a minilanguage, it being a matter of convention that ⚠ means "hazard ahead" in some countries. It is distinctive of languages that linguistic units possess meaning by convention, and linguistic meaning is very different from what is called natural meaning, exemplified in statements such as "Those clouds mean rain" and "The fall in pressure means the valve is malfunctioning".

An important characteristic of full-fledged human languages—in contrast to birdcalls and traffic signs—is their productivity. A productive language can formulate an unlimited variety of sentences.

It is relatively easy to write computer programs that seem able, in severely restricted contexts, to respond fluently in a human language to questions and statements. Although none of these programs actually understands language, they may, in principle, reach the point where their command of a language is indistinguishable from that of a normal human. What, then, is involved in genuine understanding, if even a computer that uses language like a native human speaker is not acknowledged to understand? There is no universally agreed upon answer to this difficult question. According to one theory, whether or not one understands depends not only on one's behaviour but also on one's history: in order to be said to understand, one must have learned the language and have been trained to take one's place in the linguistic community by means of interaction with other language users.

Methods and Goals in AI

Symbolic vs. Connectionist Approaches

AI research follows two distinct, and to some extent competing, methods, the symbolic (or "top-down") approach, and the connectionist (or "bottom-up") approach. The top-down approach seeks to replicate intelligence by analyzing cognition independent of the biological structure of the brain, in terms of the processing of symbols—whence the symbolic label. The bottom-up approach, on the other hand, involves creating artificial neural networks in imitation of the brain's structure—whence the connectionist label.

To illustrate the difference between these approaches, consider the task of building a system, equipped with an optical scanner that recognizes the letters of the alphabet. A bottom-up approach typically involves training an artificial neural network by presenting letters to it one by one, gradually improving performance by "tuning" the network. (Tuning adjusts the responsiveness of different neural pathways to different stimuli.) In contrast, a top-down approach typically involves writing a computer program that compares each letter with geometric descriptions. Simply put, neural activities are the basis of the bottom-up approach, while symbolic descriptions are the basis of the top-down approach.

This hypothesis states that processing structures of symbols is sufficient, in principle, to produce artificial intelligence in a digital computer and that, moreover, human intelligence is the result of the same type of symbolic manipulations.

During the 1950s and '60s the top-down and bottom-up approaches were pursued simultaneously, and both achieved noteworthy, if limited, results. During the 1970s, however, bottom-up AI was neglected, and it was not until the 1980s that this approach again became prominent. Nowadays both approaches are followed, and both are acknowledged as facing difficulties. Symbolic techniques work in simplified realms but typically break down when confronted with the real world; meanwhile, bottom-up researchers have been unable to replicate the nervous systems of even the simplest living things. Caenorhabditis elegans, a much-studied worm, has approximately 300 neurons whose pattern of interconnections is perfectly known. Yet connectionist models have failed to mimic even this worm. Evidently, the neurons of connectionist theory are gross oversimplifications of the real thing.

Expert Systems

Expert systems occupy a type of microworld—for example, a model of a ship's hold and its cargo—that is self-contained and relatively uncomplicated. For such AI systems every effort is made to incorporate all the information about some narrow field that an expert (or group of experts) would know, so that a good expert system can often outperform any single human expert. There are many commercial expert systems, including programs for medical diagnosis, chemical analysis, credit authorization, financial management, corporate planning, financial document routing, oil and mineral prospecting, genetic engineering, automobile design and manufacture, camera lens design, computer installation design, airline scheduling, cargo placement, and automatic help services for home computer owners.

Knowledge and Inference

The basic components of an expert system are a knowledge base, or KB, and an inference engine. The information to be stored in the KB is obtained by interviewing people who are expert in the area in question. The interviewer, or knowledge engineer, organizes the information elicited from the experts into a collection of rules, typically of an "if-then" structure. Rules of this type are called production rules. The inference engine enables the expert system to draw deductions from the rules in the KB. For example, if the KB contains the production rules "if x, then y" and "if y, then z," the inference engine is able to deduce "if x, then z." The expert system might then query its user, "Is x true in the situation that we are considering?" If the answer is affirmative, the system will proceed to infer z.

Some expert systems use fuzzy logic. In standard logic there are only two truth values, true and false. This absolute precision makes vague attributes or situations difficult to characterize. (When, precisely, does a thinning head of hair become a bald head?) Often the rules that human experts use contain vague expressions, and so it is useful for an expert system's inference engine to employ fuzzy logic.

Dendral

In 1965 the AI researcher Edward Feigenbaum and the geneticist Joshua Lederberg, both of Stanford University, began work on Heuristic DENDRAL (later shortened to DENDRAL), a chemical-analysis expert system. The substance to be analyzed might, for example, be a complicated compound of carbon, hydrogen, and nitrogen. Starting from spectrographic data obtained from the substance, DENDRAL would hypothesize the substance's molecular structure. DENDRAL's performance rivaled that of chemist's expert at this task, and the program was used in industry and in academia.

Mycin

Work on MYCIN, an expert system for treating blood infections, began at Stanford University in 1972. MYCIN would attempt to diagnose patients based on reported symptoms and medical test results. The program could request further information concerning the patient, as well as suggest additional laboratory tests, to arrive at a probable diagnosis, after which it would recommend a course of treatment. If requested, MYCIN would explain the reasoning that led to its diagnosis and recommendation. Using about 500 production rules, MYCIN operated at roughly the same level of competence as human specialists in blood infections and rather better than general practitioners.

Nevertheless, expert systems have no common sense or understanding of the limits of their expertise. For instance, if MYCIN were told that a patient who had received a gunshot wound was bleeding to death, the program would attempt to diagnose a bacterial cause for the patient's symptoms. Expert systems can also act on absurd clerical errors, such as prescribing an obviously incorrect dosage of a drug for a patient whose weight and age data were accidentally transposed.

The CYC Project

CYC is a large experiment in symbolic AI. The project began in 1984 under the auspices of the Microelectronics and Computer Technology Corporation, a consortium of computer, semiconductor, and electronics manufacturers. In 1995 Douglas Lenat, the CYC project director, spun off the project as Cycorp, Inc., based in Austin, Texas. The most ambitious goal of Cycorp was to build a KB containing a significant percentage of the commonsense knowledge of a human being. Millions of commonsense assertions, or rules, were coded into CYC. The expectation was that this "critical mass" would allow the system itself to extract further rules directly from ordinary prose and eventually serve as the foundation for future generations of expert systems.

With only a fraction of its commonsense KB compiled, CYC could draw inferences that would defeat simpler systems. For example, CYC could infer, "Garcia is wet," from the statement, "Garcia is finishing a marathon run," by employing its rules that running a marathon entails high exertion, that people sweat at high levels of exertion, and that when something sweats it is wet. Among the outstanding remaining problems are issues in searching and problem solving—for example, how to search the KB automatically for information that is relevant to a given problem. AI researchers call the problem of updating, searching, and otherwise manipulating a large structure of symbols in realistic amounts of time the frame problem. Some critics of symbolic AI believe that the frame problem is largely unsolvable and so maintain that the symbolic approach will never yield genuinely intelligent systems. It is possible that CYC, for example, will succumb to the frame problem long before the system achieves human levels of knowledge.

Connectionism

Connectionism, or neuronlike computing, developed out of attempts to understand how the human brain works at the neural level and, in particular, how people learn and remember. In 1943 the neurophysiologist Warren McCulloch of the University of Illinois and the mathematician Walter Pitts of the University of Chicago published an influential treatise on neural nets and automatons, according to which each neuron in the brain is a simple digital processor and the brain as a whole is a form of computing machine. As McCulloch put it subsequently, "What we thought we were doing was treating the brain as a Turing machine."

Creating an Artificial Neural Network

It was not until 1954, however, that Belmont Farley and Wesley Clark of MIT succeeded in running the first artificial neural network—albeit limited by computer memory to no more than 128 neurons. They were able to train their networks to recognize simple patterns. In addition, they discovered that the random destruction of up to 10 percent of the neurons in a trained network did not affect the network's performance—a feature that is reminiscent of the brain's ability to tolerate limited damage inflicted by surgery, accident, or disease.

The simple neural network depicted in the figure illustrates the central ideas of connectionism. Four of the network's five neurons are for input and the fifth—to which each of the others is connected—is for output. Each of the neurons is either firing (1) or not firing (0). Each connection leading to N, the output neuron has a "weight." What is called the total weighted input into N is calculated by adding up the weights of all the connections leading to N from neurons that are firing. For example, suppose that only two of the input neurons, X and Y, are firing. Since the weight of the connection from X to N is 1.5 and the weight of the connection from Y to N is 2, it follows that the total weighted input to N is 3.5. As shown in the figure, N has a firing threshold of 4. That is to say, if N's total weighted input equals or exceeds 4, then N fires; otherwise, N does not fire. So, for example, N does not fire if the only input neurons to fire are X and Y, but N does fire if X, Y, and Z all fire.

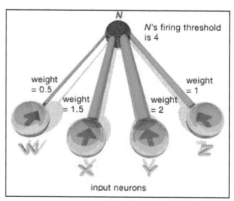

A section of an artificial neural network.

In the figure the weight, or strength, of each input is indicated by the relative size of its connection. The firing threshold for the output neuron, N, is 4 in this example. Hence, N is quiescent unless a combination of input signals is received from W, X, Y, and Z that exceeds a weight of 4.

Training the network involves two steps. First, the external agent inputs a pattern and observes the behaviour of *N*. Second, the agent adjusts the connection weights in accordance with the rules:

- If the actual output is 0 and the desired output is 1, increase by a small fixed amount the weight of each connection leading to *N* from neurons that are firing (thus making it more likely that *N* will fire the next time the network is given the same pattern);

- If the actual output is 1 and the desired output is 0, decrease by that same small amount the weight of each connection leading to the output neuron from neurons that are firing (thus making it less likely that the output neuron will fire the next time the network is given that pattern as input).

The external agent—actually a computer program—goes through this two-step procedure with each pattern in a training sample, which is then repeated a number of times. During these many repetitions, a pattern of connection weights is forged that enables the network to respond correctly to each pattern. The striking thing is that the learning process is entirely mechanical and requires no human intervention or adjustment. The connection weights are increased or decreased automatically by a constant amount, and exactly the same learning procedure applies to different tasks.

Perceptrons

In 1957 Frank Rosenblatt of the Cornell Aeronautical Laboratory at Cornell University in Ithaca, New York, began investigating artificial neural networks that he called perceptrons. He made major contributions to the field of AI, both through experimental investigations of the properties of neural networks (using computer simulations) and through detailed mathematical analysis. Rosenblatt was a charismatic communicator, and there were soon many research groups in the United States studying perceptrons. Rosenblatt and his followers called their approach connectionist to emphasize the importance in learning of the creation and modification of connections between neurons. Modern researchers have adopted this term.

One of Rosenblatt's contributions was to generalize the training procedure that Farley and Clark had applied to only two-layer networks so that the procedure could be applied to multilayer networks. Rosenblatt used the phrase "back-propagating error correction" to describe his method. The method, with substantial improvements and extensions by numerous scientists, and the term back-propagation are now in everyday use in connectionism.

Conjugating Verbs

In one famous connectionist experiment conducted at the University of California at San Diego, David Rumelhart and James McClelland trained a network of 920 artificial neurons, arranged in two layers of 460 neurons, to form the past tenses of English verbs. Root forms of verbs—such as come, look, and sleep—were presented to one layer of neurons, the input layer. A supervisory computer program observed the difference between the actual response at the layer of output neurons and the desired response—came, say—and then mechanically adjusted the connections throughout the network in accordance with the procedure described above to give the network a slight push in the direction of the correct response. About 400 different verbs were presented one by one to the network, and the connections were adjusted after each presentation. This whole procedure was repeated about 200 times using the same verbs, after which the network could correctly form the past tense of many unfamiliar verbs as well as of the original verbs. For example, when presented for the first time with guard, the network responded guarded; with weep, wept; with cling, clung; and with drip, dripped (complete with double p). This is a striking example of learning involving generalization. (Sometimes, though, the peculiarities of English were too much for the network, and it formed squawked from squat, shipped from shape, and membled from mail).

Another name for connectionism is parallel distributed processing, which emphasizes two important features. First, a large number of relatively simple processors—the neurons—operate in parallel. Second, neural networks store information in a distributed fashion, with each individual connection participating in the storage of many different items of information. The know-how that enabled the past-tense network to form wept from weep, for example, was not stored in one specific location in the network but was spread throughout the entire pattern of connection weights that was forged during training. The human brain also appears to store information in a distributed fashion, and connectionist research is contributing to attempts to understand how it does so.

Other Neural Networks

Other work on neuronlike computing includes the following:

- Visual perception: Networks can recognize faces and other objects from visual data. A neural network designed by John Hummel and Irving Biederman at the University of Minnesota can identify about 10 objects from simple line drawings. The network is able to recognize the objects—which include a mug and a frying pan—even when they are drawn from different angles. Networks investigated by Tomaso Poggio of MIT are able to recognize bent-wire shapes drawn from different angles, faces photographed from different angles and showing different expressions, and objects from cartoon drawings with gray-scale shading indicating depth and orientation.

- Language processing: Neural networks are able to convert handwritten and typewritten material to electronic text. The U.S. Internal Revenue Service has commissioned a neuronlike system that will automatically read tax returns and correspondence. Neural networks also convert speech to printed text and printed text to speech.

- Financial analysis: Neural networks are being used increasingly for loan risk assessment, real estate valuation, bankruptcy prediction, share price prediction, and other business applications.

- Medicine: Medical applications include detecting lung nodules and heart arrhythmias and predicting adverse drug reactions.

- Telecommunications: Telecommunications applications of neural networks include control of telephone switching networks and echo cancellation in modems and on satellite links.

Artificial Intelligence Pros and Cons

Advantages of Artificial Intelligence

- To 'err' is human, so why not use AI? - Machine take decision based on previous data records. With algorithms, the chances of errors are reduced. This is an achievement, as solving complex problems require difficult calculation that can be done without any error. Business organizations use digital assistants to interact with their users, this helps them to save an ample amount of time. The demand for user's businesses is fulfilled and thus they don't have to wait. They are programmed to give the best possible assistance to a user.

- For example: Heard of Mars Orbiter Mission, or the movie Mission Mangal, which is based on it? How are they reaching to such great heights? The first reason is the human brain and the second being artificial intelligence. There is no room for error with artificial intelligence. The robots are fed with information that is sent to explore space. Metal bodies have more resistant and a great ability to endure the space and hostile atmosphere. They are created and used in such a way that they cannot be modified or get disfigured or breakdown in a hostile environment.

- AI doesn't get tired and wear out easily: Artificial Intelligence and the science of robotics is used in mining and other fuel exploration processes. These complex machines help to explore the ocean floor and overcome human limitations. Due to the programming of the robots, they can perform a more laborious task with extra hard work and with greater responsibility. Moreover, they do not wear out easily.

- Digital assistance helps in day to day chores: Siri listens to us and performs the task in one tap. GPS helps you to travel the world. How can I forget the basic necessity? Food, clothing, shelter and smartphone. They are the ones that predict what we are going to type, in short, they know us better than anyone. The best is the autocorrect feature, it understands what you are trying to say and present you the sentence in the best way possible. Have you observed that while you post a picture on social media, you tag people, but the machine automatically detects the person's face and tags that individuals? Same is when you work on Google Photos. Automatically, a folder is created of the people with the help of their faces. Artificial Intelligence is widely employed by financial institutions and banking institutions because it helps to organize and manage data. Also, detection of fraud uses artificial intelligence in a smart card-based system.

- Rational decision maker: Highly advanced organizations have digital assistants which help them to interact with the users and save the need for human resources.

- Right program decisions can be taken if they are worked upon rationally. But, with humans, emotions come along. When artificial thinkers, there is no distraction at all. They don't have an emotional side, and that makes robots think logically. Emotions are not associated with them and therefore the mood doesn't hamper the efficiency. Thus they are always productive.

- Repetitive jobs: The same old task, a task that doesn't add value is of no use. Also, repetitive jobs are monotonous in nature and can be carried out with the help of machine intelligence. Machines think faster than humans and can perform various functions at the same time. It can be employed to carry out dangerous tasks and its parameters are adjusted. This is not possible with humans as their speed and time can't be calculated on the basis of parameters.

- Medical applications: This is the best thing that artificial intelligence has done to humans. It's said that time and tide waits for none but, with medical applications of artificial intelligence, a wide scope application is present. Doctors assess patients and their health risks with the help of artificial machine intelligence. The applications help to educate the machine about the side effects of various medicines. Nowadays, medical professionals are trained with artificial surgery simulators. It uses application which helps in detecting and monitoring neurological disorders and stimulate the brain functions. This also helps in the radiosurgery. Radiosurgery is used in operating tumors and help in the operation without damaging the surrounding tissues.

- Tireless, selfless and with no breaks: A machine doesn't require breaks like the way humans do. They are programmed for long hours and can continuously perform without getting bored or distracted. The machine does not get tired, even if it has to work for consecutive hours. This is a major benefit over humans, who need a rest from time to time to be efficient. However, in the case of machines, their efficiency is not affected by any external factor and it does not get in the way of continuous work.

- Right decision making: The complete absence of emotions from a machine makes it more efficient as they are able to make the right decisions in a short span of time. The best example of this is its usage in healthcare. The integration of AI tools in the healthcare sector has improved the efficiency of treatments by minimizing the risk of false diagnosis.

- Implementing AI in risky situations: Human safety is taken care of by machines. Safety is vulnerable and with machines that are fitted with predefined algorithms, this can be used. Scientists use complex machines to study the ocean floor where human survival becomes difficult. This is the level of AI. It reaches the place where humans can't reach. Thus, helps to solve issues in a jiffy.

Disadvantages of Artificial Intelligence

As it is always said, every coin has two sides and so does AI.

- High cost: It's true that AI comes with a high cost, but there is no such thing as a free lunch too. It requires huge costs as it is a complex machine. Apart from the installation cost, its repair and maintenance also require huge costs. The software programs need frequent upgradation and cater to the needs of the changing environment.

- Also, if there is a breakdown, the cost of procurement is very high. With that, recovery requires huge time too.

- No human replication: No matter how smart a machine becomes, it can never replicate a human. Machines are rational but, very inhuman as they don't possess emotions and moral values. They don't know what is ethical and what's legal and because of this, don't have their own judgment making skills. They do what they are told to do and therefore the judgment of right or wrong is nil for them. If they encounter a situation that is unfamiliar to them then they perform incorrectly or else break down in such situations.

- No improvement with Experience: Artificial intelligence cannot be improved with experience; they can perform the same function again if no different command is given to them.

With time, it can lead to wear and tear. It stores a lot of data but the way it can be accessed and used is very different from human intelligence.

- Also, they can't cope up with the dynamic environment and so they are unable to alter their responses to changing environments. We are constantly bombarded by the question of whether it is really exciting to replace humans with machines.

- Artificial intelligence doesn't have feelings and because of which there is nothing like working with a whole heart or with full passion for them. There is no sense of belonging or togetherness or a human touch. They fail to distinguish between a hardworking individual and an inefficient individual.

- Creativity is not the key for AI: Machines can't be creative. They can only do what they are being taught or commanded. Though they help in designing and creating, they can't match the power of a human brain.

- Humans are sensitive and intellectuals and they are very creative too. They can generate ideas; can think out of the box. They see, hear, think and feel which machine can't. Their thoughts are guided by the feelings which completely lacks in machines. No matter how much a machine outgrows, it can't inherent intuitive abilities of the human brain and can't replicate it.

- Unemployment: This one is the riskiest and can have severe effects. With capital intensive technologies, human-intensive requirements have decreased in some industries. If in the future, human beings don't add to their skills, then in no time, we can see that they will be replaced with machines. The major issue of the GDP being stagnant or not growing at the expected rate is unemployment. People don't possess the required skills that are in demand. There is a huge demand and supply gap because of this.

Types of AI

Artificial Intelligence can be divided in various types, there are mainly two types of main categorization which are based on capabilities and based on functionally of AI. Following is flow diagram which explain the types of AI.

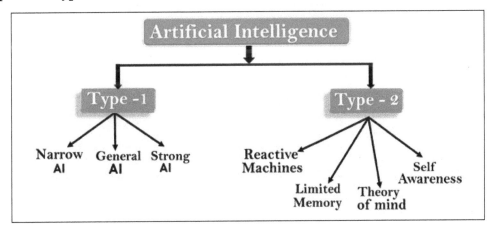

Artificial Intelligence type-1: Based on Capabilities

Weak AI or Narrow AI

- Narrow AI is a type of AI which is able to perform a dedicated task with intelligence. The most common and currently available AI is Narrow AI in the world of Artificial Intelligence.

- Narrow AI cannot perform beyond its field or limitations, as it is only trained for one specific task. Hence it is also termed as weak AI. Narrow AI can fail in unpredictable ways if it goes beyond its limits.

- Apple Siri is a good example of Narrow AI, but it operates with a limited pre-defined range of functions.

- IBM's Watson supercomputer also comes under Narrow AI, as it uses an Expert system approach combined with Machine learning and natural language processing.

- Some Examples of Narrow AI are playing chess, purchasing suggestions on e-commerce site, self-driving cars, speech recognition, and image recognition.

General AI

- General AI is a type of intelligence which could perform any intellectual task with efficiency like a human.

- The idea behind the general AI to make such a system which could be smarter and think like a human by its own.

- Currently, there is no such system exist which could come under general AI and can perform any task as perfect as a human.

- The worldwide researchers are now focused on developing machines with General AI.

- As systems with general AI are still under research, and it will take lots of efforts and time to develop such systems.

Super AI

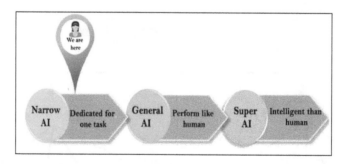

- Super AI is a level of Intelligence of Systems at which machines could surpass human intelligence, and can perform any task better than human with cognitive properties. It is an outcome of general AI.

- Some key characteristics of strong AI include capability include the ability to think, to reason, solve the puzzle, make judgments, plan, learn, and communicate by its own.

- Super AI is still a hypothetical concept of Artificial Intelligence. Development of such systems in real is still world changing task.

Artificial Intelligence type-2: Based on functionality

Reactive Machines

- Purely reactive machines are the most basic types of Artificial Intelligence.

- Such AI systems do not store memories or past experiences for future actions.

- These machines only focus on current scenarios and react on it as per possible best action.

- IBM's Deep Blue system is an example of reactive machines.

- Google's AlphaGo is also an example of reactive machines.

Limited Memory

- Limited memory machines can store past experiences or some data for a short period of time.

- These machines can use stored data for a limited time period only.

- Self-driving cars are one of the best examples of Limited Memory systems. These cars can store recent speed of nearby cars, the distance of other cars, speed limit, and other information to navigate the road.

Theory of Mind

- Theory of Mind AI should understand the human emotions, people, beliefs, and be able to interact socially like humans.

- This type of AI machines are still not developed, but researchers are making lots of efforts and improvement for developing such AI machines.

Self-awareness

- Self-awareness AI is the future of Artificial Intelligence. These machines will be super intelligent, and will have their own consciousness, sentiments, and self-awareness.

- These machines will be smarter than human mind.

- Self-Awareness AI does not exist in reality still and it is a hypothetical concept.

Artificial General Intelligence

Artificial general intelligence (AGI) is the representation of generalized human cognitive abilities in software so that, faced with an unfamiliar task, the AI system could find a solution. An AGI system could perform any task that a human is capable of.

AGI, sometimes referred to as strong AI, involves a system with comprehensive knowledge and cognitive computing capabilities such that its performance is indistinguishable from that of a human, at least in those terms. However, the broad intellectual capacities of AGI would be boosted far beyond human capacities by its ability to access and process huge amounts of data at incredible speeds.

AGI doesn't exist, but has featured in science-fiction stories for more than a century, and been popularized in modern times by films such as 2001: A Space Odyssey.

Fictional depictions of AGI vary widely, although tend more towards the dystopian vision of intelligent machines eradicating or enslaving humanity, as seen in films like The Matrix or The Terminator. In such stories, AGI is often cast as either indifferent to human suffering or even bent on mankind's destruction.

In contrast, utopian imaginings, such as Iain M Banks' Culture civilization novels, cast AGI as benevolent custodians, running egalitarian societies free of suffering, where inhabitants can pursue their passions and technology advances at a breathless pace.

Whether these ideas would bear any resemblance to real-world AGI is unknowable since nothing of the sort has been created, or, according to many working in the field of AI, is even close to being created.

Work of Artificial General Intelligence

In theory, an artificial general intelligence could carry out any task a human could, and likely many that a human couldn't. At the very least, an AGI would be able to combine human-like, flexible thinking and reasoning with computational advantages, such as near-instant recall and split-second number crunching.

Using this intelligence to control robots at least as dextrous and mobile as a person would result in a new breed of machines that could perform any human task. Over time these intelligences would be able to take over every role performed by humans. Initially, humans might be cheaper than machines, or humans working alongside AI might be more effective than AI on their own. But the advent of AGI would likely render human labor obsolete.

Effectively ending the need for human labor would have huge social ramifications, impacting both the population's ability to feed themselves and the sense of purpose and self-worth employment can bring.

Even today, the debate over the eventual impact on jobs of the very different, narrow AI that currently exist has led some to call for the introduction of Universal Basic Income (UBI).

Under UBI everyone in society would receive a regular payment from the government with no strings attached. The approach is divisive, with some advocates arguing it would provide a universal safety net and reduce bureaucratic costs. However, some anti-poverty campaigners have produced economic models showing such a scheme could worsen deprivation among vulnerable groups if it replaced existing social security systems in Europe.

Beyond the impact on social cohesion, the advent of artificial general intelligence could be profound. The ability to employ an army of intelligences equal to the best and brightest humans could help develop new technologies and approaches for mitigating intractable problems such as climate change. On a more mundane level, such systems could perform everyday tasks, from surgery and medical diagnosis to driving cars, at a consistently higher level than humans -- which in aggregate could be a huge positive in terms of time, money and lives saved.

The downside is that this combined intelligence could also have a profoundly negative effect: empowering surveillance and control of populations, entrenching power in the hands of a small group of organizations, underpinning fearsome weapons, and removing the need for governments to look after the obsolete populace.

Yes, not only would such an intelligence have the same general capabilities as a human being, it would be augmented by the advantages that computers have over humans today -- the perfect recall, and the ability to perform calculations near instantaneously.

Invention of Artificial General Intelligence

Part of the reason it's so hard to pin down is the lack of a clear path to AGI. Today machine-learning systems underpin online services, allowing computers to recognize language, understand speech, spot faces, and describe photos and videos. These recent breakthroughs, and high-profile successes such as AlphaGo's domination of the notoriously complex game of Go, can give the impression society is on the fast track to developing AGI. Yet the systems in use today are generally rather one-note, excelling at a single task after extensive training, but useless for anything else. Their nature is very different to that of a general intelligence that can perform any task asked of it, and as such these narrow AIs aren't necessarily stepping stones to developing an AGI.

The limited abilities of today's narrow AI was highlighted in a recent report, co-authored by Yoav Shoham of Stanford Artificial Intelligence Laboratory.

"While machines may exhibit stellar performance on a certain task, performance may degrade dramatically if the task is modified even slightly," it states.

"For example, a human who can read Chinese characters would likely understand Chinese speech, know something about Chinese culture and even make good recommendations at Chinese restaurants. In contrast, very different AI systems would be needed for each of these tasks".

Michael Woolridge, head of the computer science department at the University of Oxford, picked up on this point in the report, stressing "neither I nor anyone else would know how to measure progress" towards AGI.

Despite this uncertainty, there are some highly vocal advocates of near-future AGI. Perhaps the most famous is Ray Kurzweil, Google's director of engineering, who predicts an AGI capable of passing the Turing Test will exist by 2029 and that by the 2040s affordable computers will perform the same number of calculations per second as the combined brains of the entire human race.

Kurzweil's supporters point to his successful track record in forecasting technological advancement, with Kurzweil estimating that by the end of 2009 just under 80% of the predictions he made in the 1990s had come true.

Kurzweil's confidence in the rate of progress stems from what he calls the law of accelerating returns. In 2001 he said the exponential nature of technological change, where each advance accelerates the rate of future breakthroughs, means the human race will experience the equivalent of 20,000 years of technological progress in the 21st century. These rapid changes in areas such as computer processing power and brain-mapping technologies are what underpins Kurzweil's confidence in the near-future development of the hardware and software needed to support an AGI.

Requirements

Various criteria for intelligence have been proposed (most famously the Turing test) but to date, there is no definition that satisfies everyone. However, there *is* wide agreement among artificial intelligence researchers that intelligence is required to do the following:

- Reason, use strategy, solve puzzles, and make judgments under uncertainty;

- Represent knowledge, including commonsense knowledge;

- Plan;

- Learn;

- Communicate in natural language;

- And integrate all these skills towards common goals.

Other important capabilities include the ability to sense (e.g. see) and the ability to act (e.g. move and manipulate objects) in the world where intelligent behaviour is to be observed. This would include an ability to detect and respond to hazard. Many interdisciplinary approaches to intelligence (e.g. cognitive science, computational intelligence and decision making) tend to emphasise the need to consider additional traits such as imagination (taken as the ability to form mental images and concepts that were not programmed in) and autonomy. Computer based systems that exhibit many of these capabilities do exist (e.g. see computational creativity, automated reasoning, decision support system, robot, evolutionary computation, intelligent agent), but not yet at human levels.

Tests for Confirming Human-level AGI

The Turing Test (Turing): A machine and a human both converse sight unseen with a second human, who must evaluate which of the two is the machine, which passes the test if it can fool the evaluator a significant fraction of the time. Note: Turing does not prescribe what should qualify as intelligence, only that knowing that it is a machine should disqualify it.

- The Coffee Test (*Wozniak*): A machine is required to enter an average American home and figure out how to make coffee: find the coffee machine, find the coffee, add water, find a mug, and brew the coffee by pushing the proper buttons.

- The Robot College Student Test (*Goertzel*): A machine enrolls in a university, taking and passing the same classes that humans would, and obtaining a degree.

- The Employment Test (*Nilsson*): A machine works an economically important job, performing at least as well as humans in the same job.

- The flat pack furniture test (*Tony Severyns*): A machine is required to unpack and assemble an item of flat-packed furniture. It has to read the instructions and assemble the item as described, correctly installing all fixtures.

- The Mirror Test (*Tanvir Zawad*): A machine should distinguish a real object and its reflected image from a mirror.

IQ-tests AGI

Chinese researchers Feng Liu, Yong Shi and Ying Liu conducted intelligence tests in the summer of 2017 with publicly available and freely accessible weak AI such as Google AI or Apple's Siri and others. At the maximum, these AI reached a value of about 47, which corresponds approximately to a six-year-old child in first grade. An adult comes to about 100 on average. In 2014, similar tests were carried out in which the AI reached a maximum value of 27.

Problems Requiring AGI to Solve

The most difficult problems for computers are informally known as "AI-complete" or "AI-hard", implying that solving them is equivalent to the general aptitude of human intelligence, or strong AI, beyond the capabilities of a purpose-specific algorithm.

AI-complete problems are hypothesised to include general computer vision, natural language understanding, and dealing with unexpected circumstances while solving any real world problem.

AI-complete problems cannot be solved with current computer technology alone, and also require human computation. This property could be useful, for example, to test for the presence of humans, as CAPTCHAs aim to do; and for computer security to repel brute-force attacks.

AGI Research

Classical AI

Modern AI research began in the mid-1950s. The first generation of AI researchers was convinced that artificial general intelligence was possible and that it would exist in just a few decades. As AI pioneer Herbert A. Simon wrote: "machines will be capable, within twenty years, of doing any work a man can do." Their predictions were the inspiration for Stanley Kubrick and Arthur C. Clarke's character HAL 9000, who embodied what AI researchers believed they could create by the year 2001. AI pioneer Marvin Minsky was a consultant on the project of making HAL 9000 as realistic as possible according to the consensus predictions of the time; Crevier quotes him as having said on the subject, "Within a generation ... the problem of creating 'artificial intelligence' will substantially be solved," although Minsky states that he was misquoted.

However, in the early 1970s, it became obvious that researchers had grossly underestimated the difficulty of the project. Funding agencies became skeptical of AGI and put researchers under increasing pressure to produce useful "applied AI". As the 1980s began, Japan's Fifth

Generation Computer Project revived interest in AGI, setting out a ten-year timeline that included AGI goals like "carry on a casual conversation". In response to this and the success of expert systems, both industry and government pumped money back into the field. However, confidence in AI spectacularly collapsed in the late 1980s, and the goals of the Fifth Generation Computer Project were never fulfilled. For the second time in 20 years, AI researchers who had predicted the imminent achievement of AGI had been shown to be fundamentally mistaken. By the 1990s, AI researchers had gained a reputation for making vain promises. They became reluctant to make predictions at all and to avoid any mention of "human level" artificial intelligence for fear of being labeled "wild-eyed dreamers."

Narrow AI Research

In the 1990s and early 21st century, mainstream AI has achieved far greater commercial success and academic respectability by focusing on specific sub-problems where they can produce verifiable results and commercial applications, such as artificial neural networks, computer vision or data mining. These "applied AI" systems are now used extensively throughout the technology industry, and research in this vein is very heavily funded in both academia and industry. Currently, the development on this field is considered an emerging trend, and a mature stage is expected to happen in more than 10 years.

Most mainstream AI researchers hope that strong AI can be developed by combining the programs that solve various sub-problems using an integrated agent architecture, cognitive architecture or subsumption architecture. Hans Moravec wrote in 1988:

> "I am confident that this bottom-up route to artificial intelligence will one day meet the traditional top-down route more than half way, ready to provide the real world competence and the commonsense knowledge that has been so frustratingly elusive in reasoning programs. Fully intelligent machines will result when the metaphorical golden spike is driven uniting the two efforts."

However, even this fundamental philosophy has been disputed; for example, Stevan Harnad of Princeton concluded his 1990 paper on the Symbol Grounding Hypothesis by stating:

> "The expectation has often been voiced that "top-down" (symbolic) approaches to modeling cognition will somehow meet "bottom-up" (sensory) approaches somewhere in between. If the grounding considerations in this paper are valid, then this expectation is hopelessly modular and there is really only one viable route from sense to symbols: from the ground up. A free-floating symbolic level like the software level of a computer will never be reached by this route (or vice versa) – nor is it clear why we should even try to reach such a level, since it looks as if getting there would just amount to uprooting our symbols from their intrinsic meanings (thereby merely reducing ourselves to the functional equivalent of a programmable computer)."

Modern Artificial General Intelligence Research

Artificial general intelligence (AGI) describes research that aims to create machines capable of general intelligent action. The term was used as early as 1997, by Mark Gubrud in a discussion of the implications of fully automated military production and operations. The term was re-introduced and popularized by Shane Legg and Ben Goertzel. The research objective is much older, for example Doug Lenat's Cyc project, and Allen Newell's Soar project are regarded as within the scope of AGI. AGI research activity in 2006 was described by Pei Wang and Ben Goertzel as "producing publications and preliminary results". The first summer school in AGI was organized in Xiamen, China in 2009 by the Xiamen university's Artificial Brain Laboratory and OpenCog. The first university course was given in 2010 and 2011 at Plovdiv University, Bulgaria by Todor Arnaudov. MIT presented a course in AGI in 2018, organized by Lex Fridman and featuring a number of guest lecturers. However, as yet, most AI researchers have devoted little attention to AGI, with some claiming that intelligence is too complex to be completely replicated in the near term. However, a small number of computer scientists are active in AGI research, and many of this group are contributing to a series of AGI conferences. The research is extremely diverse and often pioneering in nature. In the introduction to his book, Goertzel says that estimates of the time needed before a truly flexible AGI is built vary from 10 years to over a century, but the consensus in the AGI research community seems to be that the timeline discussed by Ray Kurzweil.

However, most mainstream AI researchers doubt that progress will be this rapid. Organizations explicitly pursuing AGI include the Swiss AI lab IDSIA, Nnaisense, Vicarious, Maluuba, the OpenCog Foundation, Adaptive AI, LIDA, and Numenta and the associated Redwood Neuroscience Institute. In addition, organizations such as the Machine Intelligence Research Institute and OpenAI have been founded to influence the development path of AGI. Finally, projects such as the Human Brain Project have the goal of building a functioning simulation of the human brain.

In 2019, video game programmer and aerospace engineer John Carmack announced plans to research AGI.

Namely DeepMind with their success in Human Player Simulation for e.g. AlphaGo made use of new concepts:

- Reinforcement learning to improve already trained networks with new data.

- Unsupervised learning, e.g. by Generative adversarial network to get improved networks by competition.

Processing Power Needed to Simulate a Brain

Whole Brain Emulation

A popular approach discussed to achieving general intelligent action is whole brain emulation. A low-level brain model is built by scanning and mapping a biological brain in detail and copying its state into a computer system or another computational device. The computer runs a simulation model so faithful to the original that it will behave in essentially the same way as the original brain, or for all practical purposes, indistinguishably. Whole brain emulation is discussed in computational neuroscience and neuroinformatics, in the context of brain simulation for medical research purposes. It is discussed in artificial intelligence research as an approach to strong AI.

Early Estimates

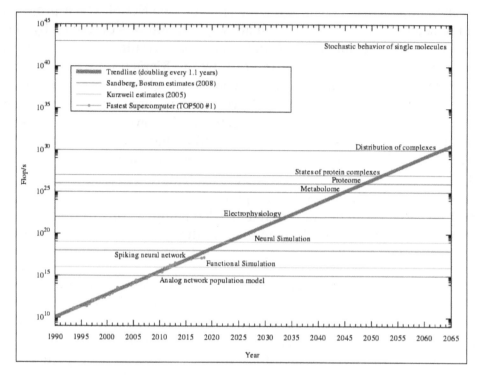

Estimates of how much processing power is needed to emulate a human brain at various levels, along with the fastest supercomputer from TOP500 mapped by year. Note the logarithmic scale and exponential trendline, which assumes the computational capacity, doubles every 1.1 years. Kurzweil believes that mind uploading will be possible at neural simulation.

For low-level brain simulation, an extremely powerful computer would be required. The human brain has a huge number of synapses. Each of the 10^{11} (one hundred billion) neurons has on average 7,000 synaptic connections to other neurons. It has been estimated that the brain of a three-year-old child has about 10^{15} synapses (1 quadrillion). This number declines with age, stabilizing by adulthood. Estimates vary for an adult, ranging from 10^{14} to 5×10^{14} synapses (100 to 500 trillion). An estimate of the brain's processing power, based on a simple switch model for neuron activity, is around 10^{14} (100 trillion) synaptic updates per second (SUPS). In 1997 Kurzweil looked at various estimates for the hardware required to equal the human brain and adopted a figure of 10^{16} computations per second (cps). He used this figure to predict the necessary hardware would be available sometime between 2015 and 2025, if the exponential growth in computer power at the time of writing continued.

Modelling the Neurons in more Detail

The artificial neuron model assumed by Kurzweil and used in many current artificial neural network implementations is simple compared with biological neurons. A brain simulation would likely have to capture the detailed cellular behaviour of biological neurons, presently understood only in the broadest of outlines. The overhead introduced by full modeling of the biological, chemical, and physical details of neural behaviour (especially on a molecular scale) would require computational powers several orders of magnitude larger than Kurzweil's estimate. In addition the estimates do not account for glial cells, which are at least as numerous as neurons, and which may outnumber neurons by as much as 10:1, and are now known to play a role in cognitive processes.

Current Research

There are some research projects that are investigating brain simulation using more sophisticated neural models, implemented on conventional computing architectures. The Artificial Intelligence System project implemented non-real time simulations of a "brain" (with 10^{11} neurons) in 2005. It took 50 days on a cluster of 27 processors to simulate 1 second of a model. The Blue Brain project used one of the fastest supercomputer architectures in the world, IBM's Blue Gene platform, to create a real time simulation of a single rat neocortical column consisting of approximately 10,000 neurons and 10^8 synapses in 2006. A longer term goal is to build a detailed, functional simulation of the physiological processes in the human brain: "It is not impossible to build a human brain and we can do it in 10 years," Henry Markram, director of the Blue Brain Project said. There have also been controversial claims to have simulated a cat brain. Neuro-silicon interfaces have been proposed as an alternative implementation strategy that may scale better.

Hans Moravec addressed the above arguments ("brains are more complicated", "neurons have to be modeled in more detail") "When will computer hardware match the human brain?". He measured the ability of existing software to simulate the functionality of neural tissue, specifically the retina. His results do not depend on the number of glial cells, nor on what kinds of processing neurons perform where.

The actual complexity of modeling biological neurons has been explored in OpenWorm project that was aimed on complete simulation of a worm that has only 302 neurons in its neural network (among about 1000 cells in total). The animal's neural network has been well documented before the start of the project. However, although the task seemed simple at the beginning, the models based on a generic neural network didn't work. Currently, the efforts are focused on precise emulation of biological neurons (partly on the molecular level), but the result can't be called a total success yet. Even if the number of issues to be solved in a human-brain-scale model is not proportional to the number of neurons, the amount of work along this path is obvious.

Criticisms of Simulation-based Approaches

A fundamental criticism of the simulated brain approach derives from embodied cognition where human embodiment is taken as an essential aspect of human intelligence. Many researchers believe that embodiment is necessary to ground meaning. If this view is correct, any fully functional brain model will need to encompass more than just the neurons (i.e., a robotic body). Goertzel proposes virtual embodiment (like Second Life), but it is not yet known whether this would be sufficient.

Desktop computers using microprocessors capable of more than 10^9 cps have been available. According to the brain power estimates used by Kurzweil (and Moravec), this computer should be capable of supporting a simulation of a bee brain, but despite some interest no such simulation exists. There are at least three reasons for this:

- The neuron model seems to be oversimplified.

- There is insufficient understanding of higher cognitive processes to establish accurately what the brain's neural activity, observed using techniques such as functional magnetic resonance imaging, correlates with.

- Even if our understanding of cognition advances sufficiently, early simulation programs are likely to be very inefficient and will, therefore, need considerably more hardware.

- The brain of an organism, while critical, may not be an appropriate boundary for a cognitive model. To simulate a bee brain, it may be necessary to simulate the body, and the environment. The Extended Mind thesis formalizes the philosophical concept, and research into cephalopods has demonstrated clear examples of a decentralized system.

In addition, the scale of the human brain is not currently well-constrained. One estimate puts the human brain at about 100 billion neurons and 100 trillion synapses. Another estimate is 86 billion neurons of which 16.3 billion are in the cerebral cortex and 69 billion in the cerebellum. Glial cell synapses are currently unquantified but are known to be extremely numerous.

Artificial Consciousness Research

Although the role of consciousness in strong AI/AGI is debatable, many AGI researchers regard research that investigates possibilities for implementing consciousness as vital. In an early effort Igor Aleksander argued that the principles for creating a conscious machine already existed but that it would take forty years to train such a machine to understand language.

Relationship to "Strong AI"

In 1980, philosopher John Searle coined the term "strong AI". He wanted to distinguish between two different hypotheses about artificial intelligence:

- An artificial intelligence system can *think* and have a *mind*. (The word "mind" has a specific meaning for philosophers, as used in "the mind body problem" or "the philosophy of mind").

- An artificial intelligence system can (only) *act like* it thinks and has a mind.

The first one is called "the strong AI hypothesis" and the second is "the weak AI hypothesis" because the first one makes the stronger statement: it assumes something special has happened to the machine that goes beyond all its abilities that we can test. Searle referred to the "strong AI hypothesis" as "strong AI". This usage is also common in academic AI research and textbooks.

The weak AI hypothesis is equivalent to the hypothesis that artificial general intelligence is possible. According to Russell and Norvig, "Most AI researchers take the weak AI hypothesis for granted, and don't care about the strong AI hypothesis."

In contrast to Searle, Kurzweil uses the term "strong AI" to describe any artificial intelligence system that acts like it has a mind, regardless of whether a philosopher would be able to determine if it actually has a mind or not.

Possible Explanations for the Slow Progress of AI Research

Since the launch of AI research in 1956, the growth of this field has slowed down over time and has stalled the aims of creating machines skilled with intelligent action at the human level. A possible explanation for this delay is that computers lack a sufficient scope of memory or processing power. In addition, the level of complexity that connects to the process of AI research may also limit the progress of AI research.

While most AI researchers believe strong AI can be achieved in the future, there are some individuals like Hubert Dreyfus and Roger Penrose who deny the possibility of achieving strong AI. John McCarthy was one of various computer scientists who believe human-level AI will be accomplished, but a date cannot accurately be predicted.

Conceptual limitations are another possible reason for the slowness in AI research. AI researchers may need to modify the conceptual framework of their discipline in order to provide a stronger base and contribution to the quest of achieving strong AI. As William Clocksin wrote: "the framework starts from Weizenbaum's observation that intelligence manifests itself only relative to specific social and cultural contexts".

Furthermore, AI researchers have been able to create computers that can perform jobs that are complicated for people to do, but conversely they have struggled to develop a computer that is capable of carrying out tasks that are simple for humans to do (Moravec's paradox). A problem described by David Gelernter is that some people assume thinking and reasoning are equivalent. However, the idea of whether thoughts and the creator of those thoughts are isolated individually has intrigued AI researchers.

The problems that have been encountered in AI research over the past decades have further impeded the progress of AI. The failed predictions that have been promised by AI researchers and the lack of a complete understanding of human behaviors have helped diminish the primary idea of human-level AI. Although the progress of AI research has brought both improvement and disappointment, most investigators have established optimism about potentially achieving the goal of AI in the 21st century.

Other possible reasons have been proposed for the lengthy research in the progress of strong AI. The intricacy of scientific problems and the need to fully understand the human brain through psychology and neurophysiology have limited many researchers from emulating the function of the human brain into a computer hardware. Many researchers tend to underestimate any doubt that is involved with future predictions of AI, but without taking those issues seriously can people then overlook solutions to problematic questions.

Clocksin says that a conceptual limitation that may impede the progress of AI research is that people may be using the wrong techniques for computer programs and implementation of equipment. When AI researchers first began to aim for the goal of artificial intelligence, a main interest was human reasoning. Researchers hoped to establish computational models of human knowledge through reasoning and to find out how to design a computer with a specific cognitive task.

The practice of abstraction, which people tend to redefine when working with a particular context in research, provides researchers with a concentration on just a few concepts. The most productive use of abstraction in AI research comes from planning and problem solving. Although the aim is to increase the speed of a computation, the role of abstraction has posed questions about the involvement of abstraction operators.

A possible reason for the slowness in AI relates to the acknowledgement by many AI researchers that heuristics is a section that contains a significant breach between computer performance and human performance. The specific functions that are programmed to a computer may be able to account for many of the requirements that allow it to match human intelligence. These explanations are not necessarily guaranteed to be the fundamental causes for the delay in achieving strong AI, but they are widely agreed by numerous researchers.

There have been many AI researchers that debate over the idea whether machines should be created with emotions. There are no emotions in typical models of AI and some researchers say programming emotions into machines allows them to have a mind of their own. Emotion sums up the experiences of humans because it allows them to remember those experiences. David Gelernter writes, "No computer will be creative unless it can simulate all the nuances of human emotion." This concern about emotion has posed problems for AI researchers and it connects to the concept of strong AI as its research progresses into the future.

Consciousness

Searle's Chinese Room suggests a hypothetical scenario in which the philosopher is presented with a written query in an unfamiliar Chinese language. Searle is sat alone in a closed room and individual characters from each word in the query are slid under the door in order. Despite not understanding the language, Searle is able to follow the instructions given by a book in the room for manipulating the symbols and numerals fed to him. These instructions allow him to create his own series of Chinese characters that he feeds back under the door. By following the instructions Searle is able to create an appropriate response and fool the person outside the room into thinking there is a native speaker inside, despite Searle not understanding the Chinese language. In this way, Searle argued the experiment demonstrates a computer could converse with people and appear to understand a language, while having no actual comprehension of its meaning.

The experiment has been used to attack the Turing Test. Devised by the brilliant mathematician and father of computing Alan Turing, the test suggests a computer could be classed as a thinking machine if it could fool one-third of the people it was talking with into believing it was a human.

In a more recent book, Searle says this uncertainty over the true nature of an intelligent computer extends to consciousness. In his book Language and Consciousness, he says: "Just as behavior by itself is not sufficient for consciousness, so computational models of consciousness by themselves are not sufficient for consciousness" going on to give an example that: "Nobody supposes the computational model of rainstorms in London will leave us wet".

Searle creates a distinction between strong AI, where the AI can be said to have a mind, and weak AI, where the AI is instead a convincing model of a mind.

Various counterpoints have been raised to the Chinese Room and Searle's conclusions, ranging from arguments that the experiment mischaracterizes the nature of a mind, to it ignoring the fact that Searle is part of a wider system, which, as a whole, understands the Chinese language.

There is also the question of whether the distinction between a simulation of a mind and an actual mind matters, with Stuart Russell and Peter Norvig, who wrote the definitive textbook on artificial intelligence, arguing most AI researchers are more focused on the outcome than the intrinsic nature of the system.

Affective Computing

Affective computing, also known as AC or emotion AI, is an area of study within cognitive computing and artificial intelligence that is concerned with gathering data from faces, voices and body language to measure human emotion. An important business goal of AC is to build human-computer interfaces that can detect and appropriately respond to an end user's state of mind.

Affective computing has the potential to humanize digital interactions and offer benefits in an almost limitless range of applications. For example, in an e-learning situation, an AC program could detect when a student is frustrated and offer expanded explanations or additional information. In telemedicine, AC programming can help physicians quickly understand a remote patient's mood or look for signs of depression. Other business applications currently being explored include customer relationship management (CRM), human resource management (HRM), marketing and entertainment.

A computing device with emotion AI programming gathers cues about a user's emotional state from a variety of sources, including facial expressions, muscle tension, posture, hand and shoulder gestures, speech patterns, heart rate, pupil dilation and body temperature. The technology that supports emotion measurement and analysis includes sensors, cameras, big data, and deep learning analytics engines. As of this writing, RESTful APIs are available to measure human emotion from companies such as Affectiva, Humanyze, CrowdEmotion and Emotient. IBM Watson APIs include Tone Analyzer and Emotion Analysis.

The term affective computing is generally credited to Rosalind Picard, a computer scientist at MIT and founder of Affectiva. In psychology, the word affect is used to describe a patient's emotional tone.

Affective computing deals with emotions. Emotions themselves are very human matter, of which there is no clear theory or understanding. The necessary background for affective computing is the knowledge on emotions and their role in human behaviour and cognitive processes.

Emotions

Some define it as the physiological changes caused in our body, while the others treat it as purely intellectual thought-process.

Emotions are closely related to perception. We understand each other's emotions through visual, auditory and tactile senses. Lack of sensory data causes misunderstandings. Widespread use of email has caused many emotional misunderstandings when effectual meanings have been communicated via textual messages that cannot carry the affective information.

Understanding emotion also has to do with getting to know a person. We can assume the emotions of a person we know. We have built some kind of emotional model of that person on which we can reflect the situation.

Emotions and Intelligence

Emotions are much more fundamental in nature than rational intelligence. A puppy can understand the mood of your commands, and behave accordingly, but it can never think rationally about it's (much less your) world. Still, with its much bounded rationality it is nonquestionaly superior to any computer device when it comes to surviving and acting in physical reality. The current computers, with their unlimited calculating power and memory, are on the intellectual level of a limp cockroach, at their best.

The actual seat of emotion in human brain is not unambiguous, but we know something about it. Paul MacLean has modelled the human brain as three regions: neocortex, limbic systems, and reptilian brain. The neocortex is traditionally the best studied, and contains the visual cortex and auditory cortex; it is where the majority of perceptional processing has been assumed to occur. The limbic system is the primary seat of emotion, attention, and memory.

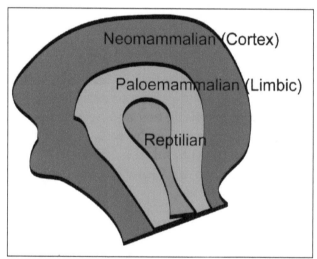

Paul MacLean's "triune brain": Although clear division between regions are shown, the functions are not disctinctly divided in reality.

Emotions are much more fundamental in human behaviour than intellect. They can hijack our rationality in situations of fear, panic, or love. They can strongly affect our decision making even in normal situations – someone might be called very emotional person.

Evidence indicates that laws and rules do not operate without emotion in two highly cognitive tasks: decision making and perception.

Decision Making

Antonio Damasio made remarkable findings for the paradigm shift for importance of emotions in thinking processes. His patients have frontal-lobe disorders, affecting a key part of the cortex that communicates with the limbic system, causing certain lack of emotional capabilities. Otherwise, the patients appear to have normal intelligence. At first encounter, they appear like Star Trek's Mr. Spock: inexpressive of emotions and unusually rational. One might expect them to be also highly intelligent, like Spock. But in real life, Damasio's patients make disastrous decisions. Losing money with an investment, a healthy people would learn it's a bad one and stop investing in it. But the patients would continue investing until all the money is gone. Moreover, this pattern appears in all fields of life, causing the people to lose their jobs, friends, family, and more. Another patient had enormous difficulties making any decisions. He would consider all the possibilities involved and continue analysing them ad infinitum, simply unable to come into any conclusion.

These findings point to an essential role of emotion in rational thinking. Humans associate judgements of value and valience with important decisions. Even the massive parallelism of the human brain cannot fully search the large spaces involved in many day-to-day decisions. There is no time to consider everything. Valience and "gut feeling" help to cope with these issues. Therefore affective computing could be able to provide better decision-making systems. Pure reasoning might be the Platonic ideal but in successful cognitive systems it's a logical howler.

Learning

Emotions play an important role in human learning. Emotions are hypothesized to provide the flexibility not present in traditional stimulus-response theories of learning. Learning is best thought as a two-step procedure, first creating an emotion for learning, before the stimulus-response. Consider a rat that learns to leave his box upon hearing a tone after being experienced that tone paired with a painful shock. First, the rat learns to fear the tone, and second, upon hearing the tone tries to reduce the fear. The emotional state of fear motivates the rat to seek methods of escape. This more flexible theory of learning explains how a rat might develop alternative solutions for the situation, but always motivated by its emotional state.

Memory

The same emotion that affects decision making and learning also influences memory retrieval. Scientists believe that emotional valence attaches to concepts, ideas, plans, and every experience stored in our memories. Good feelings likely encode knowledge of effectiveness, familiarity, opportunity, and associations with positive outcomes. Bad feelings likely encode knowledge of ineffectiveness, unfamiliarity, risk, and associations with negative outcomes. Because memory is intricately involved in decision-making and almost every aspect of cognition, it may be that the way in which emotion works so many of its influences is via its influence on memory. The findings of Bower and Cohen on mood-congruent memory retrieval and learning have influenced several models door representing emotion-memory interactions and their impact on cognitive processes.

Emotions and Computers

Affective computing consists of four related areas. For communication, computers can both recognize and express emotion. Emotions can be expressed without really having them, like an actor playing a role. Having emotions is a separate, but very profound question. Last, computers could be able to have emotional intelligence. Lately very fashionable in human psychology, it deals with reasoning and understanding of emotions.

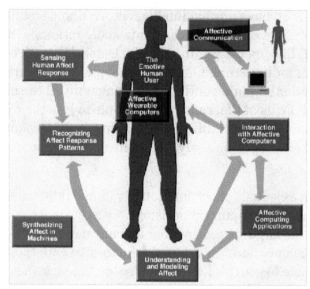

The research areas of affective computing as visualized by MIT.

Recognizing Emotions

The foundation of affective computing will be the ability to recognize emotions, to infer an emotional state from observation of emotional expressions and through reasoning about an emotion-generating situation.

For recognizing ordinary human emotions computer needs human senses like audio and video, gathering facial expressions and vocal intonations. Additionally, it can sense inputs that may not have analogs in human senses – reading infrared temperature, measuring electro thermal conductivity, and so forth. Once emotional expressions are sensed and recognized, the system can use its knowledge about emotion generation and situation to infer the underlying emotional state that most probably gave rise to the expressions.

When does a computer have this ability? One way to test it is to try replacing humans with computers in recognizing and interpreting emotions. If 70% of test persons watching a videotaped expression interpret the emotional state correctly, a computer that comes to the same conclusion with 70% probability should be regarded as able to recognize emotions.

A computer does not have to be bound to human senses when recognizing emotions. Video and audio input could be augmented with body temperature and skin conductivity, heart rate and respiration, and so forth. Wearable computers have access to lots of physiolochigal data that might be too revealing and intimate to be shared with a public computer. Computers might also be able to recognize and label affective states that do not have particular name or meaning for humans.

Giving only the ability to recognize emotions might be enough to enable computer affectively. It might be also preferred. Being able to only recognize user's emotions and adapt its behaviour accordingly makes well-behaving computer. Nobody wants the negatively-emotional computer sulking and shouting insults at the user. However, human emotional system doesn't rely only on signal recognition in interpreting emotions. Therefore also other emotional abilities should be given to a computer in order to make it emotionally fully capable.

Expressing Emotions

A computer can express emotion without actually having emotions, just as actors can express emotions that they do not have. The basic requirement for a computer to express emotions is to have channels of communication such as voice, image, and an ability to communicate affection over those channels. The ways of expressing emotion could be human, like showing a face, to easily communicate the emotion to human users. It could be also something totally different and new, as computers are not humans and don't genuinely have the same ways of expression.

Information age has brought a problem of feeding us too much information, leading to cognitive fatigue and inability to process effectively new inputs. Information presented through the affective channel, through emotions, does not usually demand our conscious attention. Affective information is processed in parallel and could be utilized to lighten the cognitive load. A computer greeting at startup could inform with voice intonation the result of previous task or its current status. Saying "Hello" in a cheerful tone is more expressive and cognitively less demanding.

Affective bandwidth is a characteristic that can be assigned to communication channels. It describes how much certain communication channel lets affective information through. With text it is minimal, increasing with voice and video. Ordinarily mediated communication channels have much less affective bandwidth than person-to-person, though in a virtual reality environment utilizing emotional data that humans cannot perceive (skin conductivity, temperature) it could be even higher.

Computer generated affective information promises to be fairly easily generated. Clark Elliott of DePaul University conducted a test on computer generated emotions. He videotaped an actor expressing different emotions while speaking, and a computer that generated facial expressions and vocal intonations to express the emotional states. In tests with human viewers, roughly 70% of the persons recognized the emotions generated by the computer, while only 50% recognized correctly those expressed by the human actor.

Another test of effectivity of affective communication is how much, if at all, a computer is able to induce emotion in its user. A computer is able to express emotions effectively if it can cheer up and make its depressed, angry user feel happy.

Computer may have unique emotional states, which call for correspondingly unique ways of expressing them. For example, a computer running out of memory may feel uncomfortable with receiving large chunks of data. These emotions can be communicated between computing machinery in their unique ways, or translated into some suitable human emotion to be expressed to the user.

A computer can express emotions without really "having" emotions, or without really "feeling", as when programmed to be cheerful. Humans on the other hand always have emotions, whether or not they can express them. Emotional state and expressing emotion is also coupled. Making a smile can make a person feel happy. A person feeling outraged can very hardly make a convincing happy face, however sincerely he tried. Having emotions affects the ability to express them. This bias-exclusion effect should be considered when designing systems with emotional capabilities.

Having Emotions

Can computers feel? Certainly this is the most profound question in the field of affective computing. Feelings are usually considered to be the division between a human and a machine. Consciousness is also a prerequisite for many human emotions, like shame and quilt – if you don't have consciousness, there's no reason to be ashamed of anything. Picard proposes s model of five components that all should be present in a system if it is to have emotions.

Picard calls the first component "emergent emotions." Emergent emotions are those which are attributed to systems based on their observable emotional behaviour, especially when the system at hand doesn't have any explicit internal mechanism or representation to emotions. Mac showing a smiling face at boot up can be seen as having "positive emotions towards serving the user". In reality the Mac doesn't really have any emotions; the user just perceives these emergent emotions.

Second component are fast primary emotions. Many animals including humans have hard-wired, innate responses, especially to potentially harmful events. We can feel startled, angry, or afraid before the signals event get to the cortex, and before becoming aware of what is happening. These primary emotions work through two communicating pattern recognizing systems: a rough system that acts fast and can hijack the cortex, and a finer system that is slower but more precise.

A third component of having emotions are cognitive emotions, involving explicit cognitive reasoning in their generation. For example, completing a difficult task can generate an intense feeling of satisfaction. In healthy human, cognitively generated emotions usually provoke an emotional experience with subjective feelings, activating limbic responses and bodily feelings.

The fourth component is emotional experience. A feeling system is able to label its emotional behaviours, and understand its own affective system. Then it can be said to have a rudimentary awareness of its emotional behaviours. Second aspect of experience is awareness of the emotions' physiological accompaniments. For humans these include heart rate, breathing, cold feet, and so forth. Most computers don't have sensors that could discern their physical state but those could be added. For computers awareness of their internal "software" state is probably more relevant. Third aspect of emotional experience are the tricky "gut feelings" that lets you know subjectively something is good or bad, that you like or dislike something.

Body-mind interactions constitute the fifth and the last component. Emotions influence decision making, perception, interest, learning, priorities, creativity, and more. Emotions influence cognition, and therefore intelligence, especially when it involves social decision making and interaction. The human emotions not only influence cognition but also physiological systems outside to brain – vocal and facial expressions, posture and movement. Emotions intricately interact with the human body and mind. Not only does emotion influence cognitive and bodily functions, but the emotion is itself affected by them. Cognitive thoughts can generate emotions. Also biochemical processes like hormones and neurotransmitters and physical drives like hunger evoke emotions. The aspects of emotion's interaction with body and mind that may be most important for computers are the influence of emotion on cognitive processes.

Emotional Intelligence

We all cognitively manage our emotions. Emotions can be powerful motivators. If you enjoy interacting with people, you may seek opportunities to do so. However, you are able to self-regulate the pursuit of pleasure and recognize that sometimes negative feelings or emotional restraints have to be tolerated in order to reach something greater.

A computer with emotional intelligence will be one that is skilled at understanding and expressing its own emotions, recognizing emotion in others, regulating affect, and using moods and emotions to motivate adaptive behaviours. Recognition of emotion in others includes reasoning about what emotion is likely to be generated in a situation, ultimately understanding what is important to other person, what are his goals, preferences and biases. Regulating one's own emotional reactions is a characteristic of a civilized adult. Ability to utilize emotions, both with self and in others, for higher cognitive goals like learning, creativity, and attention is a powerful skill.

These components of emotional intelligence rely on the three abilities of affective computing presented above: recognizing and expressing emotions, and "having" emotions. Computers that have emotions have to be aware of them, and will need to be able to regulate and utilize them.

Potential Concerns

Unfortunately, technology almost always has a darker side. The suddenly consciousness computer systems with emotionally hostile attitude towards whole human race have been regular theme of entertainment industry for decades, from HAL to Terminator. Computers start to make emotionally distorted, harmful decisions. Emotions and computers have potentially harmful outcomes which the developers of affective computing should address.

Emotional decision making has strong negative connotations. It is usually connected to non-rational, bad, non-intelligent decisions. When somebody is said to act emotionally, it usually means he's doing bad for himself and possibly for others, too. Making the computer decision making process emotional is a delicate matter. A balance should be found where the positive effects of emotionality can be utilized without slipping into unrational behaviour. A strong regulation of affection is needed.

Emotional manipulation, from TV shop sales pitches to Nazi propaganda, is a well-known activity. Like humans, emotionally capable computers will have the ability to mislead and deceive users. Computers could be also used in large-scale monitoring and manipulation of emotions, scaringly powerful tool for an authoritarian government.

Applications

Real-life applications of affective computing are still somewhat few. The field has so far been dominated by research, not applications. Nonetheless, future forms of computing can be seen to call for affective capabilities, for example wearable computers could have much use of emotional capabilities.

Affective Computing Foundations

Human emotions are communicated though sensory data. Therefore effective processing of visual and auditory data is the fundamental of getting emotions into computers. Digital signal processing is the low level recognizing of emotions. Analyzing video and audio data the computer can try to connect some input signals to emotions. The system needs also some kind of high-level, symbolic models of emotions and moods.

In building affective computers the tools of pattern recognizing and analysis are used for recognizing and synthesizing facial expressions, recognizing and synthesizing vocal inflection, recognizing physiological patterns corresponding to affective states, and modelling emotional behaviour. Research in the area is very new, but the results so far have proved promising results.

Emotion synthesis, the process of generating emotional states and communicating them, can utilize models employing both cognitive and non-cognitive mechanisms. Cognitively generated emotions have been the easiest to implement with AI based systems, since they are rule-based and lend to implementation in a computer.

Affection-to-go

Wearable computers could get to know you very well, adapt to your situation and serve you in a much more powerful way, were they enabled with emotions. Soon you could build a relationship with your computer, and, like your underwear, they come very personal and you will not want to borrow it to others.

Applications of affective wearable computers are such as a portable music player that plays music depending on your mood and listening preferences, glasses that show other people's affective state (transmitted by wearable devices) and conductor's sensor-net jacket that augments the ability to express emotion and intentionality.

Wearable computers have full access to you, and should be under total control of the human wearer not to cause any anxiety.

Persuasive Computing

Persuasive computing is a research field studying use of computers in persuading humans. The application might be from simple user-interface features to software that trains heroin-addicts out of the habit.

Technology can be made persuasive with logic and intention, but coupled with emotional capabilities of affective computing; it can really get the means of persuasion.

References

- Artificial-intelligence: britannica.com, Retrieved 05 January, 2019
- Artificial-intelligence-advantages-disadvantages: data-flair.training, Retrieved 10 February, 2019
- Types-of-artificial-intelligence: javatpoint.com, Retrieved 25 June, 2019
- Artificial-general-intelligence-AGI: searchenterpriseai.techtarget.com, Retrieved 16 April, 2019
- What-is-artificial-general-intelligence: zdnet.com, Retrieved 29 June, 2019
- Affective-computing: whatis.techtarget.com, Retrieved 26 August, 2019

Knowledge, Reasoning and Agents

Knowledge, reasoning and intelligent agents are three primary areas of study within artificial intelligence. This chapter will discuss in detail the varied types of knowledge representation, reasoning and intelligent agents along with their role in artificial intelligence.

Knowledge Representation

Humans are best at understanding, reasoning, and interpreting knowledge. Human knows things, which is knowledge and as per their knowledge they perform various actions in the real world. But how machines do all these things comes under knowledge representation and reasoning. Hence we can describe Knowledge representation as following:

- Knowledge representation and reasoning (KR, KRR) is the part of Artificial intelligence which concerned with AI agents thinking and how thinking contributes to intelligent behavior of agents.

- It is responsible for representing information about the real world so that a computer can understand and can utilize this knowledge to solve the complex real world problems such as diagnosis a medical condition or communicating with humans in natural language.

- It is also a way which describes how we can represent knowledge in artificial intelligence. Knowledge representation is not just storing data into some database, but it also enables an intelligent machine to learn from that knowledge and experiences so that it can behave intelligently like a human.

What to Represent

Following are the kind of knowledge which needs to be represented in AI systems:

- Object: All the facts about objects in our world domain. E.g., Guitars contains strings, trumpets are brass instruments.

- Events: Events are the actions which occur in our world.

- Performance: It describes behavior which involves knowledge about how to do things.

- Meta-knowledge: It is knowledge about what we know.

- Facts: Facts are the truths about the real world and what we represent.

- Knowledge-Base: The central component of the knowledge-based agents is the knowledge base. It is represented as KB. The Knowledgebase is a group of the Sentences (Here, sentences are used as a technical term and not identical with the English language).

Knowledge: Knowledge is awareness or familiarity gained by experiences of facts, data, and situations.

Relation between Knowledge and Intelligence

Knowledge of real-worlds plays a vital role in intelligence and same for creating artificial intelligence. Knowledge plays an important role in demonstrating intelligent behavior in AI agents. An agent is only able to accurately act on some input when he has some knowledge or experience about that input.

Let's suppose if you met some person who is speaking in a language which you don't know, then how you will able to act on that. The same thing applies to the intelligent behavior of the agents.

As we can see in below diagram, there is one decision maker which act by sensing the environment and using knowledge. But if the knowledge part will not present then, it cannot display intelligent behavior.

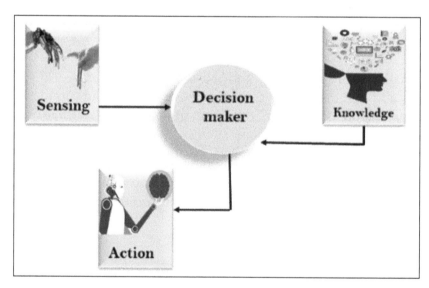

AI Knowledge Cycle

An Artificial intelligence system has the following components for displaying intelligent behavior:

- Perception,
- Learning,
- Knowledge Representation and Reasoning,
- Planning,
- Execution.

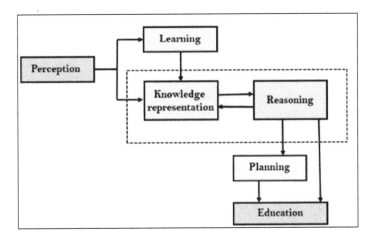

The above diagram is showing how an AI system can interact with the real world and what components help it to show intelligence. AI system has Perception component by which it retrieves information from its environment. It can be visual, audio or another form of sensory input. The learning component is responsible for learning from data captured by Perception comportment. In the complete cycle, the main components are knowledge representation and Reasoning. These two components are involved in showing the intelligence in machine-like humans. These two components are independent with each other but also coupled together. The planning and execution depend on analysis of Knowledge representation and reasoning.

Approaches to Knowledge Representation

There are mainly four approaches to knowledge representation, which are given below:

Simple relational knowledge:

- It is the simplest way of storing facts which uses the relational method, and each fact about a set of the object is set out systematically in columns.

- This approach of knowledge representation is famous in database systems where the relationship between different entities is represented.

- This approach has little opportunity for inference.

Example: The following is the simple relational knowledge representation.

Player	Weight	Age
Player1	65	23
Player2	58	18
Player3	75	24

Inheritable Knowledge:

- In the inheritable knowledge approach, all data must be stored into a hierarchy of classes.

- All classes should be arranged in a generalized form or a hierarchal manner.

- In this approach, we apply inheritance property.

- Elements inherit values from other members of a class.

- This approach contains inheritable knowledge which shows a relation between instance and class, and it is called instance relation.

- Every individual frame can represent the collection of attributes and its value.

- In this approach, objects and values are represented in Boxed nodes.

- We use Arrows which point from objects to their values.

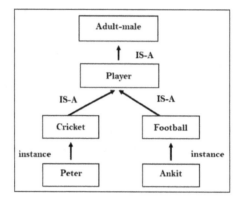

Inferential knowledge:

- Inferential knowledge approach represents knowledge in the form of formal logics.

- This approach can be used to derive more facts.

- It guaranteed correctness.

- Example: Let's suppose there are two statements:

  ○ Marcus is a man.

  ○ All men are mortal.

    Then it can represent as;
    man(Marcus)
    $\forall x = $ man (x) ----------> mortal (x)s

Procedural Knowledge:

- Procedural knowledge approach uses small programs and codes which describes how to do specific things, and how to proceed.

- In this approach, one important rule is used which is If-Then rule.

- In this knowledge, we can use various coding languages such as LISP language and Prolog language.

- We can easily represent heuristic or domain-specific knowledge using this approach.

- But it is not necessary that we can represent all cases in this approach.

Requirements for Knowledge Representation System

A good knowledge representation system must possess the following properties.

- Representational Accuracy: KR system should have the ability to represent all kind of required knowledge.

- Inferential Adequacy: KR system should have ability to manipulate the representational structures to produce new knowledge corresponding to existing structure.

- Inferential Efficiency: The ability to direct the inferential knowledge mechanism into the most productive directions by storing appropriate guides.

- Acquisitional efficiency: The ability to acquire the new knowledge easily using automatic methods.

Types of knowledge Representation

Knowledge can be represented in different ways. The structuring of knowledge and how designers might view it, as well as the type of structures used internally are considered. Different knowledge representation techniques are:

- Logic,

- Semantic Network,

- Frame,

- Conceptual Graphs,

- Conceptual Dependency,

- Script.

Logic

Logic is a formal language, with precisely defined syntax and semantics, which supports sound inference. Different logics exist, which allow you to represent different kinds of things, and which allow more or less efficient inference. The logic may be different types like propositional logic, predicate logic, temporal logic, description logic etc. But representing something in logic may not be very natural and inferences may not be efficient.

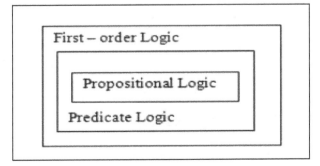

Semantic Network

A semantic network is a graphical knowledge representation technique. This knowledge representation system is primarily on network structure. The semantic networks were basically developed to model human memory. A semantic net consists of nodes connected by arcs. The arcs are defined in a variety of ways, depending upon the kind of knowledge being represented.

The main idea behind semantic net is that the meaning of a concept comes, from the ways in which it is connected to other concepts. The semantic network consists of different nodes and arcs. Each node should contain the information about objects and each arc should contain the relationship between objects. Semantic nets are used to find relationships among objects by spreading activation about from each of two nodes and seeing where the activation met this process is called intersection search.

For example: Ram is a boy.

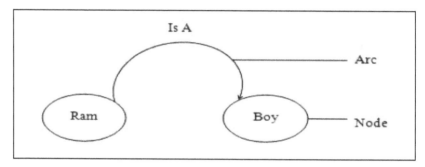

Semantic Network by using Instances

The semantic network based knowledge representation mechanism is useful where an object or concept is associated with many attributes and where relationships between objects are important. Semantic nets have also been used in natural language research to represent complex sentences expressed in English. The semantic representation is useful because it provides a standard way of analyzing the meaning of sentence. It is a natural way to represent relationships that would appear as ground instances of binary predicates in predicate logic. In this case we can create one instance of each object. In instance based semantic net representations some keywords are used like: IS A, INSTANCE, AGENT, HAS-PARTS etc.

Consider the following examples:

- Suppose we have to represent the sentence "Sima is a girl".

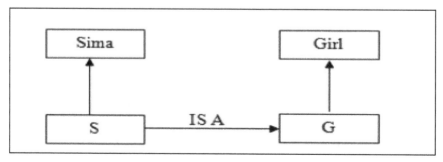

- Ram is taller than Hari.

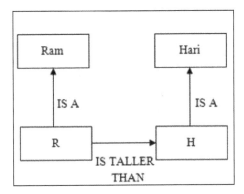

It can also be represented as,

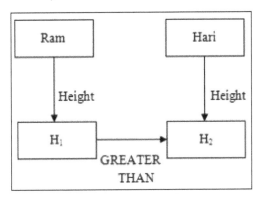

- "Mouse is a Rodent and Rodent is a mammal. Mouse has teeth and eats grass". Check whether the sentence mammal has teeth is valid or not.

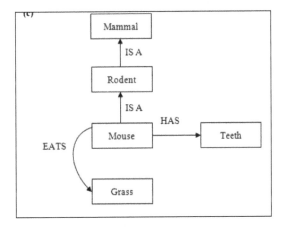

Partitioned Semantic Network

Some complex sentences are there which cannot be represented by simple semantic nets and for this we have to follow the technique partitioned semantic networks. Partitioned semantic net allow for:

- Propositions to be made without commitment to truth.

- Expressions to be quantified.

In partitioned semantic network, the network is broken into spaces which consist of groups of nodes and arcs and regard each space as a node.

Let us consider few examples.

Draw the partitioned semantic network structure for the followings:

- Sima is eating an apple.

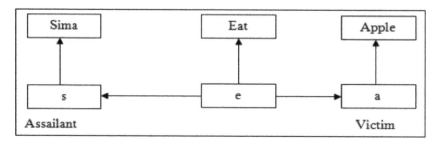

- All Sima are eating an apple.

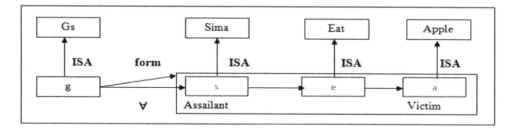

- All Sima are eating some apple.

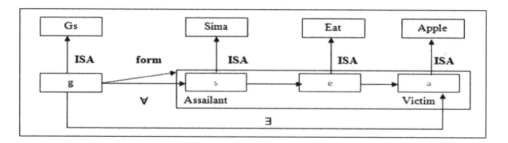

- All men are mortal.

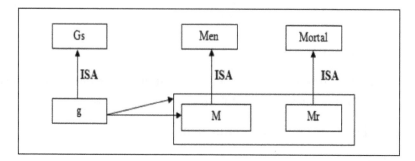

- Every dog has bitten a shopkeeper.

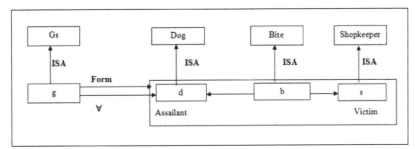

- Every dog in town has bitten a shopkeeper.

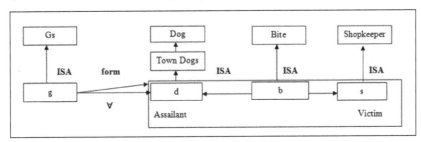

On the above semantic network structures, the instance "IS A" is used. Also two terms like assailant and victim are used. Assailant means "by which the work is done" and that of victim refers to "on which the work is applied". Another term namely GS, which refers to General Statement. For GS, make a node g which is an instance of Gs. Every element will have at least two attributes. Firstly, a form that states which a relation is being asserted. Secondly, one or more for all ($\forall$) or there exists ($\exists$) connections which represent universally quantifiable variables.

Frame

A frame is a collection of attributes and associated values that describe some entity in the world. Frames are general record like structures which consist of a collection of slots and slot values. The slots may be of any size and type. Slots typically have names and values or subfields called facets. Facets may also have names and any number of values. A frame may have any number of slots; a slot may have any number of facets, each with any number of values. A slot contains information such as attribute value pairs, default values, condition for filling a slot, pointers to other related frames and procedures that are activated when needed for different purposes. Sometimes a frame describes an entity in some absolute sense; sometimes it represents the entity from a particular point of view. A single frame taken alone is rarely useful. We build frame systems out of collection of frames that are connected to each other by virtue of the fact that the value of an attribute of one frame may be another frame. Each frame should start with an open parenthesis and closed with a closed parenthesis.

Syntax of a Frame

(<frame name>

(<slot 1> (< facet 1> < value 1> ....<value n_1>)

(<facet2> <value1> ....<value n$_2$>)

.

.

.

.

.

(<facet n> < value 1> .... < value n$_n$ >))

(<slot 2> (< facet 1> <value 1> .... < value n$_1$>)

(< facet 2> < value 2> .... < value n$_2$>)

.

.

))

Let us consider the below examples:

Create a frame of the person Ram who is a doctor. He is of 40. His wife name is Sita. They have two children Babu and Gita. They live in 100 kps street in the city of Delhi in India. The zip code is 756005.

(Ram

     (PROFESSION (VALUE Doctor))

     (AGE (VALUE 40))

     (WIFE (VALUE Sita))

     (CHILDREN (VALUE Bubu, Gita))

     (ADDRESS

          (STREET (VALUE 100 kps))

          (CITY(VALUE Delhi))

          (COUNTRY(VALUE India))

          (ZIP (VALUE 756005))))

Create a frame of the person Anand who is a chemistry professor in RD Women's College. His wife name is Sangita having two children Rupa and Shipa.

(Anand

    (PROFESSION (VALUE Chemistry Professor))

    (ADDRESS (VALUE RD Women's College))

    (WIFE (VALUE Sangita))

    (CHILDREN(VALUE RupaShipa)))

Create a frame of the person Akash who has a white maruti car of LX-400 Model. It has 5 doors. Its weight is 225kg, capacity is 8, and mileage is 15 km /lit.

(Akash

    (CAR (VALUE Maruti))

    (COLOUR (VALUE White))

    (MODEL (VALUE LX-400))

    (DOOR (VALUE 5))

    (WEIGHT (VALUE 225kg))

    (CAPACITY (VALUE 8))

    (MILAGE (VALUE 15km/lit)))

The frames can be attached with another frame and can create a network of frames. The main task of action frame is to provide the facility for procedural attachment and help in reasoning process. Reasoning using frames is done by instantiation. Instantiation process begins, when the given situation is matched with frames that are already in existence. The reasoning process tries to match the current problem state with the frame slot and assigns them values. The values assigned to the slots depict a particular situation and by this, the reasoning process moves towards a goal. The reasoning process can be defined as filling slot values in frames.

Conceptual Graphs

It is a knowledge representation technique which consists of basic concepts and the relationship between them. As the name indicates, it tries to capture the concepts about the events and represents them in the form of a graph. A concept may be individual or generic. An individual concept has a type field followed by a reference field. For example person: Ram. Here person indicates type and Ram indicates reference.

An individual concept should be represented within a rectangle in graphical representation and within a square bracket in linear representation. The generic concept should be represented within an oval in graphical representation and within a parenthesis in linear representation. Conceptual graph is a basic building block for associative network. Concepts like AGENT, OBJECT, INSTRUMENT, PART are obtained from a collection of standard concepts. New concepts and relations can be defined from these basic ones. These are also basic building block for associative network.

A linear conceptual graph is an elementary form of this structure. A single conceptual graph is roughly equivalent to a graphical diagram of a natural language sentence where the words are depicted as concepts and relationships.

Consider an example:

"Ram is eating an apple."

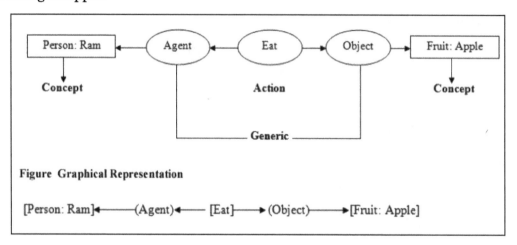

Figure Graphical Representation

[Person: Ram]◄———(Agent)◄——— [Eat]———►(Object)———►[Fruit: Apple]

Conceptual Dependency

It is an another knowledge representation technique in which we can represent any kind of knowledge. It is based on the use of a limited number of primitive concepts and rules of formation to represent any natural language statement. Conceptual dependency theory is based on the use of knowledge representation methodology was primarily developed to understand and represent natural language structures. The conceptual dependency structures were originally developed by Roger C SChank in 1977.

If a computer program is to be developed that can understand wide phenomenon represented by natural languages, the knowledge representation should be powerful enough to represent these concepts. The conceptual dependency representation captures maximum concepts to provide canonical form of meaning of sentences. Generally there are four primitives from which the conceptual dependency structure can be described. They are,

- ACTS: Actions.

- PPs: Objects (Picture Producers).

- AAs: Modifiers of Actions (Action Aiders).

- Pas: Modifiers of PPs (Picture Aiders).

- TS: Time of action.

Conceptual dependency provides both a structure and a specific set of primitives at a particular level of granularity, out of which representation of particular pieces of information can be constructed.

For example:

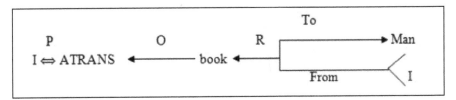

Where, ←: Direction of dependency-

- Double arrow indicates two way link between actor and action.

- P: Past Tense.

- ATRANS: One of the primitive acts used by the theory.

- O: The objective case relation.

- R: Recipient case Relation.

In CD, representation of actions are built from a set of primitive acts:

- ATRANS: Transfer of an abstract relationship (give, accept, take).

- PTRANS: Transfer the physical location of an object (Go, Come, Run, Walk).

- MTRANS: Transfer the mental information (Tell).

- PROPEL: Application of physical force to an object (push, pull, throw).

- MOVE: Movement of a body part by its owner (kick).

- GRASP: Grasping of an object by an action (clutch).

- INGEST: Ingestion of an object by an animal (eat).

- EXPEL: Expel from an animal body (cry).

- MBUILD: Building new information out of old (decide).

- SPEAK: Production of sounds (say).

ATTEND: Focusing of a sense organ towards a stimulus (Listen).

The main goal of CD representation is to capture the implicit concept of a sentence and make it explicit. In normal representation of the concepts, besides actor and object, other concepts of time, location, source and destination are also mentioned. Following conceptual tenses are used in CD representation.

- O: Object case relationship.

- R: Recipient case relationship.

- P: Past.

- F: Future.

- Nil: Present.

- T: Transition.

- Ts: Start Transition.

- Tf: Finisher Transition.

- K: Continuing.

- ?: Interrogative.

- /: Negative.

- C: Conditional.

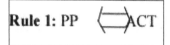

Rule 1: PP ⇐⇒ ACT

It describes the relationship between an actor and an event, he/she causes.

E.g. Ram ran.

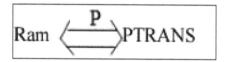

Where, P: Past Tense

Rule 2: PP ⇔ PA

It describes the relationship between a PP and PA where the PA indicates one characteristics of PP. E.g. Ram is tall.

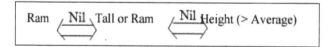

Rule 3: PP ⇔ PP

It describe the relationship between two PPs where one PP is defined by other.

E.g. Ram is a doctor.

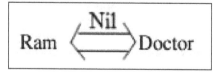

Rule 4: PP PA

  ↑ or ↓

  PA PP

It describes the relationship between the PP and PA, where PA indicates on attributes of PP.

E.g. A nice boy is doctor.

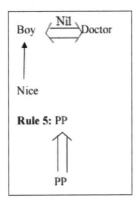

Rule 5: PP

  PP

It describes the relationship between 3 PP's where one PP is the owner of another PP.

E.g. Ram's Cat.

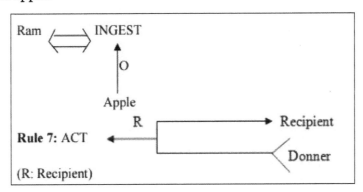

Ram

Rule 6: Act ←—^{O}—PP Where O: Object

It describes the relationship between the PP and ACT. Where PP indicates the object of that action.
E.g. Ram is eating an apple.

Here on PP describes the recipient and another PP describes the donner.

E.g. Rahul gave a book to sourav.

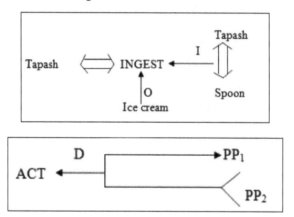

Here PP$_1$ indicates the agent and PP$_2$ indicates the object that is used in the action.

E.g. Tapash ate the ice cream with the spoon.

Here D indicates destination, PP$_1$ indicates destination and PP$_2$ indicates the source.

E.g. the bucket is filled with milk.

x indicates the average milk and the source i.e. bucket is dry which is hidden.

Rule 10:

It describes the relationship between a conceptualization and the time at which the event is described occurs.

E.g. Sita ate the apple yesterday.

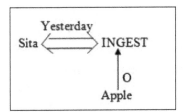

Rule 11:

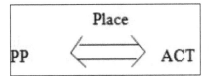

It describes the relationship between a conceptualization and the place at which it is occurred.

E.g. Shanu ate the apple at VRS hotel yesterday.

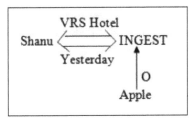

Rule 12:

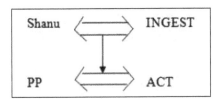

It describes the relationship between one conceptualization with another.

E.g. while I was going to college, I saw a snake.

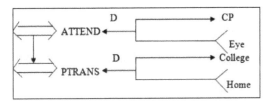

(Where CP: Conscious Processor i.e. the combination of all sense organs like eye, ear, nose, etc).

Script

It is a knowledge representation technique. Scripts are frame like structures used to represent commonly occurring experiences such as going to restaurant, visiting a doctor. A script is a structure that describes a stereotyped sequence of events in a particular context. A script consists of a set of slots. Associated with each slot may be some information about what kinds of values it may contain as well as a default value to be used if no other information is available. Scripts are useful because in the real world, there are no patterns to the occurrence of events. These patterns arise because of clausal relationships between events. The events described in a script form a giant casual chain. The beginning of the chain is the set of entry conditions which enable the first events of the script to occur. The end of the chain is the set of results which may enable later events to occur. The headers of a script can all serve as indicators that the script should be activated.

Once a script has been activated, there are a variety of ways in which it can be useful in interpreting a particular situation. A script has the ability to predict events that has not explicitly been observed. An important use of scripts is to provide a way of building a single coherent interpretation from a collection of observation. Scripts are less general structures than are frames and so are not suitable for representing all kinds of knowledge. Scripts are very useful for representing the specific kinds of knowledge for which they were designed.

A script has various components like:

- Entry condition: It must be true before the events described in the script can occur. E.g. in a restaurant script the entry condition must be the customer should be hungry and the customer has money.

- Tracks: It specifies particular position of the script e.g. In a supermarket script the tracks may be cloth gallery, cosmetics gallery etc.

- Result: It must be satisfied or true after the events described in the script have occurred. e.g. In a restaurant script the result must be true if the customer is pleased. The customer has less money.

- Probs: It describes the inactive or dead participants in the script e.g. In a supermarket script, the probes may be clothes, sticks, doors, tables, bills etc.

- Roles: It specifies the various stages of the script. E.g. In a restaurant script the scenes may be entering, ordering etc.

    Now let us look on a movie script description according to the above component.

    ○ Script name: Movie

        ▪ Track: CINEMA HALL.

        ▪ Roles: Customer(c), Ticket seller(TS), Ticket Checker(TC), Snacks.

        ▪ Sellers (SS).

        ▪ Probes: Ticket, snacks, chair, money, Ticket, chart.

        ▪ Entry condition: The customer has money.

    The customer has interest to watch movie.

- Scenes:

    ○ SCENE-1 (Entering into the cinema hall).

- CPTRANS C into the cinema hall.

- C ATTEND eyes towards the ticket counter C PTRANS C towards the ticket counters C ATTEND eyes to the ticket chart.

- C MBUILD to take which class ticket C MTRANS TS for ticket.

- C ATRANS money to TS.

- TS ATRANS ticket to C.

- SCENE-2 (Entering into the main ticket check gate):

  ○ C PTRANS C into the queue of the gate C ATRANS ticket to TC.

  ○ TC ATTEND eyes onto the ticket.

  ○ TC MBUILD to give permission to C for entering into the hall.

  ○ TC ATRANS ticket to C.

  ○ C PTRANS C into the picture hall.

- SCENE-3 (Entering into the picture hall):

  ○ CATTEND eyes into the chair.

  ○ TC SPEAK where to sit.

  ○ C PTRANS C towards the sitting position.

  ○ C ATTEND eyes onto the screen.

- SCENE-4 (Ordering snacks):

  ○ C MTRANS SS for snacks.

  ○ SS ATRANS snacks to C.

  ○ C ATRANS money to SS.

  ○ C INGEST snacks.

- SCENE-5 (Exit):

  ○ C ATTEND eyes onto the screen till the end of picture.

  ○ C MBUILD when to go out of the hall.

  ○ C PTRANS C out of the hall.

- Result:

  ○ The customer is happy.

- The customer has less money.

Example: Write a script of visiting a doctor in a hospital.

- **SCRIPT_NAME:** Visiting a doctor.

- **TRACKS:** Ent specialist.

- **ROLES:** Attendant (A), Nurse(N), Chemist (C), Gatekeeper(G), Counter clerk(CC), Receptionist(R), Patient(P), Ent specialist Doctor (D), Medicine Seller (M).

- **PROBES:** Money, Prescription, Medicine, Sitting chair, Doctor's table, Thermometer, Stetho scope, writing pad, pen, torch, stature.

- **ENTRY CONDITION:** The patient needs consultation. Doctor's visiting time on.

SCENES:

- **SCENE-1 (Entering into the hospital):**
  - PPTRANS P into hospital.
  - P   ATTEND eyes towards ENT department.
  - P PTRANS P into ENT department.
  - P PTRANS P towards the sitting chair.

- **SCENE-2 (Entering into the Doctor's Room):**
  - P PTRANS P into doctor's room.
  - P MTRANS P about the diseases.
  - P SPEAK D about the disease.
  - D MTRANS P for blood test, urine test.
  - D ATRANS prescription to P.
  - P PTRANS prescription to P.
  - P   PTRANS P for blood and urine test.

- **SCENE-3 (Entering into the Test Lab):**
  - P   PTRANS P into the test room.
  - P ATRANS blood sample at collection room.
  - P ATRANS urine sample at collection room.
  - P   ATRANS the examination reports.

- **SCENE-4 (Entering to the Doctor's room with Test reports):**

- ○ P ATRANS the report to D.
- ○ D ATTEND eyes into the report.
- ○ D MBUILD to give the medicines.
- ○ D SPEAK details about the medicine to P.
- ○ P ATRANS doctor's fee.
- ○ P PTRANS from doctor's room.
- • SCENE-5 (Entering towards medicine shop):
  - ○ P PTRANS P towards medicine counter.
  - ○ P ATRANS Prescription to M.
  - ○ M ATTEND eyes into the prescription.
  - ○ M MBUILD which medicine to give.
  - ○ M ATRANS medicines to P.
  - ○ P ATRANS money to M.
  - ○ P PTRANS P from the medicine shop.
- • RESULT:
  - ○ The patient has less money.
  - ○ Patient has prescription and medicine.

Techniques of Knowledge Representation

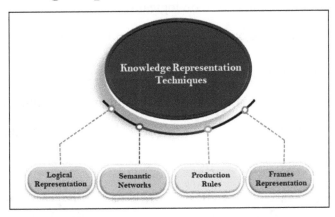

There are mainly four ways of knowledge representation which are given as follows:

- • Logical Representation,
- • Semantic Network Representation,

- Frame Representation,
- Production Rules.

Logical Representation

Logical representation is a language with some concrete rules which deals with propositions and has no ambiguity in representation. Logical representation means drawing a conclusion based on various conditions. This representation lays down some important communication rules. It consists of precisely defined syntax and semantics which supports the sound inference. Each sentence can be translated into logics using syntax and semantics.

Syntax

- Syntaxes are the rules which decide how we can construct legal sentences in the logic.
- It determines which symbol we can use in knowledge representation.
- How to write those symbols.

Semantics

- Semantics are the rules by which we can interpret the sentence in the logic.
- Semantic also involves assigning a meaning to each sentence.

Logical representation can be categorised into mainly two logics:
- Propositional Logics
- Predicate logics

Advantages of Logical Representation

- Logical representation enables us to do logical reasoning.
- Logical representation is the basis for the programming languages.

Disadvantages of Logical Representation

- Logical representations have some restrictions and are challenging to work with.
- Logical representation technique may not be very natural, and inference may not be so efficient.

Semantic Network Representation

Semantic networks are alternative of predicate logic for knowledge representation. In Semantic networks, we can represent our knowledge in the form of graphical networks. This network consists of nodes representing objects and arcs which describe the relationship between those objects. Semantic networks can categorize the object in different forms and can also link those objects. Semantic networks are easy to understand and can be easily extended.

This representation consists of mainly two types of relations:

- IS-A relation (Inheritance),
- Kind-of-relation.

Example: Following are some statements which we need to represent in the form of nodes and arcs.

Statements

- Jerry is a cat.
- Jerry is a mammal
- Jerry is owned by Priya.
- Jerry is brown colored.
- All Mammals are animal.

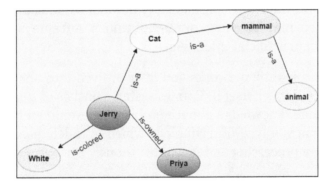

In the above diagram, we have represented the different type of knowledge in the form of nodes and arcs. Each object is connected with another object by some relation.

Drawbacks in Semantic Representation

- Semantic networks take more computational time at runtime as we need to traverse the complete network tree to answer some questions. It might be possible in the worst case scenario that after traversing the entire tree, we find that the solution does not exist in this network.

- Semantic networks try to model human-like memory (Which has 1015 neurons and links) to store the information, but in practice, it is not possible to build such a vast semantic network.

- These types of representations are inadequate as they do not have any equivalent quantifier, e.g., for all, for some, none, etc.

- Semantic networks do not have any standard definition for the link names.

- These networks are not intelligent and depend on the creator of the system.

Advantages of Semantic Network

- Semantic networks are a natural representation of knowledge.

- Semantic networks convey meaning in a transparent manner.

- These networks are simple and easily understandable.

Frame Representation

A frame is a record like structure which consists of a collection of attributes and its values to describe an entity in the world. Frames are the AI data structure which divides knowledge into substructures by representing stereotypes situations. It consists of a collection of slots and slot values. These slots may be of any type and sizes. Slots have names and values which are called facets.

Facets: The various aspects of a slot are known as Facets. Facets are features of frames which enable us to put constraints on the frames. Example: IF needed facts are called when data of any particular slot is needed. A frame may consist of any number of slots, and a slot may include any number of facets and facets may have any number of values. A frame is also known as slot-filter knowledge representation in artificial intelligence.

Frames are derived from semantic networks and later evolved into our modern-day classes and objects. A single frame is not much useful. Frames system consists of a collection of frames which are connected. In the frame, knowledge about an object or event can be stored together in the knowledge base. The frame is a type of technology which is widely used in various applications including Natural language processing and machine visions.

Example: Let's take an example of a frame for a book.

Slots	Filters
Title	Artificial Intelligence
Genre	Computer Science
Author	Peter Norvig
Edition	Third Edition
Year	1996
Page	1152

Example: Let's suppose we are taking an entity, Peter. Peter is an engineer as a profession, and his age is 25, he lives in city London, and the country is England. So following is the frame representation for this:

Slots	Filter
Name	Peter
Profession	Doctor
Age	25
Marital status	Single
Weight	78

Advantages of Frame Representation

- The frame knowledge representation makes the programming easier by grouping the related data.

- The frame representation is comparably flexible and used by many applications in AI.

- It is very easy to add slots for new attribute and relations.

- It is easy to include default data and to search for missing values.

- Frame representation is easy to understand and visualize.

Disadvantages of Frame Representation

- In frame system inference mechanism is not be easily processed.

- Inference mechanism cannot be smoothly preceded by frame representation.

- Frame representation has a much generalized approach.

Production Rules

Production rules system consist of (condition, action) pairs which mean, "If condition then action". It has mainly three parts:

- The set of production rules,

- Working Memory,

- The recognize-act-cycle.

In production rules agent checks for the condition and if the condition exists then production rule fires and corresponding action is carried out. The condition part of the rule determines which rule may be applied to a problem. And the action part carries out the associated problem-solving steps. This complete process is called a recognize-act cycle.

The working memory contains the description of the current state of problems-solving and rule can write knowledge to the working memory. This knowledge match and may fire other rules.

If there is a new situation (state) generates, then multiple production rules will be fired together, this is called conflict set. In this situation, the agent needs to select a rule from these sets, and it is called a conflict resolution.

Example:

- IF (at bus stop AND bus arrives) THEN action (get into the bus).

- IF (on the bus AND paid AND empty seat) THEN action (sit down).

- IF (on bus AND unpaid) THEN action (pay charges).

- IF (bus arrives at destination) THEN action (get down from the bus).

Advantages of Production rule

- The production rules are expressed in natural language.

- The production rules are highly modular, so we can easily remove, add or modify an individual rule.

Disadvantages of Production Rule

- Production rule system does not exhibit any learning capabilities, as it does not store the result of the problem for the future uses.

- During the execution of the program, many rules may be active hence rule-based production systems are inefficient.

Reasoning

The reasoning is the mental process of deriving logical conclusion and making predictions from available knowledge, facts, and beliefs. Or we can say, "Reasoning is a way to infer facts from existing data." It is a general process of thinking rationally, to find valid conclusions. In artificial intelligence, the reasoning is essential so that the machine can also think rationally as a human brain, and can perform like a human. Reasoning allows AI technologies to extract critical information from large sets of structured and unstructured data, perform clustering analysis, and use statistical inference in a way that starts to approach human cognition.

Types of Reasoning

Deductive Reasoning

Deductive reasoning is a logical process in which a conclusion is based on the concordance of multiple premises that are generally assumed to be true.

Deductive reasoning is sometimes referred to as top-down logic. Its counterpart, inductive reasoning, is sometimes referred to as bottom-up logic. Where deductive reasoning proceeds from general premises to a specific conclusion, inductive reasoning proceeds from specific premises to a general conclusion.

The Greek philosopher Aristotle, who is considered the father of deductive reasoning, wrote the following classic example:

- All men are mortal.

- Socrates is a man.

- Therefore, Socrates is mortal.

In Aristotle's example, sometimes referred to as a syllogism, the premises of the argument -- that all men are mortal and that Socrates is a man -- are self-evidently true. Because the premises establish that Socrates is an individual in a group whose members are all mortal, the inescapable conclusion is that Socrates must likewise be mortal.

3 Types of Deductive Reasoning

There are three common types of deductive reasoning:

Syllogism

One common type of deductive reasoning is known as a syllogism. Syllogisms almost always appear in the three-line form, with a common term that appears in both premises but not the conclusion. Here is an example:

- If a person is born in the 1970s, they're in Generation X.
- If a person is in Generation X, then they listened to music on a Walkman.
- Therefore if a person is born in the 1970s, then they listened to music on a Walkman.

Modus Ponens

Another type of deductive reasoning is known as modus ponens and it follows this pattern:

- If a person is born between 1981 and 1996, then they're a millennial.
- Miley was born in 1992.
- Therefore Miley is a millennial.

This type of reasoning is also known as "affirming the antecedent," because only the first premise is a conditional statement, and the second premise merely affirms that the first part of the previous statement (the antecedent) applies.

Modus Tollens

Yet another type of deductive reasoning is modus tollens, or "the law of contrapositive." It is the opposite of modus ponens because its second premise negates the second part (the consequent) of the previous conditional statement. For example:

- If a person is born between 1981 and 1996, then they're a millennial.
- Bruce is not a millennial.
- Therefore Bruce was not born between 1981 and 1996.

Deductive Reasoning Examples

Here are several examples to help you better understand deductive reasoning:

- My state requires all lawyers pass the bar to practice. If I do not pass the bar, then I will not be able to represent someone legally.

- My boss said the person with the highest sales would get a promotion at the end of the year. I generated the highest sales, so I am looking forward to a promotion.

- Our biggest sales come from executives who live in our company's home state. Based on this information, we have decided to allocate more of our marketing dollars to targeting executives in that state.

- One of our customers is unhappy with his experience. He does not like how long it takes for a return phone call. Therefore, if we provide a quicker response, he will be more satisfied.

- I must have 40 credits to graduate this spring. Because I only have 38 credits, I will not be graduating this spring.

- The career counseling center at my college is offering free resume reviews to students. I am a student and I plan on having my resume reviewed, so I will not have to pay anything for this service.

Each of these statements includes two accurate pieces of information and an assumption based on the first two pieces of information. So long as the first two pieces of information are correct, the assumption should also be accurate.

The Deductive Reasoning Process

Understanding the process of deductive reasoning can help you apply logic to solve challenges in your work.

Deductive thought uses only information assumed to be accurate. It does not include emotions, feelings, or assumptions without evidence because it's difficult to determine the accuracy of this information.

The process of deductive reasoning includes the following steps:

- Initial assumption: Deductive reasoning begins with an assumption. This assumption is usually a generalized statement that if something is true, then it must be true in all cases.

- Second premise: A second premise is made in relation to the first assumption. If the first statement is true, then the second related statement must also be true.

- Testing: Next, the deductive assumption is tested in a variety of scenarios.

- Conclusion: Based on the results of the test, the information is determined to be valid or invalid.

When to use Deductive Reasoning

There are many ways you can use deductive reasoning to make decisions in your professional life. Here are a few ways you can use this process to draw conclusions throughout your career:

Using Deductive Reasoning in the Workplace

Learning to apply existing deductive reasoning skills during the decision-making process will help you make better-informed choices in the workplace. You may use deductive reasoning when finding and acquiring a job, hiring employees, managing employees, working with customers, and making a variety of business or career decisions.

Deductive reasoning in the workplace requires the following skills:

- Problem-solving: Many roles require you to use problem-solving skills to overcome challenges and discover reliable resolutions. You can apply the deductive reasoning process to your problem-solving efforts by first identifying an accurate assumption you can use as a foundation for your solution. Deductive reasoning often leads to fewer errors because it reduces guesswork.

- Teamwork: Many organizations expect employees to work together in teams to achieve results. Teams are often composed of employees with varying work styles, which can hinder collaboration and reduce productivity. Using the process of deductive reasoning, you can identify where the problem lies and draw accurate conclusions and help team members align.

- Customer service: You can apply deductive reasoning skills to the customer service experience, too. Using this process, you can determine an appropriate solution to a customer's problem. By identifying what the customer is unhappy about and then connecting it to what you know about their experience, you can adequately address their concern and increase customer satisfaction.

Inductive Reasoning

Inductive reasoning is the use of evidence to propose a theory, or in other words, assuming a given outcome from past outcomes or other available data. Inductive reasoning is probabilistic or uncertain in the sense that it relies on the given data instead of other types of discovery.

In its various forms, inductive reasoning is the fundamental engine of machine learning systems. The typical machine learning system takes in data in the form of training sets, and uses that available data to produce probabilistic conclusions.

Inductive reasoning is often contrasted to deductive reasoning, which uses strong logical conditions to draw conclusions. Unlike deductive reasoning, inductive reasoning uses the evidence to postulate or theorize a conclusion, so it is not a "guaranteed reasoner." Apart from its widespread use in machine learning, inductive reasoning also plays a role in examining how neural networks mimic human cognitive ability and how the neurons or units of processing use probabilistic inputs to determine outcomes.

Types of inductive reasoning include simple induction, generalization, statistical syllogism and arguments related to contrasting analogies.

3 Ways Inductive Reasoning Is Used

Inductive reasoning is used in a number of different ways, each serving a different purpose:

- We use inductive reasoning in everyday life to build our understanding of the world.

- Inductive reasoning also underpins the scientific method: scientists gather data through observation and experiment, make hypotheses based on that data, and then test those theories further. That middle step—making hypotheses—is an inductive inference, and they wouldn't get very far without it.

- Finally, despite the potential for weak conclusions, an inductive argument is also the main type of reasoning in academic life.

6 Types of Inductive Reasoning

There are a few key types of inductive reasoning:

- Generalized: This is the simple example given above, with the white swans. It uses premises about a sample set to draw conclusions about a whole population.

- Statistical: This form uses statistics based on a large and random sample set, and its quantifiable nature makes the conclusions stronger. For example: "95% of the swans I've seen on my global travels are white, therefore 95% of the world's swans are white."

- Bayesian: This is a method of adapting statistical reasoning to take into account new or additional data. For instance, location data might allow a more precise estimate of the percentage of white swans.

- Analogical: This form notes that on the basis of shared properties between two groups, they are also likely to share some further property. For example: "Swans look like geese and geese lay eggs, therefore swans also lay eggs."

- Predictive: This type of reasoning draws a conclusion about the future based on a past sample. For instance: "There have always been swans on the lake in past summers, therefore there will be swans this summer."

- Causal inference: This type of reasoning includes a causal link between the premise and the conclusion. For instance: "There have always been swans on the lake in summer, therefore the start of summer will bring swans onto the lake."

Examples of Inductive Reasoning

In practice, inductive reasoning often appears invisible. You might not be aware that you're taking in information, recognizing a potential pattern, and then acting on your hypothesis. But, if you're a good problem solver, chances are that these examples will feel familiar:

- A teacher notices that his students learned more when hands-on activities were incorporated into lessons, and then decides to regularly include a hands-on component in his future lessons.

- An architect discerns a pattern of cost overages for plumbing materials in jobs and opts to increase the estimate for plumbing costs in subsequent proposals.

- A stockbroker observes that Intuit stock increased in value four years in a row during tax season and recommends clients buy it in March.

- A recruiter conducts a study of recent hires that have achieved success and stayed on with the organization. She finds that they graduated from three local colleges, so she decides to focus recruiting efforts on those schools.

- A salesperson presents testimonials of current customers to suggest to prospective clients that her products are high quality and worth the purchase.

- A defence attorney reviews the strategy employed by lawyers in similar cases and finds an approach that has consistently led to acquittals. She then applies this approach to her own case.

- A production manager examines cases of injuries on the line and discerns that many injuries occurred towards the end of long shifts. The manager proposes moving from 10-hour to 8-hour shifts based on this observation.

- A bartender becomes aware that customers give her higher tips when she shares personal information, so she intentionally starts to divulge personal information when it feels appropriate to do so.

- An activities leader at an assisted living facility notices that residents light up when young people visit. She decides to develop a volunteer initiative with a local high school, connecting students with residents who need cheering up.

- A market researcher designs a focus group to assess consumer responses to new packaging for a snack product. She discovers that participants repeatedly gravitate towards a label stating "15 grams of protein." The researcher recommends increasing the size and differentiating the color of that wording.

Abductive Reasoning

Abductive reasoning starts from a set of accepted facts and infers most likely, or best, explanations. The term "abduction" also sometimes only refers to the generation of hypotheses that explain observations or conclusions, but the former definition is more common both in philosophy and computing.

Aristotle discussed abductive reasoning (apagoge, Greek) in his Prior Analytics. Charles Peirce formulated abduction as a method of scientific research and introduced it into modern logic. The concept of abduction is applied beyond logic to the social sciences and the development of artificial intelligence.

Logic-based Abduction

In logic, an explanation is expressed by T, which represents a domain and a set of observations O. Abduction is the process of deriving a set of explanations of O according to T and picking out one of those explanations. For E to be an explanation of O according to T, it should satisfy two conditions:

- O follows from E and T;

- E is consistent with T.

In formal logic, O and E are assumed to be sets of literals. The two conditions for E being an explanation of O according to theory T are formalized as:

$$T \cup E \models O\ ;$$

$T \cup E$ is consistent.

Among the possible explanations E satisfying these two conditions, some other condition of minimality is usually imposed to avoid irrelevant facts (not contributing to the entailment of O) being included in the explanations. Abduction is then the process that picks out some member of E. Criteria for picking out a member representing "the best" explanations include the simplicity, the prior probability, or the explanatory power of the explanation.

A proof theoretical abduction method for first order classical logic based on sequent calculus and dual calculus, based on semantic tableaux (analytic tableaux) has been proposed. The methods are sound and complete, and they work for full first order logic without requiring any preliminary reduction of formulae into normal forms. These methods have also been extended to modal logic.

Abductive logic programming is a computational framework that extends normal logic programming with abduction. It separates the theory T into two components, one of which is a normal logic program, used to generate E by means of backward reasoning, the other of which is a set of integrity constraints, used to filter the set of candidate explanations.

Set-cover Abduction

A different formalization of abduction is based on inverting the function that calculates the visible effects of the hypotheses. Formally, one is given a set of hypotheses H and a set of manifestations M; they are related by the domain knowledge, represented by a function e that takes as an argument a set of hypotheses and gives as a result the corresponding set of manifestations. In other words, for every subset of the hypotheses $H' \subseteq H$, their effects are known to be $e(H')$.

Abduction is performed by finding a set $H' \subseteq H$ such that $M \subseteq e(H')$. In other words, abduction is performed by finding a set of hypotheses H' such that their effects $e(H')$ include all observations M.

A common assumption is that the effects of the hypotheses are independent, that is, for every $H' \subseteq H$, it holds that $e(H') = \bigcup_{h \in H'} e(\{h\})$. If this condition is met, abduction can be seen as a form of set covering.

Applications

Applications in artificial intelligence include fault diagnosis, belief revision, and automated planning. The most direct application of abduction is that of automatically detecting faults in systems. Given a theory relating faults with their effects and a set of observed effects, abduction can be used to derive sets of faults that are likely to be the cause of the problem.

Abduction can also be used to model automated planning. Given a logical theory relating action occurrences with their effects (for example, a formula of the event calculus), the problem of finding a plan for reaching a state can be modeled as the problem of abducting a set of literals implying that the final state is the goal state.

Belief revision, the process of adapting beliefs in view of new information, is another field in which abduction has been applied. The main problem of belief revision is that the new information may be inconsistent with the corpus of beliefs, while the result of the incorporation cannot be inconsistent. This process can be done by the use of abduction: Once an explanation for the observation has been found, integrating it does not generate inconsistency. This use of abduction is not straightforward, as adding propositional formulae to other propositional formulae can only make inconsistencies worse. Instead, abduction is done at the level of the ordering of preference of the possible worlds.

In the philosophy of science, abduction has been the key inference method to support scientific realism, and much of the debate about scientific realism is focused on whether abduction is an acceptable method of inference.

In historical linguistics, abduction during language acquisition is often taken to be an essential part of processes of language change such as reanalysis and analogy.

Abductive Validation

Abductive validation is the process of validating a given hypothesis through abductive reasoning. Under this principle, an explanation is valid if it is the best possible explanation of a set of known data. The best possible explanation is often defined in terms of simplicity and elegance (such as Occam's razor). Abductive validation is common practice in hypothesis formation in science.

After obtaining results from an inference procedure, we may be left with multiple assumptions, some of which may be contradictory. Abductive validation is a method for identifying the assumptions that will lead to a goal.

Commonsense Reasoning

Commonsense reasoning is one of the branches of artificial intelligence (AI) that is concerned with simulating the human ability to make presumptions about the type and essence of ordinary situations they encounter every day. These assumptions include judgments about the physical properties, purpose, intentions and behavior of people and objects, as well as possible outcomes of their actions and interactions. A device that exhibits commonsense reasoning will be capable of predicting results and drawing conclusions that are similar to humans' folk psychology (humans' innate ability to reason about people's behavior and intentions) and naive physics (humans' natural understanding of the physical world).

Commonsense Knowledge

In Artificial intelligence, commonsense knowledge is the set of background information that an individual is intended to know or assume and the ability to use it when appropriate. It is a shared knowledge (between everybody or people in a particular culture or age group only). The way to obtain commonsense is by learning it or experiencing it. In communication, it is what people don't have to say because the interlocutor is expected to know or make a presumption about.

Commonsense Knowledge Problem

The commonsense knowledge problem is a current project in the sphere of artificial intelligence to create a database that contains the general knowledge most individuals are expected to have, represented in an accessible way to artificial intelligence programs that use natural language. Due to the broad scope of the commonsense knowledge this issue is considered to be among the most difficult ones in the AI research sphere. In order for any task to be done as a human mind would manage it, the machine is required to appear as intelligent as a human being. Such tasks include object recognition, machine translation and text mining. To perform them, the machine has to be aware of the same concepts that an individual, who possess commonsense knowledge, recognizes.

Commonsense in Intelligent Tasks

In 1961, Bar Hillel first discussed the need and significance of practical knowledge for natural language processing in the context of machine translation. Some ambiguities are resolved by using simple and easy to acquire rules. Others require a broad acknowledgement of the surrounding world, thus they require more commonsense knowledge. For instance when a machine is used to translate a text, problems of ambiguity arise, which could be easily resolved by attaining a concrete and true understanding of the context. Online translators often resolve ambiguities using analogous or similar words. For example, in translating the sentences "The electrician is working" and "The telephone is working" into German, the machine translates correctly "working" in the means of "laboring" in the first one and as "functioning properly" in the second one. The machine has seen and read in the body of texts that the German words for "laboring" and "electrician" are frequently used in a combination and are found close together. The same applies for "telephone" and "function properly". However, the statistical proxy which works in simple cases often fails in complex ones. Existing computer programs carry out simple language tasks by manipulating short phrases or separate words, but they don't attempt any deeper understanding and focus on short-term results.

Computer Vision

Issues of this kind arise in computer vision. For instance when looking at the photograph of the bathroom some of the items that are small and only partly seen, such as the towels or the body lotions, are recognizable due to the surrounding objects (toilet, wash basin, bathtub), which suggest the purpose of the room. In an isolated image they would be difficult to identify. Movies prove to be even more difficult tasks. Some movies contain scenes and moments that cannot be understood by simply matching memorized templates to images. For instance, to understand the context of the movie, the viewer is required to make inferences about characters' intentions and make presumptions depending on their behavior. In the contemporary state of the art, it is impossible to build and manage a program that will perform such tasks as reasoning, i.e. predicting characters' actions. The most that can be done is to identify basic actions and track characters.

Robotic Manipulation

The need and importance of commonsense reasoning in autonomous robots that work in a real-life uncontrolled environment is evident. For instance, if a robot is programmed to perform the tasks of a waiter on a cocktail party, and it sees that the glass he had picked up is broken, the waiter-robot should not pour liquid into the glass, but instead pick up another one. Such tasks seem obvious when an individual possess simple commonsense reasoning, but to ensure that a robot will avoid such mistakes is challenging.

Successes in Automated Commonsense Reasoning

Significant progress in the field of the automated commonsense reasoning is made in the areas of the taxonomic reasoning, actions and change reasoning, reasoning about time. Each of these spheres has a well-acknowledged theory for wide range of commonsense inferences.

Taxonomic Reasoning

Taxonomy is the collection of individuals and categories and their relations. Taxonomies are often referred to as semantic networks. Three basic relations are demonstrated:

- An individual is an instance of a category. For example, the individual Tweety is an instance of the category robin.

- One category is a subset of another. For instance robin is a subset of bird.

- Two categories are disjoint. For instance robin is disjoint from penguin.

Transitivity is one type of inference in taxonomy. Since Tweety is an instance of robin and robin is a subset of bird, it follows that Tweety is an instance of bird. Inheritance is another type of inference. Since Tweety is an instance of robin, which is a subset of bird and bird is marked with property canfly, it follows that Tweety and robin have property canfly. When an individual taxonomizes more abstract categories, outlining and delimiting specific categories becomes more problematic. Simple taxonomic structures are frequently used in AI programs. For instance, WordNet is a resource including a taxonomy, whose elements are meanings of English words. Web mining systems used to collect commonsense knowledge from Web documents focus on taxonomic relations and specifically in gathering taxonomic relations.

Action and Change

The theory of action, events and change is another range of the commonsense reasoning. There are established reasoning methods for domains that satisfy the constraints listed below:

- Events are atomic, meaning one event occurs at a time and the reasoner needs to consider the state and condition of the world at the start and at the finale of the specific event, but not during the states, while there is still an evidence of on-going changes (progress).

- Every single change is a result of some event.

- Events are deterministic, meaning the world's state at the end of the event is defined by the world's state at the beginning and the specification of the event.

- There is a single actor and all events are his actions.

- The relevant state of the world at the beginning is either known or can be calculated.

Temporal Reasoning

Temporal reasoning is the ability to make presumptions about humans' knowledge of times, durations and time intervals. For example, if an individual knows that Mozart was born after Hadyn and died earlier than him, they can use their temporal reasoning knowledge to deduce that Mozart had died younger than Hadyn. The inferences involved reduce themselves to solving systems of linear inequalities. To integrate that kind of reasoning with concrete purposes, such as natural language interpretation, is more challenging, because natural language expressions have context dependent interpretation. Simple tasks such as assigning timestamps to procedures cannot be done with total accuracy.

Qualitative Reasoning

Qualitative reasoning is the form of commonsense reasoning analyzed with certain success. It is concerned with the direction of change in interrelated quantities. For instance, if the price of a stock goes up, the amount of stocks that are going to be sold will go down. If some ecosystem contains wolves and lambs and the number of wolves decreases, the death rate of the lambs will go down as well. This theory was firstly formulated by Johan de Kleer, who analyzed an object moving on a roller coaster. The theory of qualitative reasoning is applied in many spheres such as physics, biology, engineering, ecology, etc. It serves as the basis for many practical programs, analogical mapping, text understanding.

Challenges in Automating Commonsense Reasoning

As of 2014, there are some commercial systems trying to make the use of commonsense reasoning significant. However, they use statistical information as a proxy for commonsense knowledge, where reasoning is absent. Current programs manipulate individual words, but they don't attempt or offer further understanding. Five major obstacles interfere with the producing of a satisfactory "commonsense reasoner":

- First, some of the domains that are involved in commonsense reasoning are only partly understood. Individuals are far from a comprehensive understanding of domains as communication and knowledge, interpersonal interactions or physical processes.

- Second, situations that seem easily predicted or assumed about could have logical complexity, which humans' commonsense knowledge does not cover. Some aspects of similar situations are studied and are well understood, but there are many relations that are unknown, even in principle and how they could be represented in a form that is usable by computers.

- Third, commonsense reasoning involves plausible reasoning. It requires coming to a reasonable conclusion given what is already known. Plausible reasoning has been studied for many years and there are a lot of theories developed that include probabilistic reasoning and non-monotonic logic. It takes different forms that include using unreliable data and rules, whose conclusions are not certain sometimes.

- Fourth, there are many domains, in which a small number of examples are extremely frequent, whereas there is a vast number of highly infrequent examples.

- Fifth, when formulating pressumptions it is challenging to discern and determine the level of abstraction.

Compared with humans, all existing computer programs perform extremely poorly on modern "commonsense reasoning" benchmark tests such as the Winograd Schema Challenge. The problem of attaining human-level competency at "commonsense knowledge" tasks is considered to probably be "AI complete" (that is, solving it would require the ability to synthesize a human-level intelligence).

Approaches and Techniques

Commonsense's reasoning study is divided into knowledge-based approaches and approaches that are based on machine learning over and using large data corpora with limited interactions between these two types of approaches. There are also crowdsourcing approaches, attempting to construct a knowledge basis by linking the collective knowledge and the input of non-expert people. Knowledge-based approaches can be separated into approaches based on mathematical logic.

In knowledge-based approaches, the experts are analyzing the characteristics of the inferences that are required to do reasoning in a specific area or for a certain task. The knowledge-based approaches consist of mathematically grounded approaches, informal knowledge-based approaches and large-scale approaches. The mathematically grounded approaches are purely theoretical and the result is a printed paper instead of a program. The work is limited to the range of the domains and the reasoning techniques that are being reflected on. In informal knowledge-based approaches, theories of reasoning are based on anecdotal data and intuition that are results from empirical behavioral psychology. Informal approaches are common in computer programming. Two other popular techniques for extracting commonsense knowledge from Web documents involve Web mining and Crowd sourcing.

Monotonic Reasoning

In monotonic reasoning, once the conclusion is taken, then it will remain the same even if we add some other information to existing information in our knowledge base. In monotonic reasoning, adding knowledge does not decrease the set of prepositions that can be derived.

To solve monotonic problems, we can derive the valid conclusion from the available facts only, and it will not be affected by new facts. Monotonic reasoning is not useful for the real-time systems, as in real time, facts get changed, so we cannot use monotonic reasoning. Monotonic reasoning is used in conventional reasoning systems, and a logic-based system is monotonic.

Any theorem proving is an example of monotonic reasoning.

Example: Earth revolves around the Sun.

It is a true fact, and it cannot be changed even if we add another sentence in knowledge base like, "The moon revolves around the earth" Or "Earth is not round," etc.

Advantages of Monotonic Reasoning

- In monotonic reasoning, each old proof will always remain valid.

- If we deduce some facts from available facts, then it will remain valid for always.

Disadvantages of Monotonic Reasoning

- We cannot represent the real world scenarios using Monotonic reasoning.

- Hypothesis knowledge cannot be expressed with monotonic reasoning, which means facts should be true.

- Since we can only derive conclusions from the old proofs, so new knowledge from the real world cannot be added.

Non-monotonic Reasoning

In Non-monotonic reasoning, some conclusions may be invalidated if we add some more information to our knowledge base.

Logic will be said as non-monotonic if some conclusions can be invalidated by adding more knowledge into our knowledge base. Non-monotonic reasoning deals with incomplete and uncertain models.

"Human perceptions for various things in daily life," is a general example of non-monotonic reasoning.

Example: Let suppose the knowledge base contains the following knowledge:

- Birds can fly.

- Penguins cannot fly.

- Pitty is a bird.

So from the above sentences, we can conclude that Pitty can fly.

However, if we add one another sentence into knowledge base "Pitty is a penguin", which concludes "Pitty cannot fly", so it invalidates the above conclusion.

Advantages of Non-monotonic Reasoning

- For real-world systems such as Robot navigation, we can use non-monotonic reasoning.

- In Non-monotonic reasoning, we can choose probabilistic facts or can make assumptions.

Disadvantages of Non-monotonic Reasoning

- In non-monotonic reasoning, the old facts may be invalidated by adding new sentences.

- It cannot be used for theorem proving.

Probabilistic Reasoning in Artificial Intelligence

Uncertainty

Till now, we have learned knowledge representation using first-order logic and propositional logic with certainty, which means we were sure about the predicates. With this knowledge representation, we might write A→B, which means if A is true then B is true, but consider a situation where we are not sure about whether A is true or not then we cannot express this statement, this situation is called uncertainty.

So to represent uncertain knowledge, where we are not sure about the predicates, we need uncertain reasoning or probabilistic reasoning.

Causes of Uncertainty

Following are some leading causes of uncertainty to occur in the real world:

- Information occurred from unreliable sources,

- Experimental Errors,

- Equipment fault,

- Temperature variation,

- Climate change.

Probabilistic Reasoning

Probabilistic reasoning is a way of knowledge representation where we apply the concept of probability to indicate the uncertainty in knowledge. In probabilistic reasoning, we combine probability theory with logic to handle the uncertainty.

We use probability in probabilistic reasoning because it provides a way to handle the uncertainty that is the result of someone's laziness and ignorance.

In the real world, there are lots of scenarios, where the certainty of something is not confirmed, such as "It will rain today," "behavior of someone for some situations," "A match between two teams or two players." These are probable sentences for which we can assume that it will happen but not sure about it, so here we use probabilistic reasoning.

Need of Probabilistic Reasoning in AI

- When there are unpredictable outcomes.

- When specifications or possibilities of predicates becomes too large to handle.

- When an unknown error occurs during an experiment.

In probabilistic reasoning, there are two ways to solve problems with uncertain knowledge:

- Bayes' rule,

- Bayesian Statistics.

As probabilistic reasoning uses probability and related terms, so before understanding probabilistic reasoning, let's understand some common terms:

Probability: Probability can be defined as a chance that an uncertain event will occur. It is the numerical measure of the likelihood that an event will occur. The value of probability always remains between 0 and 1 that represent ideal uncertainties.

$0 \leq P(A) \leq 1$, where $P(A)$ is the probability of an event A.

$P(A) = 0$, indicates total uncertainty in an event A.

$P(A) = 1$, indicates total certainty in an event A.

We can find the probability of an uncertain event by using the below formula.

$$\text{Probability of occurrence} = \frac{\text{Number of desired outcomes}}{\text{Total number of outcomes}}$$

- $P(\neg A)$ = probability of a not happening event.

- $P(\neg A) + P(A) = 1$.

Event: Each possible outcome of a variable is called an event.

Sample space: The collection of all possible events is called sample space.

Random variables: Random variables are used to represent the events and objects in the real world.

Prior probability: The prior probability of an event is probability computed before observing new information.

Posterior Probability: The probability that is calculated after all evidence or information has taken into account. It is a combination of prior probability and new information.

Conditional Probability

Conditional probability is a probability of occurring an event when another event has already happened.

Let's suppose, we want to calculate the event A when event B has already occurred, "the probability of A under the conditions of B", it can be written as:

$$P(A|B) = \frac{P(A \wedge B)}{P(B)}$$

Where $P(A \wedge B)$ = Joint probability of a and B.

P(B) = Marginal probability of B.

If the probability of A is given and we need to find the probability of B, then it will be given as:

$$P(B|A) = \frac{P(A \wedge B)}{P(A)}$$

It can be explained by using the below Venn diagram, where B is occurred event, so sample space will be reduced to set B, and now we can only calculate event A when event B is already occurred by dividing the probability of P(A∧B) by P(B).

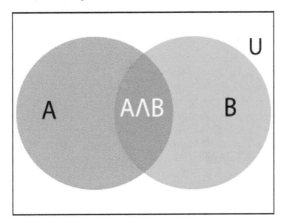

Example: In a class, there are 70% of the students who like English and 40% of the students who likes English and mathematics, and then what is the percent of students those who like English also like mathematics?

Solution: Let, A is an event that a student likes Mathematics.

B is an event that a student likes English.

$$P(A|B) = \frac{P(A \wedge B)}{P(B)} = \frac{0.4}{0.7} = 57\%$$

Hence, 57% are the students who like English also like Mathematics.

Intelligent Agents

Artificial intelligence is defined as a study of rational agents. A rational agent could be anything which makes decisions, as a person, firm, machine, or software. It carries out an action with the best outcome after considering past and current percepts(agent's perceptual inputs at a given instance). An AI system is composed of an agent and its environment. The agents act in their environment. The environment may contain other agents. An agent is anything that can be viewed as:

- Perceiving its environment through sensors and

- Acting upon that environment through actuators.

Every agent can perceive its own actions (but not always the effects).

To understand the structure of Intelligent Agents, we should be familiar with Architecture and Agent Program. Architecture is the machinery that the agent executes on. It is a device with sensors and actuators, for example: a robotic car, a camera, a PC. Agent program is an implementation of an agent function. An agent function is a map from the percept sequence(history of all that an agent has perceived till date) to an action.

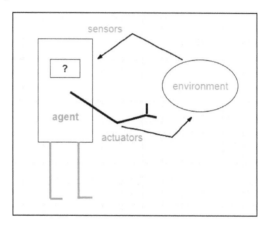

Examples of Agent

- A software agent has Keystrokes, file contents, received network packages which act as sensors and displays on the screen, files, sent network packets acting as actuators.

- A Human agent has eyes, ears, and other organs which act as sensors and hands, legs, mouth, and other body parts acting as actuators.

- A Robotic agent has Cameras and infrared range finders which act as sensors and various motors acting as actuators.

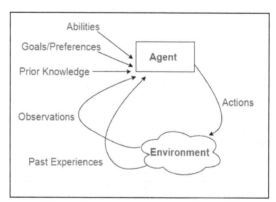

Types of AI Agents

Agents can be grouped into five classes based on their degree of perceived intelligence and capability. All these agents can improve their performance and generate better action over the time. These are given below:

Simple Reflex Agent

A simple reflex agent is the most basic of the intelligent agents out there. It performs actions based on a current situation. When something happens in the environment of a simple reflex agent, the agent quickly scans its knowledge base for how to respond to the situation at-hand based on pre-determined rules.

It would be like a home thermostat recognizing that if the temperature increases to 75 degrees in the house, the thermostat is prompted to kick on. It doesn't need to know what happened with the temperature yesterday or what might happen tomorrow. Instead, it operates based on the idea that if _____ happens, _____ is the response.

Simple reflex agents are just that - simple. They cannot compute complex equations or solve complicated problems. They work only in environments that are fully-observable in the current percept, ignoring any percept history. If you have a smart light bulb, for example, set to turn on at 6 p.m. every night, the light bulb will not recognize how the days are longer in summer and the lamp is not needed until much later. It will continue to turn the lamp on at 6 p.m. because that is the rule it follows.

Model-based Reflex Agent

Model-based reflex agents are made to deal with partial accessibility; they do this by keeping track of the part of the world it can see now. It does this by keeping an internal state that depends on what it has seen before so it holds information on the unobserved aspects of the current state.

This time out mars Lander after picking up its first sample, it stores this in the internal state of the world around it so when it come across the second same sample it passes it by and saves space for other samples.

But in order to update this internal store we need two things:

- Information on how the world evolves on its own.
  E.g. If our mars Lander picked up the rock next to the one it was going to the world around it would carry on as normal.

- How the world is affected by the agents actions.
  E.g. If our mars Lander took a sample under a precarious ledge it could displace a rock and it could be crushed.

We can predict how the world will react with facts like if you remove a supporting rock under a ledge the ledge will fall, such facts are called models, hence the name model-based agent.

Function REFLEX-AGENT-WITH-STATE (percept) return action

Static: state, a description of the current world state

rules, a set of condition-action rules

state ← UPDATE-STATE (state, percept)

rule ← RULE-MATCH (state, rules)

action ← RULE-ACTION [rule]

state ← UPDATE-STATE (state, action)

return action

Above is a written function showing the steps a model based reflex agent goes through.

In the update state section the parts of the world that the agent cannot see it put through the natural evolution algorithm, the parts that the agent can see are changed to the expected state of the world after the agents actions.

Goal-based Agents

A goal-based agent has an agenda, you might say. It operates based on a goal in front of it and makes decisions based on how best to reach that goal. Unlike a simple reflex agent that makes decisions based solely on the current environment, a goal-based agent is capable of thinking beyond the present moment to decide the best actions to take in order to achieve its goal. In this regard, a goal-based agent operates as a search and planning function, meaning it targets the goal ahead and finds the right action in order to reach it. This helps a goal-based agent to be proactive rather than simply reactive in its decision-making.

You may take a goal-based approach to tasks at work. For example, you might set a goal for yourself to become a more efficient typist, which will help you in completing assignments more quickly. A step toward that goal, then, might be to enroll in a typing course or to devote 15 minutes a day to practice in order to increase your word count per minute. Your decisions are flexible, a hallmark of goal-based agents, but the focus is always on achieving goal ahead.

Utility-based Agents

A utility-based agent is an agent that acts based not only on what the goal is, but the best way to reach that goal. In short, it is the usefulness or utility of the agent that makes itself distinct from its counterparts.

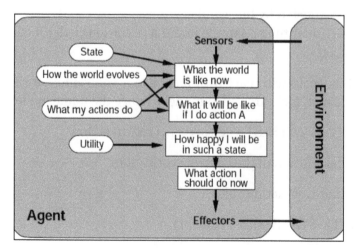

Just having goals isn't good enough because often we may have several actions which all satisfy our goal so we need some way of working out the most efficient one. A utility function maps each state after each action to a real number representing how efficiently each action achieves the goal. This is useful when we either have many actions all solving the same goal or when we have many goals that can be satisfied and we need to choose an action to perform.

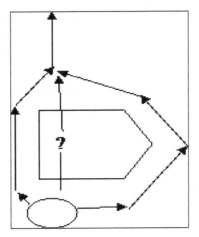

For example let's show our mars Lander on the surface of mars with an obstacle in its way. In a goal based agent it is uncertain which path will be taken by the agent and some are clearly not as efficient as others but in a utility based agent the best path will have the best output from the utility function and that path will be chosen.

Learning Agent

A learning agent is a tool in AI that is capable of learning from its experiences. It starts with some basic knowledge and is then able to act and adapt autonomously, through learning, to improve its own performance. Unlike intelligent agents that act on information provided by a programmer, learning agents are able to perform tasks, analyze performance, and look for new ways to improve on those tasks - all on their own.

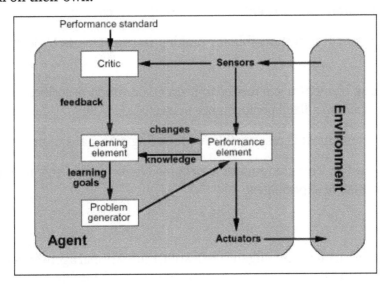

When we expand our environments we get a larger and larger amount of tasks, eventually we are going to have a very large number of actions to pre-define. Another way of going about creating an agent is to get it to learn new actions as it goes about its business, this still requires some initial knowledge but cuts down on the programming greatly. This will allow the agent to work in environments that are unknown.

A learning agent can be split into the 4 parts shown in the diagram.

The learning element is responsible for improvements this can make a change to any of the knowledge components in the agents. One way of learning is to observe pairs of successive states in the percept sequence; from this the agent can learn how the world evolves. For utility based agents an external performance standard is needed to tell the critic if the agent's action has a good or a bad effect on the world.

The performance element is responsible for selecting external actions.

The learning agent gains feedback from the critic on how well the agent is doing and determines how the performance element should be modified if at all to improve the agent. For example when you were in school you would do a test and it would be marked the test is the critic. The teacher would mark the test and see what could be improved and instructs you how to do better next time, the teacher is the learning element and you are the performance element.

The last component is the problem generator, the performance generator only suggests actions that it can already do so we need a way of getting the agent to experience new situations, and this is what the performance generator is for. This way the agent keeps on learning.

For example coming back to the school analogy, in science with your current knowledge at that time you would not have thought of placing a mass on a spring but the teacher suggested an experiment and you did it and this taught you more and added to knowledge base.

Learning Agent Components

A learning agent has mainly four conceptual components, which are:

- Learning element: It is responsible for making improvements by learning from the environment.

- Critic: Learning element takes feedback from critic which describes how well the agent is doing with respect to a fixed performance standard.

- Performance element: It is responsible for selecting external action.

- Problem Generator: This component is responsible for suggesting actions that will lead to new and informative experiences.

Rational Agents

In machine learning and artificial intelligence research, the "rational agent" is a concept that guides the use of game theory and decision theory in applying artificial intelligence to various real-world scenarios. The rational agent is a theoretical entity based on a realistic model that has preferences for advantageous outcomes, and will seek to achieve them in a learning scenario.

One of the best ways to understand rational actors is to take an example of some type of commercial artificial intelligence or machine learning project. Suppose a business wants to understand how people will use a complex navigational space like a drive-through with four lanes, or a complex restaurant layout with multiple tables and chairs. The engineers and data scientists will construct profiles and properties for the rational actors – which are modeled on real-life customers. They will then run the machine learning programs with these rational actors in mind and look at the outputs.

Rational actors can be applied in all sorts of ways to artificial intelligence projects. They help people to understand how theoretical humans might use technologies, and how the technologies can learn about human behavior to help other humans make decisions.

References

- Knowledge-representation-in-ai: javatpoint.com, Retrieved 25 February, 2019

- Types-of-Knowledge-Representation-8892: brainkart.com, Retrieved 18 June, 2019

- Ai-techniques-of-knowledge-representation: javatpoint.com, Retrieved 29 July, 2019

- What-is-deductive-reasoning-what-is-modus-ponens: masterclass.com, Retrieved 25 January, 2019

- Deductive-reasoning, career-development: indeed.com, Retrieved 20 April, 2019

- What-is-inductive-reasoning#what-is-an-example-of-inductive-reasoning: masterclass.com, Retrieved 05 May, 2019

- Abductive-reasoning: newworldencyclopedia.org,

- Rational-agent- 33315: techopedia.com, Retrieved 25 June, 2019

Problem Solving and Search Algorithms

There are many algorithms which are used in artificial intelligence in order to solve complex problems such as search algorithm. An algorithm which helps in solving search problems is referred to as a search algorithm. All the diverse principles of problem solving and search algorithms have been carefully analyzed in this chapter.

Problem Solving

In general, Problem Solving refers to as finding information one needs. Searching is the most commonly used technique of problem solving in artificial intelligence. The searching algorithm helps us to search for solution of particular problem.

The reflex agents are known as the simplest agents because they directly map states into actions. Unfortunately, these agents fail to operate in an environment where the mapping is too large to store and learn. Goal-based agent, on the other hand, considers future actions and the desired outcomes.

Problem-solving Agent

The problem-solving agent perfoms precisely by defining problems and its several solutions. Therefore, a problem-solving agent is a goal-driven agent and focuses on satisfying the goal.

Steps Performed By Problem-solving Agent

- Goal Formulation: It is the first and simplest step in problem-solving. It organizes the steps/sequence required to formulate one goal out of multiple goals as well as actions to achieve that goal. Goal formulation is based on the current situation and the agent's performance measure.

- Problem Formulation: It is the most important step of problem-solving which decides what actions should be taken to achieve the formulated goal. There are following five components involved in problem formulation:

  ○ Initial State: It is the starting state or initial step of the agent towards its goal.

  ○ Actions: It is the description of the possible actions available to the agent.

  ○ Transition Model: It describes what each action does.

  ○ Goal Test: It determines if the given state is a goal state.

○ Path cost: It assigns a numeric cost to each path that follows the goal. The problem-solving agent selects a cost function, which reflects its performance measure. Remember, an optimal solution has the lowest path cost among all the solutions.

Initial state, actions, and transition model together define the state-space of the problem implicitly. State-space of a problem is a set of all states which can be reached from the initial state followed by any sequence of actions. The state-space forms a directed map or graph where nodes are the states, links between the nodes are actions, and the path is a sequence of states connected by the sequence of actions.

- Search: It identifies all the best possible sequence of actions to reach the goal state from the current state. It takes a problem as an input and returns solution as its output.

- Solution: It finds the best algorithm out of various algorithms, which may be proven as the best optimal solution.

- Execution: It executes the best optimal solution from the searching algorithms to reach the goal state from the current state.

Example Problems

Basically, there are two types of problem approaches:

- Toy Problem: It is a concise and exact description of the problem which is used by the researchers to compare the performance of algorithms.

- Real-world Problem: It is real-world based problems which require solutions. Unlike a toy problem, it does not depend on descriptions, but we can have a general formulation of the problem.

Some Toy Problems

- 8 Puzzle Problem: Here, we have a 3×3 matrix with movable tiles numbered from 1 to 8 with a blank space. The tile adjacent to the blank space can slide into that space. The objective is to reach a specified goal state similar to the goal state, as shown in the below figure.

- In the figure, our task is to convert the current state into goal state by sliding digits into the blank space.

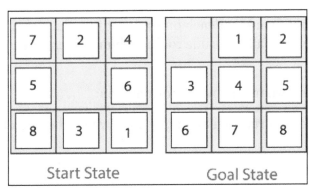

Start State   Goal State

In the above figure, our task is to convert the current(Start) state into goal state by sliding digits into the blank space.

The problem formulation is as follows:

- States: It describes the location of each numbered tiles and the blank tile.

- Initial State: We can start from any state as the initial state.

- Actions: Here, actions of the blank space is defined, i.e., either left, right, up or down

- Transition Model: It returns the resulting state as per the given state and actions.

- Goal test: It identifies whether we have reached the correct goal-state.

- Path cost: The path cost is the number of steps in the path where the cost of each step is 1.

The 8-puzzle problem is a type of sliding-block problem which is used for testing new search algorithms in artificial intelligence. The aim of this problem is to place eight queens on a chessboard in an order where no queen may attack another. A queen can attack other queens either diagonally or in same row and column.

From the following figure, we can understand the problem as well as its correct solution.

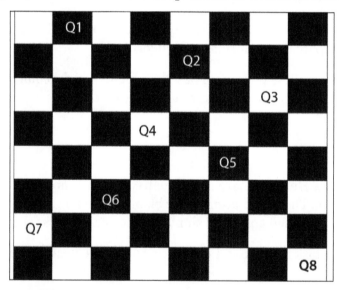

It is noticed from the above figure that each queen is set into the chessboard in a position where no other queen is placed diagonally, in same row or column. Therefore, it is one right approach to the 8-queens problem.

For this problem, there are two main kinds of formulation:

Incremental formulation: It starts from an empty state where the operator augments a queen at each step.

Following steps are involved in this formulation:

- States: Arrangement of any 0 to 8 queens on the chessboard.

- Initial State: An empty chessboard.

- Actions: Add a queen to any empty box.

- Transition model: Returns the chessboard with the queen added in a box.

- Goal test: Checks whether 8-queens are placed on the chessboard without any attack.

- Path cost: There is no need for path cost because only final states are counted.

In this formulation, there is approximately 1.8×10^{14} possible sequence to investigate.

- Complete-state formulation: It starts with all the 8-queens on the chessboard and moves them around, saving from the attacks.

Following steps are involved in this formulation:

- States: Arrangement of all the 8 queens one per column with no queen attacking the other queen.

- Actions: Move the queen at the location where it is safe from the attacks.

This formulation is better than the incremental formulation as it reduces the state space from 1.8×10^{14} to 2057, and it is easy to find the solutions.

Some Real-world Problems

- Traveling salesperson problem (TSP): It is a touring problem where the salesman can visit each city only once. The objective is to find the shortest tour and sell-out the stuff in each city.

- VLSI Layout problem: In this problem, millions of components and connections are positioned on a chip in order to minimize the area, circuit-delays, stray-capacitances, and maximizing the manufacturing yield.

The layout problem is split into two parts:

- Cell layout: Here, the primitive components of the circuit are grouped into cells, each performing its specific function. Each cell has a fixed shape and size. The task is to place the cells on the chip without overlapping each other.

- Channel routing: It finds a specific route for each wire through the gaps between the cells.

- Protein Design: The objective is to find a sequence of amino acids which will fold into 3D protein having a property to cure some disease.

Searching for Solutions

We have seen many problems. Now, there is a need to search for solutions to solve them.

For solving different kinds of problem, an agent makes use of different strategies to reach the goal by searching the best possible algorithms. This process of searching is known as search strategy.

Measuring Problem-solving Performance

Before discussing different search strategies, the performance measure of an algorithm should be measured. Consequently, there are four ways to measure the performance of an algorithm:

- Completeness: It measures if the algorithm guarantees to find a solution (if any solution exist).

- Optimality: It measures if the strategy searches for an optimal solution.

- Time Complexity: The time taken by the algorithm to find a solution.

- Space Complexity: Amount of memory required to perform a search.

The complexity of an algorithm depends on branching factor or maximum number of successors, depth of the shallowest goal node (i.e., number of steps from root to the path) and the maximum length of any path in a state space.

Search Strategies

There are two types of strategies that describe a solution for a given problem:

Uninformed Search (Blind Search)

This type of search strategy does not have any additional information about the states except the information provided in the problem definition. They can only generate the successors and distinguish a goal state from a non-goal state. This type of search does not maintain any internal state, that's why it is also known as Blind search.

There are following types of uninformed searches:

- Breadth-first search,

- Uniform cost search,

- Depth-first search,

- Depth-limited search,

- Iterative deepening search,

- Bidirectional search.

Informed Search (Heuristic Search)

This type of search strategy contains some additional information about the states beyond the problem definition. This search uses problem-specific knowledge to find more efficient solutions. This search maintains some sort of internal states via heuristic functions (which provides hints), so it is also called heuristic search.

There are following types of informed searches:

- Best first search (Greedy search),
- A* search.

Search Algorithm

Search algorithms are one of the most important areas of Artificial Intelligence. A search algorithm is the step-by-step procedure used to locate specific data among a collection of data. It is considered a fundamental procedure in computing. In computer science, when searching for data, the difference between a fast application and a slower one often lies in the use of the proper search algorithm.

All search algorithms make use of a search key in order to proceed with the procedure. Search algorithms are expected to return a success or a failure status, usually denoted by Boolean true/false. Different search algorithms are available, and the performance and efficiency of the same depend on the data and on the manner in which they are used.

A linear search algorithm is considered the most basic of all search algorithms. The best perhaps is binary search. There are other search algorithms such as the depth-first search algorithm, breadth-first algorithm, etc. The efficiency of a search algorithm is measured by the number of times a comparison of the search key is done in the worst case. The notation used in search algorithms is $O(n)$, where n is the number of comparisons done. It gives the idea of the asymptotic upper bound of execution time required for the algorithm with respect to a given condition.

Search cases in search algorithms can be categorized as best case, average case and worst case. In some algorithms, all the three cases might be asymptotically the same, whereas in some others there could be a large difference. The average behavior of the search algorithm helps in determining the usefulness of the algorithm.

Search Algorithm Terminologies

- Search: Searching is a step by step procedure to solve a search-problem in a given search space. A search problem can have three main factors:
  - Search Space: Search space represents a set of possible solutions, which a system may have.
  - Start State: It is a state from where agent begins the search.
  - Goal test: It is a function which observe the current state and returns whether the goal state is achieved or not.
- Search tree: A tree representation of search problem is called Search tree. The root of the search tree is the root node which is corresponding to the initial state.
- Actions: It gives the description of all the available actions to the agent.
- Transition model: A description of what each action do, can be represented as a transition model.

- Path Cost: It is a function which assigns a numeric cost to each path.

- Solution: It is an action sequence which leads from the start node to the goal node.

- Optimal Solution: If a solution has the lowest cost among all solutions.

Properties of Search Algorithms

Following are the four essential properties of search algorithms to compare the efficiency of these algorithms:

- Completeness: A search algorithm is said to be complete if it guarantees to return a solution if at least any solution exists for any random input.

- Optimality: If a solution found for an algorithm is guaranteed to be the best solution (lowest path cost) among all other solutions, then such a solution for is said to be an optimal solution.

- Time Complexity: Time complexity is a measure of time for an algorithm to complete its task.

- Space Complexity: It is the maximum storage space required at any point during the search, as the complexity of the problem.

Types of Search Algorithms

Informed Search Algorithms

Informed search algorithm uses the idea of heuristic, so it is also called Heuristic search.

Heuristics function: Heuristic is a function which is used in Informed Search, and it finds the most promising path. It takes the current state of the agent as its input and produces the estimation of how close agent is from the goal. The heuristic method, however, might not always give the best solution, but it guaranteed to find a good solution in reasonable time. Heuristic function estimates how close a state is to the goal. It is represented by h(n), and it calculates the cost of an optimal path between the pair of states. The value of the heuristic function is always positive.

Admissibility of the heuristic function is given as:

$$h(n) <= h*(n)$$

Here h(n) is heuristic cost, and h*(n) is the estimated cost. Hence heuristic cost should be less than or equal to the estimated cost.

Pure Heuristic Search

Pure heuristic search is the simplest form of heuristic search algorithms. It expands nodes based on their heuristic value h(n). It maintains two lists, OPEN and CLOSED list. In the CLOSED list, it places those nodes which have already expanded and in the OPEN list, it places nodes which have yet not been expanded.

On each iteration, each node n with the lowest heuristic value is expanded and generates all its successors and n is placed to the closed list. The algorithm continues unit a goal state is found.

In the informed search we will discuss two main algorithms which are given below:

- Best First Search Algorithm(Greedy search).

- A* Search Algorithm.

Best-first Search Algorithm (Greedy Search)

Greedy best-first search algorithm always selects the path which appears best at that moment. It is the combination of depth-first search and breadth-first search algorithms. It uses the heuristic function and search. Best-first search allows us to take the advantages of both algorithms. With the help of best-first search, at each step, we can choose the most promising node. In the best first search algorithm, we expand the node which is closest to the goal node and the closest cost is estimated by heuristic function, i.e.

$$f(n) = g(n).$$

Were, $h(n)$ = estimated cost from node n to the goal.

The greedy best first algorithm is implemented by the priority queue.

Best First Search Algorithm

- Step: Place the starting node into the OPEN list.

- Step: If the OPEN list is empty, Stop and return failure.

- Step: Remove the node n, from the OPEN list which has the lowest value of $h(n)$, and places it in the CLOSED list.

- Step: Expand the node n, and generate the successors of node n.

- Step: Check each successor of node n, and find whether any node is a goal node or not. If any successor node is goal node, then return success and terminate the search, else proceed to Step.

- Step: For each successor node, algorithm checks for evaluation function $f(n)$, and then check if the node has been in either OPEN or CLOSED list. If the node has not been in both list, then add it to the OPEN list.

- Step: Return to Step.

Advantages

- Best first search can switch between BFS and DFS by gaining the advantages of both the algorithms.

- This algorithm is more efficient than BFS and DFS algorithms.

Disadvantages

- It can behave as an unguided depth-first search in the worst case scenario.

- It can get stuck in a loop as DFS.

- This algorithm is not optimal.

Example: Consider the below search problem, and we will traverse it using greedy best-first search. At each iteration, each node is expanded using evaluation function f(n)=h(n), which is given in the below table.

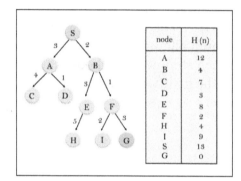

In this search example, we are using two lists which are OPEN and CLOSED Lists. Following are the iteration for traversing the above example:

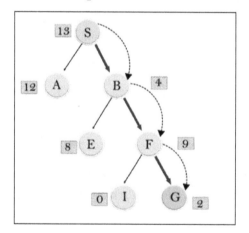

Expand the nodes of S and put in the CLOSED list

Initialization: Open [A, B], Closed [S]

Iteration 1: Open [A], Closed [S, B]

Iteration 2: Open [E, F, A], Closed [S, B]

       : Open [E, A], Closed [S, B, F]

Iteration 3: Open [I, G, E, A], Closed [S, B, F]

       : Open [I, E, A], Closed [S, B, F, G]

Hence the final solution path will be: S----> B----->F----> G.

- Time Complexity: The worst case time complexity of Greedy best first search is $O(b^m)$.

- Space Complexity: The worst case space complexity of Greedy best first search is $O(b^m)$. Where, m is the maximum depth of the search space.

- Complete: Greedy best-first search is also incomplete, even if the given state space is finite.

- Optimal: Greedy best first search algorithm is not optimal.

A* Search Algorithm

A* search is the most commonly known form of best-first search. It uses heuristic function h(n), and cost to reach the node n from the start state g(n). It has combined features of UCS and greedy best-first search, by which it solve the problem efficiently. A* search algorithm finds the shortest path through the search space using the heuristic function. This search algorithm expands less search tree and provides optimal result faster. A* algorithm is similar to UCS except that it uses g(n)+h(n) instead of g(n).

In A* search algorithm, we use search heuristic as well as the cost to reach the node. Hence we can combine both costs as following, and this sum is called as a fitness number.

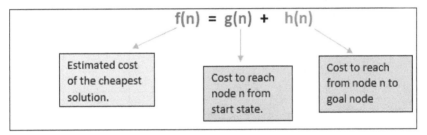

Algorithm of A* Search

- Step: Place the starting node in the OPEN list.

- Step: Check if the OPEN list is empty or not, if the list is empty then return failure and stops.

- Step: Select the node from the OPEN list which has the smallest value of evaluation function (g+h), if node n is goal node then return success and stop, otherwise

- Step: Expand node n and generate all of its successors, and put n into the closed list. For each successor n', check whether n' is already in the OPEN or CLOSED list, if not then compute evaluation function for n' and place into Open list.

- Step: Else if node n' is already in OPEN and CLOSED, then it should be attached to the back pointer which reflects the lowest g(n') value.

- Step: Return to Step 2.

Advantages

- A* search algorithm is the best algorithm than other search algorithms.

- A* search algorithm is optimal and complete.

- This algorithm can solve very complex problems.

Disadvantages

- It does not always produce the shortest path as it mostly based on heuristics and approximation.

- A* search algorithm has some complexity issues.

- The main drawback of A* is memory requirement as it keeps all generated nodes in the memory, so it is not practical for various large-scale problems.

Example: In this example, we will traverse the given graph using the A* algorithm. The heuristic value of all states is given in the below table so we will calculate the f(n) of each state using the formula f(n)= g(n) + h(n), where g(n) is the cost to reach any node from start state.

Here we will use OPEN and CLOSED list.

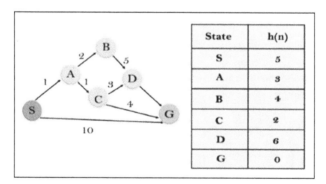

State	h(n)
S	5
A	3
B	4
C	2
D	6
G	0

Solution:

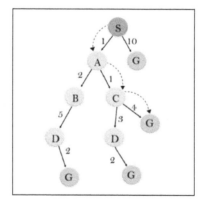

Initialization: {(S, 5)}

Iteration1: {(S--> A, 4), (S-->G, 10)}

Iteration2: {(S--> A-->C, 4), (S--> A-->B, 7), (S-->G, 10)}

Iteration3: {(S--> A-->C--->G, 6), (S--> A-->C--->D, 11), (S--> A-->B, 7), (S-->G, 10)}

Iteration 4 will give the final result, as S--->A--->C--->G it provides the optimal path with cost 6.

Uninformed Search Algorithms

Uninformed search is a class of general-purpose search algorithms which operates in brute force-way. Uninformed search algorithms do not have additional information about state or search space other than how to traverse the tree, so it is also called blind search.

Following are the various types of uninformed search algorithms:

- Breadth-first Search,
- Depth-first Search,
- Depth-limited Search,
- Iterative deepening depth-first search,
- Uniform cost search,
- Bidirectional Search.

Breadth-first Search

- Breadth-first search is the most common search strategy for traversing a tree or graph. This algorithm searches breadthwise in a tree or graph, so it is called breadth-first search.
- BFS algorithm starts searching from the root node of the tree and expands all successor nodes at the current level before moving to nodes of next level.
- The breadth-first search algorithm is an example of a general-graph search algorithm.
- Breadth-first search implemented using FIFO queue data structure.

Advantages

- BFS will provide a solution if any solution exists.
- If there is more than one solution for a given problem, then BFS will provide the minimal solution which requires the least number of steps.

Disadvantages

- It requires lots of memory since each level of the tree must be saved into memory to expand the next level.
- BFS needs lots of time if the solution is far away from the root node.

Example: In the below tree structure, we have shown the traversing of the tree using BFS algorithm from the root node S to goal node K. BFS search algorithm traverse in layers, so it will follow the path which is shown by the dotted arrow, and the traversed path will be:

S---> A--->B---->C--->D---->G--->H--->E---->F---->I---->K

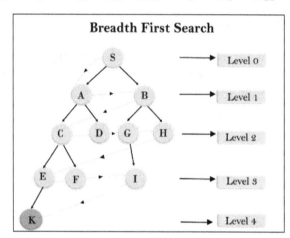

- Time Complexity: Time Complexity of BFS algorithm can be obtained by the number of nodes traversed in BFS until the shallowest Node. Where the d= depth of shallowest solution and b is a node at every state.

  $T(b) = 1 + b^2 + b^3 + \ldots\ldots + b^d = O(b^d)$

- Space Complexity: Space complexity of BFS algorithm is given by the Memory size of frontier which is $O(b^d)$.

- Completeness: BFS is complete, which means if the shallowest goal node is at some finite depth, then BFS will find a solution.

- Optimality: BFS is optimal if path cost is a non-decreasing function of the depth of the node.

Depth-first Search

- Depth-first search is a recursive algorithm for traversing a tree or graph data structure.

- It is called the depth-first search because it starts from the root node and follows each path to its greatest depth node before moving to the next path.

- DFS uses a stack data structure for its implementation.

- The process of the DFS algorithm is similar to the BFS algorithm.

Advantage

- DFS requires very less memory as it only needs to store a stack of the nodes on the path from root node to the current node.

- It takes less time to reach to the goal node than BFS algorithm (if it traverses in the right path).

Disadvantage

- There is the possibility that many states keep re-occurring, and there is no guarantee of finding the solution.

- DFS algorithm goes for deep down searching and sometime it may go to the infinite loop.

Example: In the below search tree, we have shown the flow of depth-first search, and it will follow the order as:

Root node--->Left node ----> right node.

It will start searching from root node S, and traverse A, then B, then D and E, after traversing E, it will backtrack the tree as E has no other successor and still goal node is not found. After backtracking it will traverse node C and then G, and here it will terminate as it found goal node.

- Completeness: DFS search algorithm is complete within finite state space as it will expand every node within a limited search tree.

- Time Complexity: Time complexity of DFS will be equivalent to the node traversed by the algorithm. It is given by:

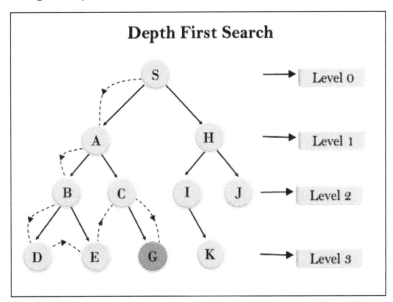

$T(n)= 1 + n2+ n3 +..........+ nm=O(nm)$

where, m= maximum depth of any node and this can be much larger than d (Shallowest solution depth).

- Space Complexity: DFS algorithm needs to store only single path from the root node, hence space complexity of DFS is equivalent to the size of the fringe set, which is O(bm).

- Optimal: DFS search algorithm is non-optimal, as it may generate a large number of steps or high cost to reach to the goal node.

Depth-limited Search Algorithm

A depth-limited search algorithm is similar to depth-first search with a predetermined limit. Depth-limited search can solve the drawback of the infinite path in the Depth-first search. In this algorithm, the node at the depth limit will treat as it has no successor nodes further.

Depth-limited search can be terminated with two Conditions of failure:

- Standard failure value: It indicates that problem does not have any solution.

- Cutoff failure value: It defines no solution for the problem within a given depth limit.

Advantages

Depth-limited search is Memory efficient.

Disadvantages

- Depth-limited search also has a disadvantage of incompleteness.

- It may not be optimal if the problem has more than one solution.

Example:

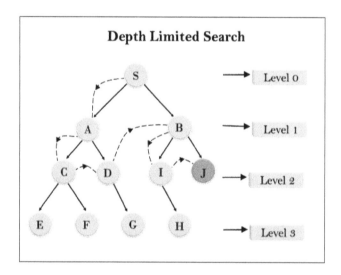

- Completeness: DLS search algorithm is complete if the solution is above the depth-limit.

- Time Complexity: Time complexity of DLS algorithm is $O(b^\ell)$.

- Space Complexity: Space complexity of DLS algorithm is $O(b \times \ell)$.

- Optimal: Depth-limited search can be viewed as a special case of DFS, and it is also not optimal even if $\ell > d$.

Uniform-cost Search Algorithm

Uniform-cost search is a searching algorithm used for traversing a weighted tree or graph. This algorithm comes into play when a different cost is available for each edge. The primary goal of the uniform-cost search is to find a path to the goal node which has the lowest cumulative cost. Uniform-cost search expands nodes according to their path costs form the root node. It can be used to solve any graph/tree where the optimal cost is in demand. A uniform-cost search algorithm is implemented by the priority queue. It gives maximum priority to the lowest cumulative cost. Uniform cost search is equivalent to BFS algorithm if the path cost of all edges is the same.

Advantages

Uniform cost search is optimal because at every state the path with the least cost is chosen.

Disadvantages

It does not care about the number of steps involve in searching and only concerned about path cost. Due to which this algorithm may be stuck in an infinite loop.

Example:

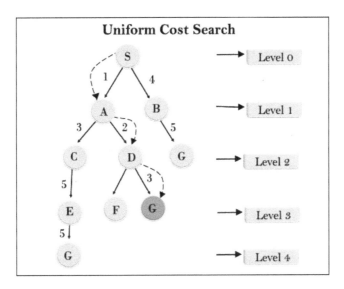

Completeness: Uniform-cost search is complete, such as if there is a solution, UCS will find it.

Time Complexity: Let C^* is Cost of the optimal solution, and ε is each step to get closer to the goal node. Then the number of steps is = $C^*/\varepsilon+1$. Here we have taken +1, as we start from state 0 and end to C^*/ε.

Hence, the worst-case time complexity of Uniform-cost search is$O(b^{1 + [C^*/\varepsilon]})/$.

Space Complexity: The same logic is for space complexity so, the worst-case space complexity of Uniform-cost search is $O(b^{1 + [C^*/\varepsilon]})$.

Optimal: Uniform-cost search is always optimal as it only selects a path with the lowest path cost.

Iterative Deepening Depth-first Search

The iterative deepening algorithm is a combination of DFS and BFS algorithms. This search algorithm finds out the best depth limit and does it by gradually increasing the limit until a goal is found.

This algorithm performs depth-first search up to a certain "depth limit", and it keeps increasing the depth limit after each iteration until the goal node is found.

This Search algorithm combines the benefits of Breadth-first search's fast search and depth-first search's memory efficiency.

The iterative search algorithm is useful uninformed search when search space is large, and depth of goal node is unknown.

Advantages

It combines the benefits of BFS and DFS search algorithm in terms of fast search and memory efficiency.

Disadvantages

The main drawback of IDDFS is that it repeats all the work of the previous phase.

Example: Following tree structure is showing the iterative deepening depth-first search. IDDFS algorithm performs various iterations until it does not find the goal node. The iteration performed by the algorithm is given as:

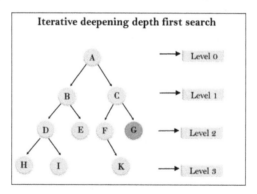

1'st Iteration-----> A

2'nd Iteration----> A, B, C

3'rd Iteration------>A, B, D, E, C, F, G

4'th Iteration------>A, B, D, H, I, E, C, F, K, G

In the fourth iteration, the algorithm will find the goal node.

Completeness: This algorithm is complete is ifthe branching factor is finite.

Time Complexity: Let's suppose b is the branching factor and depth is d then the worst-case time complexity is O(b^d).

Space Complexity: The space complexity of IDDFS will be O(b^d).

Optimal: IDDFS algorithm is optimal if path cost is a non- decreasing function of the depth of the node.

Bidirectional Search Algorithm

Bidirectional search algorithm runs two simultaneous searches, one form initial state called as forward-search and other from goal node called as backward-search, to find the goal node. Bidirectional search replaces one single search graph with two small subgraphs in which one starts the search from an initial vertex and other starts from goal vertex. The search stops when these two graphs intersect each other.

Bidirectional search can use search techniques such as BFS, DFS, DLS, etc.

Advantages

- Bidirectional search is fast.
- Bidirectional search requires less memory.

Disadvantages

- Implementation of the bidirectional search tree is difficult.
- In bidirectional search, one should know the goal state in advance.

Example: In the below search tree, bidirectional search algorithm is applied. This algorithm divides one graph/tree into two sub-graphs. It starts traversing from node 1 in the forward direction and starts from goal node 16 in the backward direction.

The algorithm terminates at node 9 where two searches meet.

Completeness: Bidirectional Search is complete if we use BFS in both searches.

Time Complexity: Time complexity of bidirectional search using BFS is $O(b^d)$.

Space Complexity: Space complexity of bidirectional search is $O(b^d)$.

Optimal: Bidirectional search is Optimal.

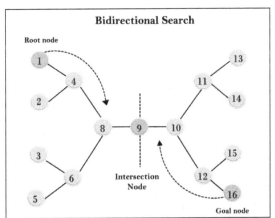

Hill Climbing Algorithm

Hill climbing is a mathematical optimization heuristic method used for solving computationally challenging problems that have multiple solutions. It is an iterative method belonging to the local search family which starts with a random solution and then iteratively improves that solution one element at a time until it arrives at a more or less optimized solution.

Hill climbing is an optimization technique that is used to find a "local optimum" solution to a computational problem. It starts off with a solution that is very poor compared to the optimal solution and then iteratively improves from there. It does this by generating "neighbor" solutions which are relatively a step better than the current solution, picks the best and then repeats the process until it arrives at the most optimal solution because it can no longer find any improvements.

Variants

- Simple: The first closest node or solution to be found is chosen.

- Steepest ascent: All available successor solutions are considered and then the closest one is selected.

- Stochastic: A neighbor solution is selected at random, and it is then decided whether or not to move on to that solution based on the amount of improvement over the current node.

Hill climbing is done iteratively — it goes through an entire procedure and the final solution is stored. If a different iteration finds a better final solution, the stored solution or state is replaced. This is also called shotgun hill climbing, as it simply tries out different paths until it hits the best one, just like how a shotgun is inaccurate but may still hit its target because of the wide spread of projectiles. This works very well in many cases because at it turns out, it is better to spend CPU resources exploring different paths than carefully optimizing from an initial condition.

Given a large set of inputs and a good heuristic function, it tries to find a sufficiently good solution to the problem. This solution may not be the global optimal maximum.

- In the above definition, mathematical optimization problems implies that hill-climbing solves the problems where we need to maximize or minimize a given real function by choosing values from the given inputs. Example-Travelling salesman problem where we need to minimize the distance traveled by the salesman.

- 'Heuristic search' means that this search algorithm may not find the optimal solution to the problem. However, it will give a good solution in reasonable time.

- A heuristic function is a function that will rank all the possible alternatives at any branching step in search algorithm based on the available information. It helps the algorithm to select the best route out of possible routes.

Features of Hill Climbing

- Variant of generate and test algorithm: It is a variant of generate and test algorithm. The generate and test algorithm is as follows:

- ○ Generate possible solutions.

- ○ Test to see if this is the expected solution.

- ○ If the solution has been found quit else go to step 1.

- Hence we call Hill climbing as a variant of generate and test algorithm as it takes the feedback from the test procedure. Then this feedback is utilized by the generator in deciding the next move in search space.

- Uses the Greedy approach: At any point in state space, the search moves in that direction only which optimizes the cost of function with the hope of finding the optimal solution at the end.

Problems in Different Regions in Hill Climbing

Hill climbing cannot reach the optimal/best state(global maximum) if it enters any of the following regions:

- Local maximum: At a local maximum all neighboring states have values which are worse than the current state. Since hill-climbing uses a greedy approach, it will not move to the worse state and terminate itself. The process will end even though a better solution may exist.

  - ○ To overcome local maximum problem: Utilize backtracking technique. Maintain a list of visited states. If the search reaches an undesirable state, it can backtrack to the previous configuration and explore a new path.

- Plateau: On plateau all neighbors have same value. Hence, it is not possible to select the best direction.

  - ○ To overcome plateaus: Make a big jump. Randomly select a state far away from the current state. Chances are that we will land at a non-plateau region

- Ridge: Any point on a ridge can look like peak because movement in all possible directions is downward. Hence the algorithm stops when it reaches this state.

  - ○ To overcome ridge: In this kind of obstacle, use two or more rules before testing. It implies moving in several directions at once.

Types of Hill Climbing Algorithm

Simple Hill Climbing

Simple hill climbing is the simplest way to implement a hill climbing algorithm. It only evaluates the neighbor node state at a time and selects the first one which optimizes current cost and set it as a current state. It only checks it's one successor state, and if it finds better than the current state, then move else be in the same state. This algorithm has the following features:

- Less time consuming.

- Less optimal solution and the solution is not guaranteed.

Algorithm for Simple Hill Climbing

- Step 1: Evaluate the initial state, if it is goal state then return success and Stop.

- Step 2: Loop Until a solution is found or there is no new operator left to apply.

- Step 3: Select and apply an operator to the current state.

- Step 4: Check new state:

    ○ If it is goal state, then return success and quit.

    ○ Else if it is better than the current state then assign new state as a current state.

    ○ Else if not better than the current state, then return to step 2.

- Step 5: Exit.

Steepest-Ascent Hill Climbing

The steepest-Ascent algorithm is a variation of simple hill climbing algorithm. This algorithm examines all the neighboring nodes of the current state and selects one neighbor node which is closest to the goal state. This algorithm consumes more time as it searches for multiple neighbors

Algorithm for Steepest-Ascent hill climbing:

- Step 1: Evaluate the initial state, if it is goal state then return success and stop, else make current state as initial state.

- Step 2: Loop until a solution is found or the current state does not change.

    ○ Let SUCC be a state such that any successor of the current state will be better than it.

    ○ For each operator that applies to the current state:

        ▪ Apply the new operator and generate a new state.

        ▪ Evaluate the new state.

        ▪ If it is goal state, then return it and quit, else compare it to the SUCC.

        ▪ If it is better than SUCC, then set new state as SUCC.

        ▪ If the SUCC is better than the current state, then set current state to SUCC.

- Step 5: Exit.

Stochastic Hill Climbing

Stochastic hill climbing does not examine for all its neighbor before moving. Rather, this search algorithm selects one neighbor node at random and decides whether to choose it as a current state or examine another state.

References

- Problem-solving-in-artificial-intelligence: tutorialandexample.com, Retrieved 06 August, 2019

- Search-algorithm- 21975: techopedia.com, Retrieved 23 July, 2019

- Search-algorithms-in-ai: javatpoint.com, Retrieved 26 June, 2019

- Ai-informed-search-algorithms: javatpoint.com, Retrieved 19 April, 2019

- Introduction-hill-climbing-artificial-intelligence: geeksforgeeks.org, Retrieved 29 March, 2019

Machine Learning and Computer Vision

The algorithms and statistical models used by computer systems to perform tasks are studied under machine learning. Computer vision aims to advance the level of understanding of computers through digital images. This chapter discusses in detail the theories and methodologies related to machine learning and computer vision.

Machine Learning

Machine Learning is a system that can learn from example through self-improvement and without being explicitly coded by programmer. The breakthrough comes with the idea that a machine can singularly learn from the data (i.e., example) to produce accurate results.

Machine learning combines data with statistical tools to predict an output. This output is then used by corporate to makes actionable insights. Machine learning is closely related to data mining and Bayesian predictive modeling. The machine receives data as input, use an algorithm to formulate answers.

A typical machine learning tasks are to provide a recommendation. For those who have a Netflix account, all recommendations of movies or series are based on the user's historical data. Tech companies are using unsupervised learning to improve the user experience with personalizing recommendation.

Machine learning is also used for a variety of task like fraud detection, predictive maintenance, portfolio optimization, automatize task and so on.

Machine Learning vs. Traditional Programming

Traditional programming differs significantly from machine learning. In traditional programming, a programmer codes all the rules in consultation with an expert in the industry for which software is being developed. Each rule is based on a logical foundation; the machine will execute an output following the logical statement. When the system grows complex, more rules need to be written. It can quickly become unsustainable to maintain.

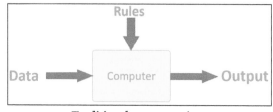

Traditional programming.

Machine learning is supposed to overcome this issue. The machine learns how the input and output data are correlated and it writes a rule. The programmers do not need to write new rules each time there is new data. The algorithms adapt in response to new data and experiences to improve efficacy over time.

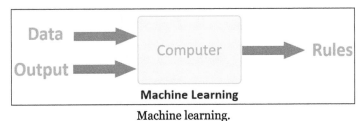

Machine learning.

Working of Machine Learning

Machine learning is the brain where all the learning takes place. The way the machine learns is similar to the human being. Humans learn from experience. The more we know, the more easily we can predict. By analogy, when we face an unknown situation, the likelihood of success is lower than the known situation. Machines are trained the same. To make an accurate prediction, the machine sees an example. When we give the machine a similar example, it can figure out the outcome. However, like a human, if it's feed a previously unseen example, the machine has difficulties to predict.

The core objective of machine learning is the learning and inference. First of all, the machine learns through the discovery of patterns. This discovery is made thanks to the data. One crucial part of the data scientist is to choose carefully which data to provide to the machine. The list of attributes used to solve a problem is called a feature vector. You can think of a feature vector as a subset of data that is used to tackle a problem.

The machine uses some fancy algorithms to simplify the reality and transform this discovery into a model. Therefore, the learning stage is used to describe the data and summarize it into a model.

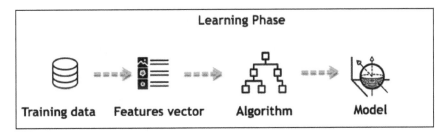

For instance, the machine is trying to understand the relationship between the wage of an individual and the likelihood to go to a fancy restaurant. It turns out the machine finds a positive relationship between wage and going to a high-end restaurant.

Inferring

When the model is built, it is possible to test how powerful it is on never-seen-before data. The new data are transformed into a features vector, go through the model and give a prediction. This is all the beautiful part of machine learning. There is no need to update the rules or train again the model. You can use the model previously trained to make inference on new data.

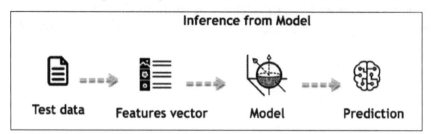

The life of Machine Learning programs is straightforward and can be summarized in the following points:

- Define a question,
- Collect data,
- Visualize data,
- Train algorithm,
- Test the Algorithm,
- Collect feedback,
- Refine the algorithm,
- Loop 4-7 until the results are satisfying,
- Use the model to make a prediction.

Once the algorithm gets good at drawing the right conclusions, it applies that knowledge to new sets of data.

Machine Learning Algorithms and their Uses

Machine learning can be grouped into two broad learning tasks: Supervised and Unsupervised. There are many other algorithms.

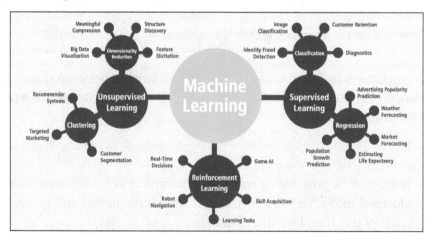

Supervised Machine Learning

An algorithm uses training data and feedback from humans to learn the relationship of given inputs to a given output. For instance, a practitioner can use marketing expense and weather forecast as input data to predict the sales of cans.

You can use supervised learning when the output data is known. The algorithm will predict new data.

There are two categories of supervised learning:

- Classification task,

- Regression task.

Classification

Imagine you want to predict the gender of a customer for a commercial. You will start gathering data on the height, weight, job, salary, purchasing basket, etc. from your customer database. You know the gender of each of your customer; it can only be male or female. The objective of the classifier will be to assign a probability of being a male or a female (i.e., the label) based on the information (i.e., features you have collected). When the model learned how to recognize male or female, you can use new data to make a prediction. For instance, you just got new information from an unknown customer, and you want to know if it is a male or female. If the classifier predicts male = 70%, it means the algorithm is sure at 70% that this customer is a male, and 30% it is a female.

The label can be of two or more classes. The above example has only two classes, but if a classifier needs to predict object, it has dozens of classes (e.g., glass, table, shoes, etc. each object represents a class).

Regression

When the output is a continuous value, the task is a regression. For instance, a financial analyst may need to forecast the value of a stock based on a range of feature like equity, previous stock performances, macroeconomics index. The system will be trained to estimate the price of the stocks with the lowest possible error.

Algorithm Name	Description	Type
Linear regression	Finds a way to correlate each feature to the output to help predict future values.	Regression
Logistic regression	Extension of linear regression that's used for classification tasks. The output variable 3is binary (e.g., only black or white) rather than continuous (e.g., an infinite list of potential colors).	Classification
Decision tree	Highly interpretable classification or regression model that splits data-feature values into branches at decision nodes (e.g., if a feature is a color, each possible color becomes a new branch) until a final decision output is made.	Regression Classification
Naive Bayes	The Bayesian method is a classification method that makes use of the Bayesian theorem. The theorem updates the prior knowledge of an event with the independent probability of each feature that can affect the event.	Regression Classification

Support vector machine	Support Vector Machine, or SVM, is typically used for the classification task. SVM algorithm finds a hyperplane that optimally divided the classes. It is best used with a non-linear solver.	Regression (not very common) Classification
Random forest	The algorithm is built upon a decision tree to improve the accuracy drastically. Random forest generates many times simple decision trees and uses the 'majority vote' method to decide on which label to return. For the classification task, the final prediction will be the one with the most vote; while for the regression task, the average prediction of all the trees is the final prediction.	Regression Classification
AdaBoost	Classification or regression technique that uses a multitude of models to come up with a decision but weighs them based on their accuracy in predicting the outcome.	Regression Classification
Gradient-boosting trees	Gradient-boosting trees is a state-of-the-art classification/regression technique. It is focusing on the error committed by the previous trees and tries to correct it.	Regression Classification

Unsupervised Machine Learning

In unsupervised learning, an algorithm explores input data without being given an explicit output variable (e.g., explores customer demographic data to identify patterns).

You can use it when you do not know how to classify the data, and you want the algorithm to find patterns and classify the data for you.

Algorithm	Description	Type
K-means clustering	Puts data into some groups (k) that each contains data with similar characteristics (as determined by the model, not in advance by humans).	Clustering
Gaussian mixture model	A generalization of k-means clustering that provides more flexibility in the size and shape of groups.	Clustering
Hierarchical clustering	Splits clusters along a hierarchical tree to form a classification system. Can be used for Cluster loyalty-card customer.	Clustering
Recommend-er system	Help to define the relevant data for making a recommendation.	Clustering
PCA/T-SNE	Mostly used to decrease the dimensionality of the data. The algorithms reduce the number of features to 3 or 4 vectors with the highest variances.	Dimension Reduction

Choosing a Machine Learning Algorithm

There are plenty of machine learning algorithms. The choice of the algorithm is based on the objective.

In the example below, the task is to predict the type of flower among the three varieties. The predictions are based on the length and the width of the petal. The picture depicts the results of ten different algorithms. The picture on the top left is the dataset. The data is classified into three categories: red, light blue and dark blue. There are some groupings. For instance, from the second image, everything in the upper left belongs to the red category, in the middle part; there is a mixture of uncertainty and light blue while the bottom corresponds to the dark category. The other images show different algorithms and how they try to classified the data.

Challenges and Limitations of Machine Learning

The primary challenge of machine learning is the lack of data or the diversity in the dataset. A machine cannot learn if there is no data available. Besides, a dataset with a lack of diversity gives the machine a hard time. A machine needs to have heterogeneity to learn meaningful insight. It is rare that an algorithm can extract information when there are no or few variations. It is recommended to have at least 20 observations per group to help the machine learn. This constraint leads to poor evaluation and prediction.

Application of Machine Learning

- Augmentation: Machine learning, which assists humans with their day-to-day tasks, personally or commercially without having complete control of the output. Such machine learning is used in different ways such as Virtual Assistant, Data analysis, software solutions. The primary user is to reduce errors due to human bias.

- Automation: Machine learning, which works entirely autonomously in any field without the need for any human intervention. For example, robots performing the essential process steps in manufacturing plants.

- Finance Industry: Machine learning is growing in popularity in the finance industry. Banks are mainly using ML to find patterns inside the data but also to prevent fraud.

- Government organization: The government makes use of ML to manage public safety and utilities. Take the example of China with the massive face recognition. The government uses Artificial intelligence to prevent jaywalker.

- Healthcare industry: Healthcare was one of the first industry to use machine learning with image detection.

- Marketing: Broad use of AI is done in marketing thanks to abundant access to data. Before the age of mass data, researchers develop advanced mathematical tools like Bayesian analysis to estimate the value of a customer. With the boom of data, marketing department relies on AI to optimize the customer relationship and marketing campaign.

Example of application of Machine Learning in Supply Chain

Machine learning gives terrific results for visual pattern recognition, opening up many potential applications in physical inspection and maintenance across the entire supply chain network.

Unsupervised learning can quickly search for comparable patterns in the diverse dataset. In turn, the machine can perform quality inspection throughout the logistics hub, shipment with damage and wear.

For instance, IBM's Watson platform can determine shipping container damage. Watson combines visual and systems-based data to track, report and make recommendations in real-time.

In past year stock manager relies extensively on the primary method to evaluate and forecast the inventory. When combining big data and machine learning, better forecasting techniques have been implemented (an improvement of 20 to 30 % over traditional forecasting tools). In term of sales, it means an increase of 2 to 3 % due to the potential reduction in inventory costs.

Example of Machine Learning Google Car

For example, everybody knows the Google car. The car is full of lasers on the roof which are telling it where it is regarding the surrounding area. It has radar in the front, which is informing the car of the speed and motion of all the cars around it. It uses all of that data to figure out not only how to drive the car but also to figure out and predict what potential drivers around the car are going to do. What's impressive is that the car is processing almost a gigabyte a second of data.

Importance of Machine Learning

Machine learning is the best tool so far to analyze, understand and identify a pattern in the data. One of the main ideas behind machine learning is that the computer can be trained to automate tasks that would be exhaustive or impossible for a human being. The clear breach from the traditional analysis is that machine learning can take decisions with minimal human intervention.

Take the following example; a retail agent can estimate the price of a house based on his own experience and his knowledge of the market.

A machine can be trained to translate the knowledge of an expert into features. The features are all the characteristics of a house, neighborhood, economic environment, etc. that make the price difference. For the expert, it took him probably some years to master the art of estimate the price of a house. His expertise is getting better and better after each sale.

For the machine, it takes millions of data, (i.e., example) to master this art. At the very beginning of its learning, the machine makes a mistake, somehow like the junior salesman. Once the machine sees all the example, it got enough knowledge to make its estimation. At the same time, with incredible accuracy. The machine is also able to adjust its mistake accordingly.

Machine Learning Methods

The process of learning begins with observations or data, such as examples, direct experience, or instruction, in order to look for patterns in data and make better decisions in the future based on the examples that we provide. The primary aim is to allow the computers learn automatically without human intervention or assistance and adjust actions accordingly.

Some Machine Learning Methods

Machine learning algorithms are often categorized as supervised or unsupervised:

- Supervised machine learning algorithms can apply what has been learned in the past to new data using labeled examples to predict future events. Starting from the analysis of a known training dataset, the learning algorithm produces an inferred function to make predictions about the output values. The system is able to provide targets for any new input after sufficient training. The learning algorithm can also compare its output with the correct, intended output and find errors in order to modify the model accordingly.

- In contrast, unsupervised machine learning algorithms are used when the information used to train is neither classified nor labeled. Unsupervised learning studies how systems can infer a function to describe a hidden structure from unlabeled data. The system doesn't figure out the right output, but it explores the data and can draw inferences from datasets to describe hidden structures from unlabeled data.

- Semi-supervised machine learning algorithms fall somewhere in between supervised and unsupervised learning, since they use both labeled and unlabeled data for training – typically a small amount of labeled data and a large amount of unlabeled data. The systems that use this method are able to considerably improve learning accuracy. Usually, semi-supervised learning is chosen when the acquired labeled data requires skilled and relevant resources in order to train it/learn from it. Otherwise, acquiring unlabeled data generally doesn't require additional resources.

- Reinforcement machine learning algorithms is a learning method that interacts with its environment by producing actions and discovers errors or rewards. Trial and error search and delayed reward are the most relevant characteristics of reinforcement learning. This method allows machines and software agents to automatically determine the ideal behavior within a specific context in order to maximize its performance. Simple reward feedback is required for the agent to learn which action is best; this is known as the reinforcement signal.

Machine learning enables analysis of massive quantities of data. While it generally delivers faster, more accurate results in order to identify profitable opportunities or dangerous risks, it may also require additional time and resources to train it properly. Combining machine learning with AI and cognitive technologies can make it even more effective in processing large volumes of information.

Supervised Machine Learning Algorithm

Supervised machine learning algorithms uncover insights, patterns, and relationships from a labeled training dataset – that is, a dataset that already contains a known value for the target variable for each record. Because you provide the machine learning algorithm with the correct answers for a problem during training, the algorithm is able to "learn" how the rest of the features relate to the target, enabling you to uncover insights and make predictions about future outcomes based on historical data.

Examples of Supervised Machine Learning Techniques

- Regression, in which the algorithm returns a numerical target for each example, such as how much revenue will be generated from a new marketing campaign.

- Classification, in which the algorithm attempts to label each example by choosing between two or more different classes. Choosing between two classes is called binary classification, such as determining whether or not someone will default on a loan. Choosing between more than two classes is referred to as multiclass classification.

Algorithm Choice

A wide range of supervised learning algorithms are available, each with its strengths and weaknesses. There is no single learning algorithm that works best on all supervised learning problems.

There are four major issues to consider in supervised learning:

Bias-variance Tradeoff

A first issue is the tradeoff between *bias* and *variance*. Imagine that we have available several different, but equally good, training data sets. A learning algorithm is biased for a particular input x if, when trained on each of these data sets, it is systematically incorrect when predicting the correct output for x. A learning algorithm has high variance for a particular input x if it predicts different output values when trained on different training sets. The prediction error of a learned classifier is related to the sum of the bias and the variance of the learning algorithm. Generally, there is a tradeoff between bias and variance. A learning algorithm with low bias must be "flexible" so that it can fit the data well. But if the learning algorithm is too flexible, it will fit each training data set differently, and hence have high variance. A key aspect of many supervised learning methods is that they are able to adjust this tradeoff between bias and variance (either automatically or by providing a bias/variance parameter that the user can adjust).

Function Complexity and Amount of Training Data

The second issue is the amount of training data available relative to the complexity of the "true" function (classifier or regression function). If the true function is simple, then an "inflexible" learning algorithm with high bias and low variance will be able to learn it from a small amount of data. But if the true function is highly complex (e.g., because it involves complex interactions among many different input features and behaves differently in different parts of the input space), then the function will only be able to learn from a very large amount of training data and using a "flexible" learning algorithm with low bias and high variance.

Dimensionality of the Input Space

A third issue is the dimensionality of the input space. If the input feature vectors have very high dimension, the learning problem can be difficult even if the true function only depends on a small number of those features. This is because the many "extra" dimensions can confuse the learning algorithm and cause it to have high variance. Hence, high input dimensional typically requires tuning the classifier to have low variance and high bias. In practice, if the engineer can manually remove irrelevant features from the input data, this is likely to improve the accuracy of the learned function. In addition, there are many algorithms for feature selection that seek to identify the relevant features and discard the irrelevant ones. This is an instance of the more general strategy of dimensionality reduction, which seeks to map the input data into a lower-dimensional space prior to running the supervised learning algorithm.

Noise in the Output Values

A fourth issue is the degree of noise in the desired output values (the supervisory target variables). If the desired output values are often incorrect (because of human error or sensor errors), then the learning algorithm should not attempt to find a function that exactly matches the training examples. Attempting to fit the data too carefully leads to overfitting. You can overfit even when there are no measurement errors (stochastic noise) if the function you are trying to learn is too complex for your learning model. In such a situation, the part of the target function that cannot be modeled "corrupts" your training data - this phenomenon has been called deterministic noise. When either type of noise is present, it is better to go with a higher bias, lower variance estimator.

In practice, there are several approaches to alleviate noise in the output values such as early stopping to prevent overfitting as well as detecting and removing the noisy training examples prior to training the supervised learning algorithm. There are several algorithms that identify noisy training examples and removing the suspected noisy training examples prior to training has decreased generalization error with statistical significance.

Other Factors to Consider

Other factors to consider when choosing and applying a learning algorithm include the following:

- Heterogeneity of the data: If the feature vectors include features of many different kinds (discrete, discrete ordered, counts, continuous values), some algorithms are easier to apply than others. Many algorithms, including Support Vector Machines, linear regression, logistic regression, neural networks, and nearest neighbor methods, require that the input features be numerical and scaled to similar ranges (e.g., to the [-1,1] interval). Methods that employ a distance function, such as nearest neighbor methods and support vector machines with Gaussian kernels, are particularly sensitive to this. An advantage of decision trees is that they easily handle heterogeneous data.

- Redundancy in the data: If the input features contain redundant information (e.g., highly correlated features), some learning algorithms (e.g., linear regression, logistic regression, and distance based methods) will perform poorly because of numerical instabilities. These problems can often be solved by imposing some form of regularization.

- Presence of interactions and non-linearities: If each of the features makes an independent contribution to the output, then algorithms based on linear functions (e.g., linear regression, logistic regression, Support Vector Machines, naive Bayes) and distance functions (e.g., nearest neighbor methods, support vector machines with Gaussian kernels) generally perform well. However, if there are complex interactions among features, then algorithms such as decision trees and neural networks work better, because they are specifically designed to discover these interactions. Linear methods can also be applied, but the engineer must manually specify the interactions when using them.

When considering a new application, the engineer can compare multiple learning algorithms and experimentally determine which one works best on the problem at hand. Tuning the performance of a learning algorithm can be very time-consuming. Given fixed resources, it is often better to spend more time collecting additional training data and more informative features than it is to spend extra time tuning the learning algorithms.

Algorithms

The most widely used learning algorithms are:

- Support vector machines,

- Linear regression,

- Logistic regression,

- Naive bayes,

- Linear discriminant analysis,

- Decision trees,

- k-nearest neighbor algorithm,

- Neural networks (multilayer perceptron),

- Similarity learning.

Working of Supervised Learning Algorithms

Given a set of N training examples of the form $\{(x_1, y_1),..,(x_N, y_N)\}$ such that x_i is the feature vector of the i-th example and y_i is its label (i.e., class), a learning algorithm seeks a function $g : X \to Y$, where X is the input space and Y is the output space. The function g is an element of some space of possible functions G, usually called the *hypothesis space*. It is sometimes convenient to represent g using a scoring function $f : X \times Y \to \mathbb{R}$ such that g is defined as returning the y value that gives the highest score: $g(x) = \arg\max_y f(x, y)$. Let F denote the space of scoring functions.

Although G and F can be any space of functions, many learning algorithms are probabilistic models where g takes the form of a conditional probability model $g(x) = P(y \mid x)$, or f takes the form of a joint probability model $f(x, y) = P(x, y)$. For example, naive Bayes and linear discriminant analysis are joint probability models, whereas logistic regression is a conditional probability model.

There are two basic approaches to choosing f or g : empirical risk minimization and structural risk minimization. Empirical risk minimization seeks the function that best fits the training data. Structural risk minimization includes a *penalty function* that controls the bias/variance tradeoff.

In both cases, it is assumed that the training set consists of a sample of independent and identically distributed pairs, (x_i, y_i). In order to measure how well a function fits the training data, a loss function $L : Y \times Y \to \mathbb{R}^{\geq 0}$ is defined. For training example (x_i, y_i), the loss of predicting the value $\hat{y}$ is $L(y_i, \hat{y})$.

The *risk* $R(g)$ of function g is defined as the expected loss of g. This can be estimated from the training data as:

$$R_{emp}(g) = \frac{1}{N} \sum_i L(y_i, g(x_i)).$$

Empirical Risk Minimization

In empirical risk minimization, the supervised learning algorithm seeks the function g that minimizes $R(g)$. Hence, a supervised learning algorithm can be constructed by applying an optimization algorithm to find g.

When g is a conditional probability distribution $P(y|x)$ and the loss function is the negative log likelihood: $L(y,\hat{y}) = -\log P(y|x)$, then empirical risk minimization is equivalent to maximum likelihood estimation.

When G contains many candidate functions or the training set is not sufficiently large, empirical risk minimization leads to high variance and poor generalization. The learning algorithm is able to memorize the training examples without generalizing well. This is called overfitting.

Structural Risk Minimization

Structural risk minimization seeks to prevent overfitting by incorporating a regularization penalty into the optimization. The regularization penalty can be viewed as implementing a form of Occam's razor that prefers simpler functions over more complex ones.

A wide variety of penalties have been employed that correspond to different definitions of complexity. For example, consider the case where the function g is a linear function of the form,

$$g(x) = \sum_{j=1}^{d} \beta_j x_j.$$

A popular regularization penalty is $\sum_j \beta_j^2$, which is the squared Euclidean norm of the weights, also known as the L_2 norm. Other norms include the L_1 norm, $\sum_j |\beta_j|$, and the L_0 norm, which is the number of non-zero β_j s. The penalty will be denoted by $C(g)$.

The supervised learning optimization problem is to find the function g that minimizes,

$$J(g) = R_{emp}(g) + \lambda C(g).$$

The parameter λ controls the bias-variance tradeoff. When $\lambda = 0$, this gives empirical risk minimization with low bias and high variance. When λ is large, the learning algorithm will have high bias and low variance. The value of λ can be chosen empirically via cross validation.

The complexity penalty has a Bayesian interpretation as the negative log prior probability of $g, -\log P(g)$, in which case $J(g)$ is the posterior probabability of g.

Generative Training

The training methods described above are discriminative training methods, because they seek to find a function g that discriminates well between the different output values. For the special case where $f(x,y) = P(x,y)$ is a joint probability distribution and the loss function is the negative log likelihood $-\sum_i \log P(x_i, y_i)$, a risk minimization algorithm is said to perform generative training, because f can be regarded as a generative model that explains how the data were generated. Generative training algorithms are often simpler and more computationally efficient than discriminative training algorithms. In some cases, the solution can be computed in closed form as in naive Bayes and linear discriminant analysis.

Generalizations

There are several ways in which the standard supervised learning problem can be generalized:

- Semi-supervised learning: In this setting, the desired output values are provided only for a subset of the training data. The remaining data is unlabeled.

- Weak supervision: In this setting, noisy, limited, or imprecise sources are used to provide supervision signal for labeling training data.

- Active learning: Instead of assuming that all of the training examples are given at the start, active learning algorithms interactively collect new examples, typically by making queries to a human user. Often, the queries are based on unlabeled data, which is a scenario that combines semi-supervised learning with active learning.

- Structured prediction: When the desired output value is a complex object, such as a parse tree or a labeled graph, then standard methods must be extended.

- Learning to rank: When the input is a set of objects and the desired output is a ranking of those objects, then again the standard methods must be extended.

Challenges in Supervised Machine Learning

Here, are challenges faced in supervised machine learning:

- Irrelevant input feature present training data could give inaccurate results.

- Data preparation and pre-processing is always a challenge.

- Accuracy suffers when impossible, unlikely, and incomplete values have been inputted as training data.

- If the concerned expert is not available, then the other approach is "brute-force." It means you need to think that the right features (input variables) to train the machine on. It could be inaccurate.

Advantages of Supervised Learning

- Supervised learning allows you to collect data or produce a data output from the previous experience.

- Helps you to optimize performance criteria using experience.

- Supervised machine learning helps you to solve various types of real-world computation problems.

Disadvantages of Supervised Learning

- Decision boundary might be overtrained if your training set which doesn't have examples that you want to have in a class.

- You need to select lots of good examples from each class while you are training the classifier.

- Classifying big data can be a real challenge.

- Training for supervised learning needs a lot of computation time.

Unsupervised Machine Learning Algorithm

Unsupervised machine learning algorithms infer patterns from a dataset without reference to known, or labeled, outcomes. Unlike supervised machine learning, unsupervised machine learning methods cannot be directly applied to a regression or a classification problem because you have no idea what the values for the output data might be, making it impossible for you to train the algorithm the way you normally would. Unsupervised learning can instead be used to discover the underlying structure of the data.

Importance of Unsupervised Machine Learning

Unsupervised machine learning purports to uncover previously unknown patterns in data, but most of the time these patterns are poor approximations of what supervised machine learning can achieve. Additionally, since you do not know what the outcomes should be, there is no way to determine how accurate they are, making supervised machine learning more applicable to real-world problems.

The best time to use unsupervised machine learning is when you do not have data on desired outcomes, such as determining a target market for an entirely new product that your business has never sold before. However, if you are trying to get a better understanding of your existing consumer base, supervised learning is the optimal technique.

Some applications of unsupervised machine learning techniques include:

- Clustering allows you to automatically split the dataset into groups according to similarity. Often, however, cluster analysis overestimates the similarity between groups and doesn't treat data points as individuals. For this reason, cluster analysis is a poor choice for applications like customer segmentation and targeting.

- Anomaly detection can automatically discover unusual data points in your dataset. This is useful in pinpointing fraudulent transactions, discovering faulty pieces of hardware, or identifying an outlier caused by a human error during data entry.

- Association mining identifies sets of items that frequently occur together in your dataset. Retailers often use it for basket analysis, because it allows analysts to discover goods often purchased at the same time and develop more effective marketing and merchandising strategies.

- Latent variable models are commonly used for data preprocessing, such as reducing the number of features in a dataset (dimensionality reduction) or decomposing the dataset into multiple components.

The patterns you uncover with unsupervised machine learning methods may also come in handy when implementing supervised machine learning methods later on. For example, you might use an unsupervised technique to perform cluster analysis on the data, and then use the cluster to which each row belongs as an extra feature in the supervised learning model. Another example is a fraud detection model that uses anomaly detection scores as an extra feature.

Neural Networks

The classical example of unsupervised learning in the study of neural networks is Donald Hebb's principle, that is, neurons that fire together wire together. In Hebbian learning, the connection is reinforced irrespective of an error, but is exclusively a function of the coincidence between action potentials between the two neurons. A similar version that modifies synaptic weights takes into account the time between the action potentials (spike-timing-dependent plasticity or STDP). Hebbian Learning has been hypothesized to underlie a range of cognitive functions, such as pattern recognition and experiential learning.

Among neural network models, the self-organizing map (SOM) and adaptive resonance theory (ART) are commonly used in unsupervised learning algorithms. The SOM is a topographic organization in which nearby locations in the map represent inputs with similar properties. The ART model allows the number of clusters to vary with problem size and lets the user control the degree of similarity between members of the same clusters by means of a user-defined constant called the vigilance parameter. ART networks are used for many pattern recognition tasks, such as automatic target recognition and seismic signal processing.

Method of Moments

One of the statistical approaches for unsupervised learning is the method of moments. In the method of moments, the unknown parameters (of interest) in the model are related to the moments of one or more random variables, and thus, these unknown parameters can be estimated given the moments. The moments are usually estimated from samples empirically. The basic moments are first and second order moments. For a random vector, the first order moment is the mean vector, and the second order moment is the covariance matrix (when the mean is zero). Higher order moments are usually represented using tensors which are the generalization of matrices to higher orders as multi-dimensional arrays.

In particular, the method of moments is shown to be effective in learning the parameters of latent variable models. Latent variable models are statistical models where in addition to the observed variables, a set of latent variables also exists which is not observed. A highly practical example of latent variable models in machine learning is the topic modeling which is a statistical model for generating the words (observed variables) in the document based on the topic (latent variable) of the document. In the topic modeling, the words in the document are generated according to different statistical parameters when the topic of the document is changed. It is shown that method of moments (tensor decomposition techniques) consistently recover the parameters of a large class of latent variable models under some assumptions.

The Expectation–maximization algorithm (EM) is also one of the most practical methods for learning latent variable models. However, it can get stuck in local optima, and it is not guaranteed that the algorithm will converge to the true unknown parameters of the model. In contrast, for the method of moments, the global convergence is guaranteed under some conditions.

Semi-supervised Machine Learning Algorithm

Semi-supervised machine learning is a combination of supervised and unsupervised machine learning methods.

With more common supervised machine learning methods, you train a machine learning algorithm on a "labeled" dataset in which each record includes the outcome information. This allows the algorithm to deduce patterns and identify relationships between your target variable and the rest of the dataset based on information it already has. In contrast, unsupervised machine learning algorithms learn from a dataset without the outcome variable. In semi-supervised learning, an algorithm learns from a dataset that includes both labeled and unlabeled data, usually mostly unlabeled.

Importance of Semi-supervised Machine Learning

When you don't have enough labeled data to produce an accurate model and you don't have the ability or resources to get more data, you can use semi-supervised techniques to increase the size of your training data. For example, imagine you are developing a model intended to detect fraud for a large bank. Some fraud you know about, but other instances of fraud are slipping by without your knowledge. You can label the dataset with the fraud instances you're aware of, but the rest of your data will remain unlabelled:

Name	Loan Amount	Loan Repaid	Fraud
Ashley	100000	1	1
Chuck	25000	0	0
Tim	4000	1	1
Mike	150000	1	1
Colin	200000000	0	
Libby	400400	1	0
Sheila	3200	1	1
Mandi	34850	1	
Gareth	6570	0	0

You can use a semi-supervised learning algorithm to label the data, and retrain the model with the newly labeled dataset:

Name	Loan Amount	Load Repaid	Fraud
Ashley	100000	1	1
Chuck	25000	0	0
Tim	4000	1	1
Mike	150000	1	1
Colin	200000000	0	0

Libby	400400	1	0
Sheila	3200	1	1
Mandi	34850	1	1
Gareth	6570	0	0

Then, you apply the retrained model to new data, more accurately identifying fraud using supervised machine learning techniques. However, there is no way to verify that the algorithm has produced labels that are 100% accurate, resulting in less trustworthy outcomes than traditional supervised techniques.

Assumptions Used

In order to make any use of unlabeled data, we must assume some structure to the underlying distribution of data. Semi-supervised learning algorithms make use of at least one of the following assumptions.

Continuity Assumption

Points which are close to each other are more likely to share a label. This is also generally assumed in supervised learning and yields a preference for geometrically simple decision boundaries. In the case of semi-supervised learning, the smoothness assumption additionally yields a preference for decision boundaries in low-density regions, so that there are fewer points close to each other but in different classes.

Cluster Assumption

The data tend to form discrete clusters, and points in the same cluster are more likely to share a label (although data sharing a label may be spread across multiple clusters). This is a special case of the smoothness assumption and gives rise to feature learning with clustering algorithms.

Manifold Assumption

The data lie approximately on a manifold of much lower dimension than the input space. In this case we can attempt to learn the manifold using both the labeled and unlabeled data to avoid the curse of dimensionality. Then learning can proceed using distances and densities defined on the manifold.

The manifold assumption is practical when high-dimensional data are being generated by some process that may be hard to model directly, but which only has a few degrees of freedom. For instance, human voice is controlled by a few vocal folds, and images of various facial expressions are controlled by a few muscles. We would like in these cases to use distances and smoothness in the natural space of the generating problem, rather than in the space of all possible acoustic waves or images respectively.

The heuristic approach of self-training (also known as self-learning or self-labeling) is historically the oldest approach to semi-supervised learning, with examples of applications starting in the 1960s.

The transductive learning framework was formally introduced by Vladimir Vapnik in the 1970s. Interest in inductive learning using generative models also began in the 1970s. A *probably approximately correct* learning bound for semi-supervised learning of a Gaussian mixture was demonstrated by Ratsaby and Venkatesh in 1995.

Semi-supervised learning has recently become more popular and practically relevant due to the variety of problems for which vast quantities of unlabeled data are available—e.g. text on websites, protein sequences, or images.

Methods

Generative Models

Generative approaches to statistical learning first seek to estimate $p(x \mid y)$, the distribution of data points belonging to each class. The probability $p(y \mid x)$ that a given point x has label y is then proportional to $p(x \mid y)p(y)$ by Bayes' rule. Semi-supervised learning with generative models can be viewed either as an extension of supervised learning (classification plus information about $p(x)$) or as an extension of unsupervised learning (clustering plus some labels).

Generative models assume that the distributions take some particular form $p(x \mid y, \theta)$ parameterized by the vector θ. If these assumptions are incorrect, the unlabeled data may actually decrease the accuracy of the solution relative to what would have been obtained from labeled data alone. However, if the assumptions are correct, then the unlabeled data necessarily improves performance.

The unlabeled data are distributed according to a mixture of individual-class distributions. In order to learn the mixture distribution from the unlabeled data, it must be identifiable, that is, different parameters must yield different summed distributions. Gaussian mixture distributions are identifiable and commonly used for generative models.

The parameterized joint distribution can be written as $p(x, y \mid \theta) = p(y \mid \theta)p(x \mid y, \theta)$ by using the Chain rule. Each parameter vector θ is associated with a decision function $f_\theta(x) = \underset{y}{\operatorname{argmax}}\ p(y \mid x, \theta)$. The parameter is then chosen based on fit to both the labeled and unlabeled data, weighted by λ :

$$\underset{\Theta}{\operatorname{argmax}} \left(\log p(\{x_i, y_i\}_{i=1}^{l} \mid \theta) + \lambda \log p(\{x_i\}_{i=l+1}^{l+u} \mid \theta) \right).$$

Low-density Separation

Another major class of methods attempts to place boundaries in regions where there are few data points (labeled or unlabeled). One of the most commonly used algorithms is the transductive support vector machine, or TSVM (which, despite its name, may be used for inductive learning as well). Whereas support vector machines for supervised learning seek a decision boundary with maximal margin over the labeled data, the goal of TSVM is a labeling of the unlabeled data such that the decision boundary has maximal margin over all of the data. In addition to the standard hinge loss $(1 - yf(x))_+$ for labeled data, a loss function $(1 - \mid f(x) \mid)_+$ is introduced over the unlabeled data by letting $y = \operatorname{sign} f(x)$. TSVM then selects $f^*(x) = h^*(x) + b$ from a reproducing kernel Hilbert space $\mathcal{H}$ by minimizing the regularized empirical risk:

$$f^* = \underset{f}{\arg\min}\left(\sum_{i=1}^{l}(1 - y_i f(x_i))_+ + \lambda_1 \parallel h \parallel_{\mathcal{H}}^2 + \lambda_2 \sum_{i=l+1}^{l+u}(1 - |f(x_i)|)_+ \right).$$

An exact solution is intractable due to the non-convex term $(1 - |f(x)|)_+$, so research has focused on finding useful approximations.

Other approaches that implement low-density separation include Gaussian process models, information regularization, and entropy minimization (of which TSVM is a special case).

Graph-based Methods

Graph-based methods for semi-supervised learning use a graph representation of the data, with a node for each labeled and unlabeled example. The graph may be constructed using domain knowledge or similarity of examples; two common methods are to connect each data point to its k nearest neighbors or to examples within some distance ε. The weight W_{ij} of an edge between x_i and x_j is then set to $e^{\frac{-\|x_i - x_j\|^2}{\epsilon}}$.

Within the framework of manifold regularization, the graph serves as a proxy for the manifold. A term is added to the standard Tikhonov regularization problem to enforce smoothness of the solution relative to the manifold (in the intrinsic space of the problem) as well as relative to the ambient input space. The minimization problem becomes

$$\underset{f \in \mathcal{H}}{\arg\min}\left(\frac{1}{l}\sum_{i=1}^{l}V(f(x_i), y_i) + \lambda_A \parallel f \parallel_{\mathcal{H}}^2 + \lambda_I \int_{\mathcal{M}} \parallel \nabla_{\mathcal{M}} f(x) \parallel^2 dp(x) \right)$$

where $\mathcal{H}$ is a reproducing kernel Hilbert space and $\mathcal{M}$ is the manifold on which the data lie. The regularization parameters λ_A and λ_I control smoothness in the ambient and intrinsic spaces respectively. The graph is used to approximate the intrinsic regularization term. Defining the graph Laplacian $L = D - W$ where $D_{ii} = \sum_{j=1}^{l+u} W_{ij}$ and f the vector $[f(x_1) \ldots f(x_{l+u})]$, we have

$$\mathbf{f}^T L \mathbf{f} = \sum_{i,j=1}^{l+u} W_{ij}(f_i - f_j)^2 \approx \int_{\mathcal{M}} \parallel \nabla_{\mathcal{M}} f(x) \parallel^2 dp(x).$$

The Laplacian can also be used to extend the supervised learning algorithms: regularized least squares and support vector machines (SVM) to semi-supervised versions Laplacian regularized least squares and Laplacian SVM.

Heuristic Approaches

Some methods for semi-supervised learning are not intrinsically geared to learning from both unlabeled and labeled data, but instead make use of unlabeled data within a supervised learning framework. For instance, the labeled and unlabeled examples $x_1, \ldots, x_{l+u}$ may inform a choice of representation, distance metric, or kernel for the data in an unsupervised first step. Then supervised learning proceeds from only the labeled examples.

Self-training is a wrapper method for semi-supervised learning. First a supervised learning algorithm is trained based on the labeled data only. This classifier is then applied to the unlabeled data to generate more labeled examples as input for the supervised learning algorithm. Generally only the labels the classifier is most confident of are added at each step.

Co-training is an extension of self-training in which multiple classifiers are trained on different (ideally disjoint) sets of features and generate labeled examples for one another.

In Human Cognition

Human responses to formal semi-supervised learning problems have yielded varying conclusions about the degree of influence of the unlabeled data. More natural learning problems may also be viewed as instances of semi-supervised learning. Much of human concept learning involves a small amount of direct instruction (e.g. parental labeling of objects during childhood) combined with large amounts of unlabeled experience (e.g. observation of objects without naming or counting them, or at least without feedback).

Human infants are sensitive to the structure of unlabeled natural categories such as images of dogs and cats or male and female faces. More recent work has shown that infants and children take into account not only the unlabeled examples available, but the sampling process from which labeled examples arise.

Practical Applications of Semi-supervised Learning

- Speech Analysis: Since labeling of audio files is a very intensive task, Semi-Supervised learning is a very natural approach to solve this problem.

- Internet Content Classification: Labeling each webpage is an impractical and unfeasible process and thus uses Semi-Supervised learning algorithms. Even the Google search algorithm uses a variant of Semi-Supervised learning to rank the relevance of a webpage for a given query.

- Protein Sequence Classification: Since DNA strands are typically very large in size, the rise of Semi-Supervised learning has been imminent in this field.

Reinforcement Machine Learning Algorithm

Reinforcement learning is the training of machine learning models to make a sequence of decisions. The agent learns to achieve a goal in an uncertain, potentially complex environment. In reinforcement learning, an artificial intelligence faces a game-like situation. The computer employs trial and error to come up with a solution to the problem. To get the machine to do what the programmer wants, the artificial intelligence gets either rewards or penalties for the actions it performs. Its goal is to maximize the total reward.

Although the designer sets the reward policy–that is, the rules of the game–he gives the model no hints or suggestions for how to solve the game. It's up to the model to figure out how to perform the task to maximize the reward, starting from totally random trials and finishing with sophisticated tactics and superhuman skills. By leveraging the power of search and many trials, reinforcement learning is currently the most effective way to hint machine's creativity. In contrast to human beings, artificial intelligence can gather experience from thousands of parallel gameplays if a reinforcement learning algorithm is run on a sufficiently powerful computer infrastructure.

Examples of Reinforcement Learning

Applications of reinforcement learning were in the past limited by weak computer infrastructure. However, as Gerard Tesauro's backgamon AI superplayer developed in 1990's shows, progress did happen. That early progress is now rapidly changing with powerful new computational technologies opening the way to completely new inspiring applications.

Training the models that control autonomous cars is an excellent example of a potential application of reinforcement learning. In an ideal situation, the computer should get no instructions on driving the car. The programmer would avoid hard-wiring anything connected with the task and allow the machine to learn from its own errors. In a perfect situation, the only hard-wired element would be the reward function.

For example, in usual circumstances we would require an autonomous vehicle to put safety first, minimize ride time, reduce pollution, offer passengers comfort and obey the rules of law. With an autonomous race car, on the other hand, we would emphasize speed much more than the driver's comfort. The programmer cannot predict everything that could happen on the road. Instead of building lengthy "if-then" instructions, the programmer prepares the reinforcement learning agent to be capable of learning from the system of rewards and penalties. The agent (another name for reinforcement learning algorithms performing the task) gets rewards for reaching specific goals.

Another example: Deepsense.ai took part in the "Learning to run" project, which aimed to train a virtual runner from scratch. The runner is an advanced and precise musculoskeletal model designed by the Stanford Neuromuscular Biomechanics Laboratory. Learning the agent how to run is a first step in building a new generation of prosthetic legs, ones that automatically recognize people's walking patterns and tweak themselves to make moving easier and more effective. While it is possible and has been done in Stanford's labs, hard-wiring all the commands and predicting all possible patterns of walking requires a lot of work from highly skilled programmers.

Challenges with Reinforcement Learning

The main challenge in reinforcement learning lays in preparing the simulation environment, which is highly dependent on the task to be performed. When the model has to go superhuman in Chess, Go or Atari games, preparing the simulation environment is relatively simple. When it comes to building a model capable of driving an autonomous car, building a realistic simulator is crucial before letting the car ride on the street. The model has to figure out how to brake or avoid a collision in a safe environment, where sacrificing even a thousand cars comes at a minimal cost. Transferring the model out of the training environment and into to the real world is where things get tricky.

Scaling and tweaking the neural network controlling the agent is another challenge. There is no way to communicate with the network other than through the system of rewards and penalties. This in particular may lead to catastrophic forgetting, where acquiring new knowledge causes some of the old to be erased from the network.

Yet another challenge is reaching a local optimum – that is the agent performs the task as it is, but not in the optimal or required way. A "jumper" jumping like a kangaroo instead of doing the thing that was expected of it-walking-is a great example.

Finally, there are agents that will optimize the prize without performing the task it was designed for.

What Distinguishes Reinforcement Learning from Deep Learning and Machine Learning?

In fact, there should be no clear divide between machine learning, deep learning and reinforcement learning. It is like a parallelogram – rectangle – square relation, where machine learning is the broadest category and the deep reinforcement learning the most narrow one.

In the same way, reinforcement learning is a specialized application of machine and deep learning techniques, designed to solve problems in a particular way.

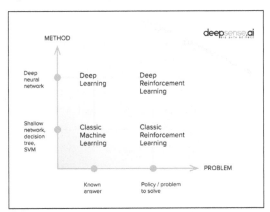

Although the ideas seem to differ, there is no sharp divide between these subtypes. Moreover, they merge within projects, as the models are designed not to stick to a "pure type" but to perform the task in the most effective way possible. So "what precisely distinguishes machine learning, deep learning and reinforcement learning" is actually a tricky question to answer.

Machine learning is a form of AI in which computers are given the ability to progressively improve the performance of a specific task with data, without being directly programmed (this is Arthur Lee Samuel's definition. He coined the term "machine learning", of which there are two types, supervised and unsupervised machine learning

Supervised machine learning happens when a programmer can provide a label for every training input into the machine learning system.

By analyzing the historical data taken from coal mines, deepsense.ai prepared an automated system for predicting dangerous seismic events up to 8 hours before they occur. The records of seismic events were taken from 24 coal mines that had collected data for several months. The model was able to recognize the likelihood of an explosion by analyzing the readings from the previous 24 hours.

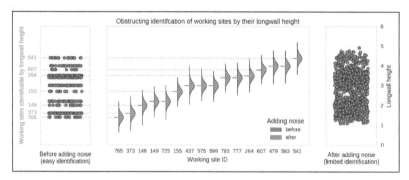

From the AI point of view, a single model was performing a single task on a clarified and normalized dataset.

Unsupervised learning takes place when the model is provided only with the input data, but no explicit labels. It has to dig through the data and find the hidden structure or relationships within. The designer might not know what the structure is or what the machine learning model is going to find.

- An example we employed was for churn prediction. We analyzed customer data and designed an algorithm to group similar customers. However, we didn't choose the groups ourselves. Later on, we could identify high-risk groups (those with a high churn rate) and our client knew which customers they should approach first.

- Another example of unsupervised learning is anomaly detection, where the algorithm has to spot the element that doesn't fit in with the group. It may be a flawed product, potentially fraudulent transaction or any other event associated with breaking the norm.

Deep learning consists of several layers of neural networks, designed to perform more sophisticated tasks. The construction of deep learning models was inspired by the design of the human brain, but simplified. Deep learning models consist of a few neural network layers which are in principle responsible for gradually learning more abstract features about particular data.

Although deep learning solutions are able to provide marvelous results, in terms of scale they are no match for the human brain. Each layer uses the outcome of a previous one as an input and the whole network is trained as a single whole. The core concept of creating an artificial neural network is not new, but only recently has modern hardware provided enough computational power to effectively train such networks by exposing a sufficient number of examples. Extended adoption has brought about frameworks like TensorFlow, Keras and PyTorch, all of which have made building machine learning models much more convenient.

Example: Deepsense.ai designed a deep learning-based model for the National Oceanic and Atmospheric Administration (NOAA). It was designed to recognize Right whales from aerial photos taken by researchers. From a technical point of view, recognizing a particular specimen of whales from aerial photos is pure deep learning. The solution consists of a few machine learning models performing separate tasks. The first one was in charge of finding the head of the whale in the photograph while the second normalized the photo by cutting and turning it, which ultimately provided a unified view (a passport photo) of a single whale.

The third model was responsible for recognizing particular whales from photos that had been prepared and processed earlier. A network composed of 5 million neurons located the blowhead bonnet-tip. Over 941,000 neurons looked for the head and more than 3 million neurons were used to classify the particular whale. That's over 9 million neurons performing the task, which may seem like a lot, but pales in comparison to the more than 100 billion neurons at work in the human brain. We later used a similar deep learning-based solution to diagnose diabetic retinopathy using images of patients' retinas.

Reinforcement learning, as stated above employs a system of rewards and penalties to compel the computer to solve a problem by itself. Human involvement is limited to changing the environment and tweaking the system of rewards and penalties. As the computer maximizes the reward, it is prone to seeking unexpected ways of doing it. Human involvement is focused on preventing it from exploiting the system and motivating the machine to perform the task in the way expected. Reinforcement learning is useful when there is no "proper way" to perform a task, yet there are rules the model has to follow to perform its duties correctly. Take the road code, for example.

Example: By tweaking and seeking the optimal policy for deep reinforcement learning, we built an agent that in just 20 minutes reached a superhuman level in playing Atari games. Similar algorithms in principal can be used to build AI for an autonomous car or a prosthetic leg. In fact, one of the best ways to evaluate the reinforcement learning approach is to give the model an Atari video game to play, such as Arkanoid or Space Invaders. According to Google Brain's Marc G. Bellemare, who introduced Atari video games as a reinforcement learning benchmark, "although challenging, these environments remain simple enough that we can hope to achieve measurable progress as we attempt to solve them".

In particular, if artificial intelligence is going to drive a car, learning to play some Atari classics can be considered a meaningful intermediate milestone. A potential application of reinforcement learning in autonomous vehicles is the following interesting case. A developer is unable to predict all future road situations, so letting the model train itself with a system of penalties and rewards in a varied environment is possibly the most effective way for the AI to broaden the experience it both has and collects.

Algorithms for Control Learning

Even if the issue of exploration is disregarded and even if the state was observable (assumed here-after), the problem remains to use past experience to find out which actions are good.

Criterion of Optimality

Policy

The agent's action selection is modeled as a map called *policy*:

$$\pi : A \times S \to [0,1]$$

$$\pi(a,s) = \Pr(a_t = a | s_t = s)$$

The policy map gives the probability of taking action a when in state s. There are also non-proba-bilistic policies.

State-value Function

Value function $V_\pi(s)$ is defined as the *expected return* starting with state s, i.e. $s_0 = s$, and succes-sively following policy π. Hence, roughly speaking, the value function estimates "how good" it is to be in a given state:

$$V_\pi(s) = E[R] = E\left[\sum_{t=0}^{\infty} \gamma^t r_t | s_0 = s \right],$$

where the random variable R denotes the return, and is defined as the sum of future discounted rewards.

$$R = \sum_{t=0}^{\infty} \gamma^t r_t,$$

where r_t is the reward at step t, $\gamma \in [0,1]$ is the discount-rate.

The algorithm must find a policy with maximum expected return. From the theory of MDPs it is known that, without loss of generality, the search can be restricted to the set of so-called stationary policies. A policy is stationary if the action-distribution returned by it depends only on the last state visited (from the observation agent's history). The search can be further restricted to deterministic stationary policies. A deterministic stationary policy deterministically selects actions based on the current state. Since any such policy can be identified with a mapping from the set of states to the set of actions, these policies can be identified with such mappings with no loss of generality.

Brute Force

The brute force approach entails two steps:

- For each possible policy, sample returns while following it.
- Choose the policy with the largest expected return.

One problem with this is that the number of policies can be large, or even infinite. Another is that variance of the returns may be large, which requires many samples to accurately estimate the return of each policy.

These problems can be ameliorated if we assume some structure and allow samples generated from one policy to influence the estimates made for others. The two main approaches for achieving this are value function estimation and direct policy search.

Value Function

Value function approaches attempt to find a policy that maximizes the return by maintaining a set of estimates of expected returns for some policy (usually either the "current" [on-policy] or the optimal [off-policy] one).

These methods rely on the theory of MDPs, where optimality is defined in a sense that is stronger than the above one: A policy is called optimal if it achieves the best expected return from *any* initial state (i.e., initial distributions play no role in this definition). Again, an optimal policy can always be found amongst stationary policies.

To define optimality in a formal manner, define the value of a policy π by,

$$V^\pi(s) = E[R|s, \pi],$$

where R stands for the return associated with following π from the initial state s. Defining $V^*(s)$ as the maximum possible value of $V^\pi(s)$, where π is allowed to change,

$$V^*(s) = \max_\pi V^\pi(s).$$

A policy that achieves these optimal values in each state is called optimal. Clearly, a policy that is optimal in this strong sense is also optimal in the sense that it maximizes the expected return ρ^π, since $\rho^\pi = E[V^\pi(S)]$, where S is a state randomly sampled from the distribution π.

Although state-values suffice to define optimality, it is useful to define action-values. Given a state s, an action a and a policy π, the action-value of the pair (s, a) under π is defined by

$$Q^\pi(s, a) = E[R|s, a, \pi],$$

Where R now stands for the random return associated with first taking action in state s and following π, thereafter.

The theory of MDPs states that if π^* is an optimal policy, we act optimally (take the optimal action) by choosing the action from $Q^{\pi^*}(s, \cdot)$ with the highest value at each state, s. The *action-value function* of such an optimal policy $\left(Q^{\pi^*}\right)$ is called the *optimal action-value function* and is commonly denoted by Q^*. In summary, the knowledge of the optimal action-value function alone suffices to know how to act optimally.

Assuming full knowledge of the MDP, the two basic approaches to compute the optimal action-value function are value iteration and policy iteration. Both algorithms compute a sequence of functions Q_k ($k = 0,1,2,\dots$) that converge to Q^*. Computing these functions involves computing expectations over the whole state-space, which is impractical for all but the smallest (finite) MDPs. In reinforcement learning methods, expectations are approximated by averaging over samples and using function approximation techniques to cope with the need to represent value functions over large state-action spaces.

Monte Carlo Methods

Monte Carlo methods can be used in an algorithm that mimics policy iteration. Policy iteration consists of two steps: *policy evaluation* and *policy improvement*.

Monte Carlo is used in the policy evaluation step. In this step, given a stationary, deterministic policy π, the goal is to compute the function values $Q^\pi(s,a)$ (or a good approximation to them) for all state-action pairs (s,a). Assuming (for simplicity) that the MDP is finite, that sufficient memory is available to accommodate the action-values and that the problem is episodic and after each episode a new one starts from some random initial state. Then, the estimate of the value of a given state-action pair (s,a) can be computed by averaging the sampled returns that originated from (s,a) over time. Given sufficient time, this procedure can thus construct a precise estimate Q of the action-value function Q^π. This finishes the description of the policy evaluation step.

In the policy improvement step, the next policy is obtained by computing a *greedy* policy with respect to Q: Given a state s, this new policy returns an action that maximizes $Q(s,\cdot)$. In practice lazy evaluation can defer the computation of the maximizing actions to when they are needed.

Problems with this procedure include:

- The procedure may spend too much time evaluating a suboptimal policy.

- It uses samples inefficiently in that a long trajectory improves the estimate only of the *single* state-action pair that started the trajectory.

- When the returns along the trajectories have *high variance*, convergence is slow.

- It works in episodic problems only.

- It works in small, finite MDPs only.

Temporal Difference Methods

The first problem is corrected by allowing the procedure to change the policy (at some or all states) before the values settle. This too may be problematic as it might prevent convergence. Most current algorithms do this, giving rise to the class of *generalized policy iteration* algorithms . Many *actor critic* methods belong to this category.

The second issue can be corrected by allowing trajectories to contribute to any state-action pair in them. This may also help to some extent with the third problem, although a better solution when returns have high variance is Sutton's temporal difference (TD) methods that are based on the recursive Bellman equation. The computation in TD methods can be incremental (when after each transition the memory is changed and the transition is thrown away), or batch (when the transitions are batched and the estimates are computed once based on the batch). Batch methods, such as the least-squares temporal difference method, may use the information in the samples better, while incremental methods are the only choice when batch methods are infeasible due to their high computational or memory complexity. Some methods try to combine the two approaches. Methods based on temporal differences also overcome the fourth issue.

In order to address the fifth issue, function approximation methods are used. Linear function approximation starts with a mapping ϕ that assigns a finite-dimensional vector to each state-action pair. Then, the action values of a state-action pair (s, a) are obtained by linearly combining the components of $\phi(s, a)$ with some weights θ:

$$Q(s, a) = \sum_{i=1}^{d} \theta_i \phi_i(s, a).$$

The algorithms then adjust the weights, instead of adjusting the values associated with the individual state-action pairs. Methods based on ideas from nonparametric statistics (which can be seen to construct their own features) have been explored.

Value iteration can also be used as a starting point, giving rise to the Q-learning algorithm and its many variants.

The problem with using action-values is that they may need highly precise estimates of the competing action values that can be hard to obtain when the returns are noisy. Though this problem is mitigated to some extent by temporal difference methods. Using the so-called compatible function approximation method compromises generality and efficiency. Another problem specific to TD comes from their reliance on the recursive Bellman equation. Most TD methods have a so-called λ parameter $(0 \leq \lambda \leq 1)$ that can continuously interpolate between Monte Carlo methods that do not rely on the Bellman equations and the basic TD methods that rely entirely on the Bellman equations. This can be effective in palliating this issue.

Direct Policy Search

An alternative method is to search directly in (some subset of) the policy space, in which case the problem becomes a case of stochastic optimization. The two approaches available are gradient-based and gradient-free methods.

Gradient-based methods (policy gradient methods) start with a mapping from a finite-dimensional (parameter) space to the space of policies: given the parameter vector θ, let π_θ denote the policy associated to θ. Defining the performance function by,

$$\rho(\theta) = \rho^{\pi_\theta},$$

under mild conditions this function will be differentiable as a function of the parameter vector θ. If the gradient of ρ was known, one could use gradient ascent. Since an analytic expression for the gradient is not available, only a noisy estimate is available. Such an estimate can be constructed in many ways, giving rise to algorithms such as Williams' REINFORCE method (which is known as the likelihood ratio method in the simulation-based optimization literature). Policy search methods have been used in the robotics context. Many policy search methods may get stuck in local optima (as they are based on local search).

A large class of methods avoids relying on gradient information. These include simulated annealing, cross-entropy search or methods of evolutionary computation. Many gradient-free methods can achieve (in theory and in the limit) a global optimum.

Policy search methods may converge slowly given noisy data. For example, this happens in episodic problems when the trajectories are long and the variance of the returns is large. Value-function based methods that rely on temporal differences might help in this case. In recent years, *actor–critic methods* have been proposed and performed well on various problems.

Theory

Both the asymptotic and finite-sample behavior of most algorithms is well understood. Algorithms with provably good online performance (addressing the exploration issue) are known.

Efficient exploration of large MDPs is largely unexplored (except for the case of bandit problems). Although finite-time performance bounds appeared for many algorithms, these bounds are expected to be rather loose and thus more work is needed to better understand the relative advantages and limitations.

For incremental algorithms, asymptotic convergence issues have been settled. Temporal-difference-based algorithms converge under a wider set of conditions than was previously possible (for example, when used with arbitrary, smooth function approximation).

Various Practical Applications of Reinforcement Learning

- RL can be used in robotics for industrial automation.

- RL can be used in machine learning and data processing.

- RL can be used to create training systems that provide custom instruction and materials according to the requirement of students.

RL can be used in Large Environments in the Following Situations

- A model of the environment is known, but an analytic solution is not available;

- Only a simulation model of the environment is given (the subject of simulation-based optimization);

- The only way to collect information about the environment is to interact with it.

Machine Learning and Artificial Intelligence

Machine Learning and Artificial Intelligence are creating a huge buzz worldwide. The plethora of applications in Artificial Intelligence have changed the face of technology. These terms Machine Learning and Artificial Intelligence are often used interchangeably. However, there is a stark difference between the two that is still unknown to the industry professionals.

Let's start by taking an example of Virtual Personal Assistants which have been familiar to most of us from quite some time now.

Working of Virtual Personal Assistants

Siri(part of Apple Inc.'s iOS, watchOS, macOS, and tvOS operating systems), Google Now (a feature of Google Search offering predictive cards with information and daily updates in the Google app for Android and iOS.), Cortana (Cortana is a virtual assistant created by Microsoft for Windows 10) are intelligent digital personal assistants on the platforms like iOS, Android and Windows respectively. To put it plainly, they help to find relevant information when requested using voice. For instance, for answering queries like 'What's the temperature today?' or 'What is the way to the nearest supermarket' etc. and the assistant will react by searching information, transferring that information from the phone or sending commands to various other applications.

AI is critical in these applications, as they gather data on the user's request and utilize that data to perceive speech in a better manner and serve the user with answers that are customized to his inclination. Microsoft says that Cortana "consistently finds out about its user" and that it will in the end build up the capacity to anticipate users' needs and cater to them. Virtual assistants process a tremendous measure of information from an assortment of sources to find out about users and be more compelling in helping them arrange and track their data. Machine learning is a vital part of these personal assistants as they gather and refine the data based on user's past participation with them. Thereon, this arrangement of information is used to render results that are custom-made to user's inclinations.

Roughly speaking, Artificial Intelligence (AI) is when a computer algorithm does intelligent work. On the other hand, Machine Learning is a part of AI that learns from the data that also involves the information gathered from the previous experiences and allows the computer program to change its behavior accordingly. Artificial Intelligence is the superset of Machine Learning i.e. all the Machine Learning is Artificial Intelligence but not all the AI is Machine Learning.

Artificial Intelligence	Machine Learning
AI manages more comprehensive issues of automating a system. This computerization should be possible by utilizing any field such as image processing, cognitive science, neural systems, machine learning etc.	Machine Learning (ML) manages influencing user's machine to gain from the external environment. This external environment can be sensors, electronic segments, external storage gadgets and numerous other devices.
AI manages the making of machines, frameworks and different gadgets savvy by enabling them to think and do errands as all people generally do.	What ML does, depends on the user input or a query requested by the client, the framework checks whether it is available in the knowledge base or not. If it is available, it will restore the outcome to the user related with that query, however if it isn't stored initially, the machine will take in the user input and will enhance its knowledge base, to give a better value to the end user

Computer Vision

Computer vision is a field of computer science that works on enabling computers to see, identify and process images in the same way that human vision does, and then provide appropriate output. It is like imparting human intelligence and instincts to a computer. In reality though, it is a difficult task to enable computers to recognize images of different objects.

Computer vision is closely linked with artificial intelligence, as the computer must interpret what it sees, and then perform appropriate analysis or act accordingly.

Computer vision's goal is not only to see, but also process and provide useful results based on the observation. For example, a computer could create a 3D image from a 2D image, such as those in cars, and provide important data to the car and/or driver. For example, cars could be fitted with computer vision which would be able to identify and distinguish objects on and around the road such as traffic lights, pedestrians, traffic signs and so on, and act accordingly. The intelligent device could provide inputs to the driver or even make the car stop if there is a sudden obstacle on the road.

When a human who is driving a car sees someone suddenly move into the path of the car, the driver must react instantly. In a split second, human vision has completed a complex task, that of identifying the object, processing data and deciding what to do. Computer vision's aim is to enable computers to perform the same kind of tasks as humans with the same efficiency.

Computer vision permits computers, and in this manner robots, other computer-controlled vehicles, and everything from processing plants and farm equipment to semi-independent cars and drones, to run all the more productively and shrewdly and even securely. In any case, computer vision's significance has turned out to be considerably increasingly evident in a world deluged with digital pictures. Since the advent of camera-prepared smartphones, we've been accumulating amazing measures of visual symbolism that, without somebody or something to process everything, is far less valuable and usable than it ought to be. We're now witnessing computer vision enable purchasers to compose and get access to their photograph gallery without expecting to include labels in, say, Google Photos, yet how to remain over the billions of pictures shared online consistently which is around 3 billion, as indicated by Mary Meeker.

To get a thought of the amount we're discussing here, a year ago photograph printing service Photoworld did the math and discovered it would take an individual 10 whole years to try and take a look at all the photographs shared on Snapchat, in simply the most recent hour. What's more, obviously, in those 10 years, an additional 880,000 years' worth of photographs would have been as of now been produced if things proceed at a similar rate. Basically, our reality has turned out to be progressively loaded up with digital pictures and we require computers to understand everything. It's as of now well past human capacities to keep up.

The determined computer vision ventures we have seen in 2018 connote that the innovation is finally making up for lost time with the applications that developers have since a long time ago longed to make. It additionally implies that it will further be less expensive to create customized computer vision applications.

ModiFace gives clients a chance to attempt on cosmetics utilizing just their cell phones. Topology does likewise for eyewear. MTailor makes especially custom fitted pants and shirts utilizing a similar procedure. Outside of fashion, Pottery Barn gives clients a chance to perceive what new furniture may look like in their homes, and Hover transforms clients' photos of their homes into completely estimated 3D models. None of these tasks is as muddled as self-driving vehicles and cashier less supermarkets, yet that is the thing that qualifies the present era of computer vision products as a harbinger for monstrous deployment in the following couple of years: Once it ends up being feasible for little organizations to create working computer vision products for a mass audience, the innovation will start invading pretty much all aspects of our lives.

Microsoft as of late made an algorithm that inaccurately identified what was in pictures simply 3.5% of the time. That implies it was right 96.5% of the time. Luckily, a portion of the masters at Google brainstormed another option: Back in 2012, they bolstered a computer loads and heaps of pictures and let it make sense of patterns all alone and see what occurred, a procedure named deep learning. Turns out that, with adequate algorithms, computers can discover patterns individually and start to deal with pictures without expecting people to handhold en route. Today, some deep learning calculations are shockingly exact.

There is no end of uses for computer vision. Think about any modern circumstance, and there's possible a computer vision-related solution that can or will sometime be deployed. Take those extravagant Tesla cars we've heard so much about: They depend on a large group of cameras and in addition sonar, that not just keep your vehicle from floating out of a path, however, can perceive what different objects and vehicles are around you and furthermore pursue signs and traffic signals. Truth be told, Tesla's vehicles really look under the vehicle before you to the vehicle ahead to consider traffic patterns. So also, as dependent on innovation as the present medicinal services as of now seems to be, computer vision will empower better approaches for doing diagnostics that are nearer to Star Trek to analyze X-rays, MRI, CAT, mammography, and different outputs. All things considered, nearly 90% of every medical data is picture based.

The recent leaps forward that Amazon, Microsoft, and Google displayed in 2018 have been the impetus that will drive computer vision over the tipping point. Product developers and AI engineers are now chipping away at new solutions that make use of computer vision and augmented reality. Hardware makers are enhancing component execution and expanding cost efficiencies to improve this innovation and make it more accessible. One of the greatest not so distant future advancements will be tied in with training data. Currently, people still need to prepare computer vision AI with manually named pictures. If you've at any point filled out a web form that expected you to pick a couple of pictures from a grid appearing basic articles like a storefront or a vehicle, you've really taken an interest in making labeled data for computer vision ventures. Be that as it may, as the innovation enhances, AI will figure out how to prepare AI, further streamlining the procedure and accelerating the rate of enhancement.

The market for computer vision is developing nearly as fast as the capacities. It's anticipated to reach $26.2 billion by 2025, developing more than 30% for every year. Artificial intelligence is the future, and computer vision is the most amazing appearance of that future. Before long, it will be anyplace and all over the place, to such an extent that you won't even notice it.

Examples of Computer Vision

Autonomous Vehicles

Computer vision is necessary to enable self-driving cars. Manufacturers such as Tesla, BMW,

Volvo, and Audi use multiple cameras, lidar, radar, and ultrasonic sensors to acquire images from the environment so that their self-driving cars can detect objects, lane markings, signs and traffic signals to safely drive.

Google Translate App

All you need to do to read signs in a foreign language is to point your phone's camera at the words and let the Google Translate app tell you what it means in your preferred language almost instantly. By using optical character recognition to see the image and augmented reality to overlay an accurate translation, this is a convenient tool that uses computer vision.

Facial Recognition

China is definitely on the cutting edge of using facial recognition technology, and they use it for police work, payment portals and security checkpoints at the airport and even to dispense toilet paper and prevent theft of the paper at Tiantan Park in Beijing, among many other applications.

Healthcare

Since 90 percent of all medical data is image based there is a plethora of uses for computer vision in medicine. From enabling new medical diagnostic methods to analyze X-rays, mammography and other scans to monitoring patients to identify problems earlier and assist with surgery, expect that our medical institutions and professionals and patients will benefit from computer vision today and even more in the future as its rolled out in healthcare.

Real-time Sports Tracking

Ball and puck tracking on televised sports has been common for a while now, but computer vision is also helping play and strategy analysis, player performance and ratings, as well as to track the brand sponsorship visibility in sports broadcasts.

Agriculture

At CES 2019, John Deere featured a semi-autonomous combine harvester that uses artificial intelligence and computer vision to analyze grain quality as it gets harvested and to find the optimal route through the crops. There's also great potential for computer vision to identify weeds so that herbicides can be sprayed directly on them instead of on the crops. This is expected to reduce the amount of herbicides needed by 90 percent.

Manufacturing

Computer vision is helping manufacturers run more safely, intelligently and effectively in a variety of ways. Predictive maintenance is just one example where equipment is monitored with computer vision to intervene before a breakdown would cause expensive downtime. Packaging and product quality are monitored, and defective products are also reduced with computer vision.

Related Areas of Computer Vision

Computer vision, or from here forward, just vision, is a broad and complex field of study that touches upon many classical fields, and many new areas of inquiry. There are many opinions about what sort of background is necessary for computer vision, but one thing is certain–inspirations for new computer vision methods have come from fields as diverse as psychology, neuroscience, physics, robotics, and statistics. To get a sense of where computer vision lies in relation to some other areas.

Optics, Photograph and Photogrammetry

Vision deals with light and its interaction with surfaces, so of course optics plays a role in understanding computer vision systems. Cameras, lenses, focussing, binocular vision, depth-of-field, sensor sensitivity, time of exposure, and other concepts from optics and photography are all relevant to computer vision. Traditionally, when computer vision focused heavily on precise measurments of the world through camera systems, understanding optics was of paramount importance. The focus on precise measurement using computer vision systems has subsided somewhat, and today the field is more focused on working with uncalibrated systems and noisy measurements.

Computer Graphics and Art

Computer graphics and art are about making images, whether realistic or fantastic, from knowledge of the world. For example, given a geometric description of a pair of dice, computer graphics algorithms render an image of the dice.

Often referred to as the "inverse" of computer graphics, computer vision attempts to make inferences about the world from images. Given a picture of two objects, we would like to infer that they are roughly cubical, and that they are likely to be dice, although we can never be completely sure.

Computer graphics and notions from art can teach us a lot that is useful in computer vision, by making it clear just what cues we use to make inferences about the world. For example, any good portrait artist knows that if a human eye is painted without a "highlight" showing a reflected light in the eye, the person's face can appear lifeless and inanimate. Conversely, a vision system may pick up on subtle specular highlights to conclude that a surface is wet, transparent, or reflective, features associated with living creatures, rather than inanimate objects. By understanding the importance of such cues in making art life-like, we gain insight into the cues that vision systems might use to categorize objects.

Neuroscience and Physiology

The human eye, the central nervous system, and the brain are all marvels of complex structure and bewildering performance. Studying these systems often provides insight, inspiration, and clues about artificial vision system design. How can a vision system be designed with no external calibration, with no direct measurement of "camera" direction, with no up-front specification of features? The human visual system seems to do all of these things. Even if we are born with sophisticated vision capabilities (which is a source of current debate), we can still ask how the relatively "dumb" process of evolution managed to produce such an extraordinary vision system. Like other evolved capabilities such as flight, we expect to see in simpler organisms precursors of our most sophisticated capabilities that use similar designs, so that evolution or learning could make a small step to produce our current system. These arguments invite a type of analysis that may ultimately lead to more sophisticated artificial vision systems.

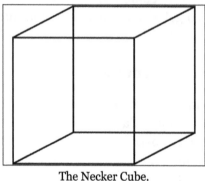

The Necker Cube.

This classic illustration demonstrates that the same image can result from different real-world objects. In particular, the image shown could result from a wire-frame object in which the viewer's eyes are above the object or a different object in which the viewer's eyes are below the object. If you are having trouble seeing both interpretations of the object, the act of blinking one's eyes often helps to see the other interpretation. Figure gives additional cues to see the two possible orientations of the cube.

Psychology and Psychophysics

Understanding the limits and capabilities of humans in performing visual tasks can offer important insights into the design of artificial vision systems. Where human vision systems fail dramatically, for example in the presence of certain visual illusions, is a particularly fascinating subject. Human responses to visual illusions can provide insight into processing (such as center-surround filters), deficits (such as the "blind spot" on the retina, and the difference between high level and low-level visual processing (Kanisza triangle). Psychophysics, a sub-field of psychology that studies how stimuli are perceived by humans and animals, can also offer insights into the structure of processing and assumptions that may be made by humans and other animals. For example, just recording the speed at which a human responds in a particular task, like reading a word, may rule out certain theories as to how certain visual stimuli are processed.

Probability, Statistics and Machine Learning

The mathematical subfield of probability, the field of statistics, and the computer science discipline of machine learning have become essential tools in computer vision. Each of these areas plays a major role in computer vision. Here, we make a few introductory comments about the role of these areas of study in computer vision.

The Ill-posed Nature of Vision

We can never be completely sure of what we are seeing, although it certainly doesn't feel that way.

The task of vision can be seen as trying to infer the state of the world, or the future state of the world, from the images that fall upon our retinas.

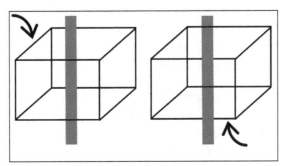

Disambiguating the Necker Cube.

One cue that can disambiguate the geometry behind an ambiguous image is occlusion. On the left, the occlusions imply a certain orientation of the Necker cube in which the observer is looking down on the top of a cube. On the right, the occlusions suggest that we are looking up into the bottom of a cube.

Since there are many different states of the world that could produce the same images on our retinas, there is no fool-proof way of distinguishing among the various structures or objects that might have created a particular image. Thus, if our goal is to infer the state of the world with certainty, then we are defeated from the start. In mathematical terms, vision is an ill-posed problem, since there does not exist a single, correct answer to the question of questions like "What kind of object is pictured in this image?" This, like many other phenomena in computer vision, is highlighted by certain classical visual illusions like the Necker cube.

Because there are multiple potential causes of each image we see, it is helpful to be able to select some notion of the "best" one. While there are many potential methods for deciding which one is best, a common approach is to try to follow the following approach:

- Develop a simplified statistical model of the experimental setting.

- Using the statistical model, evaluate the probability of each outcome.

- Choose the outcome that is consistent with our observations whose probability is highest under the statistical model.

Following these steps is a complex process that embodies much of the work done by computer vision researchers today. There is no "best" statistical model for a particular problem. Different models make different assumptions in an attempt to run faster, give more accurate answers, be applicable in more general settings, or satisfy various other requirements.

Limitations of Probability and Statistics

While techniques of probability and statistics may appear to be useful in computer vision, they are certainly not a panacea. A variety of troubling questions remain for which there are not yet any good answers. Some of these questions include the following:

- The stationarity assumption: Many machine learning methods assume that the distributions from which we are "trained" are the same distributions on which we are "tested". In other words, they assume that the probability of something occurring in the past is the same as that of it occurring in the future. We will refer to this as the stationarity assumption, since stationarity is the property of a random process, informally speaking, that its parameters do not vary in time. However, it is rare to encounter a true process that is stationary, or even approximately stationary. Thus, some of the fundamental assumptions that are behind many learning algorithms appear to be false.

- Insufficient training data: If we are to base our decisions on visual experience, it would appear that we should estimate the probabilities of complex events that we see in images. But the number of degrees of freedom in complex stimuli, such as faces, is enormous, and the number of examples needed to estimate distributions of quantities with large numbers of degrees of freedom is enormous. It frequently appears as though there is not enough data to estimate the probabilities of interest well. If these probabilities are estimated poorly, then we expect the decisions based on them to be poor as well. What is the resolution of this paradox?

Developing models with limited degrees of freedom appears to be one possible route out of this quagmire. Techniques such as regularization, sparseness priors, manifold learning, and feature selection, some of which are addressed in this text, are all attempts to deal with this problem. But up to now, they are mostly quite unsatisfying. We still do not understand how humans are capable of learning from data as efficiently as they do.

References

- Machine-learning-definition: expertsystem.com, Retrieved 06 August, 2019
- Supervised-machine-learning: datarobot.com, Retrieved 25 January, 2019
- Ml-semi-supervised-learning: geeksforgeeks.org, Retrieved 15 May, 2019
- What-is-reinforcement-learning-the-complete-guide: deepsense.ai, Retrieved 29 July, 2019
- Computer-vision- 32309: techopedia.com, Retrieved 18 August, 2019
- Computer-vision-the-future-of-artificial-intelligence: analyticsinsight.net, Retrieved 23 April, 2019
- Amazing-examples-of-computer-and-machine-vision-in-practice: forbes.com, Retrieved 16 June, 2019

Fuzzy Logic and Artificial Intelligence

The form of logic in which the truth values vary between the real numbers of 0 and 1 is known as fuzzy logic. It is primarily applied in artificial intelligence. This chapter discusses the use of fuzzy logic in this field.

The term fuzzy mean things which are not very clear or vague. In real life, we may come across a situation where we can't decide whether the statement is true or false. At that time, fuzzy logic offers very valuable flexibility for reasoning. We can also consider the uncertainties of any situation.

One legacy artificial and machine learning technology is fuzzy logic. Traditional and classical logic typically categorize information into binary patterns such as: yes/no, true/false, or day/night.

Fuzzy logic is a form of many-valued logic in which the truth values of variables may be any real number between 0 and 1, considered to be "fuzzy". By contrast, in Boolean logic, the truth values of variables may only be the "crisp" values 0 or 1. Fuzzy logic has been employed to handle the concept of partial truth, where the truth value may range between completely true and completely false. The fuzzy logic works on the levels of possibilities of input to achieve the definite output. What fuzzy sets typically bring to AI is a mathematical framework for capturing guardedness in reasoning devices. The concept of fuzzy logic is based near the human thinking and natural activities. It presents predicates which are present in nature and similar to those either big or small. This theory mimics human psychology as to how a person makes the decision faster Move over guardedness can take various forms: similarity between propositions, levels of uncertainty, and degrees of preference. In the present competitive scenario the fuzzy logic system are being adopted by the automotive manufacturers for the improvement of quality and reduction of cost as well as development time. Fuzzy logic was conceived as a better method for sorting and handling data but has proven to be an excellent choice for many control system applications.

The term "fuzzy logic" often refers to a particular control engineering methodology that exploits a numerical representation of common sense control rules, in order to synthetize, via interpolation, a control law. This approach has many common features with neural networks. It is now mainly concerned with the efficient encoding and approximation of numerical functions, and has currently less and less relationships to knowledge representation issues. This is however a very narrow view of fuzzy logic that has little to do with AI. Scanning the fuzzy set literature, one realizes that fuzzy logic may also refer to two other AI-related topics: multiple-valued logics, and approximate reasoning. There are many misconceptions about fuzzy logic. To begin with, fuzzy logic is not fuzzy. In large measure, fuzzy logic is precise. Another source of confusion is the duality of meaning of fuzzy logic. In a narrow sense, fuzzy logic is a logical system. But in much broader sense which is in dominant use today, fuzzy logic, or FL for short, is much more than a logical system. Fuzzy Logic provides a simple way to arrive at a definite conclusion based upon vague, ambiguous, imprecise, noisy, or missing input information. It is a type of logic that recognizes more than simple true and false values. With fuzzy logic, propositions can be represented with degrees of truthfulness and falsehood. For example, the statement, today is sunny, might be 100% true if there are no clouds, 80% true if there are a few clouds, 50% true if it's hazy and 0% true if it rains all day. Fuzzy logic is useful for commercial and practical purposes.

- It can control machines and consumer products.

- It may not give accurate reasoning, but acceptable reasoning.

- Fuzzy logic helps to deal with the uncertainty in engineering.

A fuzzy control system is a control system based on fuzzy logic—a mathematical system that analyzes analog input values in terms of logical variables that take on continuous values between 0 and 1, in contrast to classical or digital logic, which operates on discrete values of either 1 or 0 (true or false, respectively).

Fuzzy Expert System

A fuzzy expert system is an expert system that uses fuzzy logic instead of Boolean logic. In other words, a fuzzy expert system is a collection of membership functions and rules that are used to reason about data. Unlike conventional expert systems, which are mainly symbolic reasoning engines, fuzzy expert systems are oriented toward numerical processing.

The rules in a fuzzy expert system are usually of a form similar to the following:

If x is low and y is high then z = medium.

Where x and y are input variables (names for now data values), z is an output variable (a name for a data value to be computed), low is a membership function (fuzzy subset) defined on x, high is a membership function defined on y, and medium is a membership function defined on z. The part of the rule between the "if" and "then" is the rule's _premise_ or _antecedent_. This is a fuzzy logic expression that describes to what degree the rule is applicable. The part of the rule following the "then" is the rule's _conclusion_ or _consequent_. This part of the rule assigns a membership function to each of one or more output variables. Most tools for working with fuzzy expert systems allow more than one conclusion per rule.

A typical fuzzy expert system has more than one rule. The entire group of rules is collectively known as a _rulebase_ or _knowledge base_.

Where the Fuzzy Logic System Used?

To date, fuzzy expert systems are the most common use of fuzzy logic. They are used in several wide-ranging fields, including:

- Linear and nonlinear control,

- Pattern recognition,

- Financial systems.

Working of Fuzzy Logic System

It has four main parts:

- Knowledge Base: Every system which works on Artificial Intelligence has a Knowledge-base. The Fuzzy logic system is also an AI-based system, and thus it also has its own knowledge base where all the information and data for the reference by the agent is stored. In the Knowledge Base of Fuzzy Logic system, the rules of the Fuzzy Logic set theory are stored. Their rules are present in the form of an if-else ladder. So, whenever the system tries to solve any problem, this if-else ladder is executed and the system then works on the rule that it gets from the matched condition.

- Fuzzification Module: The fuzzification module performs the conversion of the input information. The information is converted into a form which the system can search for in its Knowledge Base. This is done by splitting the sentences into simpler terms and extracting the main terms out of it which are then sent to the inference engine for further processing.

- Inference Engine: The Inference engine is the main component of the Fuzzy Logic System. If compared with the computer parts, our inference engine is the same as the processor of the computer. All the processing of the information takes place inside it. The task of the inference engine is to draw a valid result by analyzing and concluding all the information that it gets from the fuzzification module. This is again done by referring to the rules and prior information present in the Knowledge Base. The final conclusions made are then sent for further modification to the defuzzification module.

- Defuzzification Module: The Defuzzification Module receives the processed information from the Inference Engine. This information contains the conclusion, but still, it is not in the form in which it was received, i.e. user-understandable form. So, the defuzzification module again converts this information into a form which is well accepted by the user.

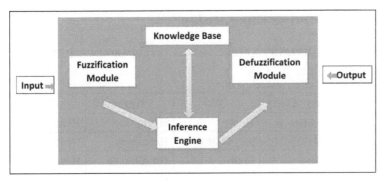

Algorithm

- Define linguistic Variables and terms (start).

- Construct membership functions for them (start).

- Construct knowledge base of rules (start).

- Convert crisp data into fuzzy data sets using membership functions (fuzzification).

- Evaluate rules in the rule base (Inference Engine).

- Combine results from each rule (Inference Engine).

- Convert output data into non-fuzzy values (defuzzification).

Development

Step 1: Define Linguistic Variables and Terms

Linguistic variables are input and output variables in the form of simple words or sentences. For room temperature, cold, warm, hot, etc., are linguistic terms.

Temperature (t) = {very-cold, cold, warm, very-warm, hot}

Every member of this set is a linguistic term and it can cover some portion of overall temperature values.

Step 2: Construct Membership Functions for them

The membership functions of temperature variable are as shown:

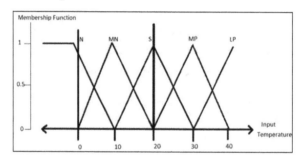

Step3: Construct Knowledge Base Rules

Create a matrix of room temperature values versus target temperature values that an air conditioning system is expected to provide.

RoomTemp./Target	Very_Cold	Cold	Warm	Hot	Very_Hot
Very_Cold	No_Change	Heat	Heat	Heat	Heat
Cold	Cool	No_Change	Heat	Heat	Heat
Warm	Cool	Cool	No_Change	Heat	Heat
Hot	Cool	Cool	Cool	No_Change	Heat
Very_Hot	Cool	Cool	Cool	Cool	No_Change

Build a set of rules into the knowledge base in the form of IF-THEN-ELSE structures.

Sr. No.	Condition	Action
1	IF temperature = (Cold OR Very_Cold) AND target = Warm THEN	Heat
2	IF temperature = (Hot OR Very_Hot) AND target = Warm THEN	Cool
3	IF (temperature = Warm) AND (target = Warm) THEN	No_Change

Step 4: Obtain Fuzzy Value

Fuzzy set operations perform evaluation of rules. The operations used for OR and AND are Max and Min respectively. Combine all results of evaluation to form a final result. This result is a fuzzy value.

Step 5: Perform Defuzzification

Defuzzification is then performed according to membership function for output variable.

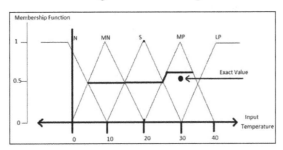

Application Areas of Fuzzy Logic

The Below given table shows how famous companies using fuzzy logic in their products.

Product	Company	Fuzzy Logic
Anti-lock brakes	Nissan	Use fuzzy logic to controls brakes in hazardous cases depend on car speed, acceleration, wheel speed, and acceleration.
Auto transmission	NOK/Nissan	Fuzzy logic is used to control the fuel injection and ignition based on throttle setting, cooling water temperature, RPM, etc.
Auto engine	Honda, Nissan	Use to select geat based on engine load, driving style, and road conditions.
Copy machine	Canon	Using for adjusting drum voltage based on picture density, humidity, and temperature.
Cruise control	Nissan, Isuzu, Mitsubishi	Use it to adjusts throttle setting to set car speed and acceleration
Dishwasher	Matsushita	Uses for adjusting the cleaning cycle, rinse and wash strategies based depend upon the number of dishes and the amount of food served on the dishes.
Elevator control	Fujitec, Mitsubishi Electric, Toshiba	Use it to reduce waiting for time-based on passenger traffic.
Golf diagnostic system	Maruman Golf	Selects golf club based on golfer's swing and physique.
Fitness management	Omron	Fuzzy rules implied by them to check the fitness of their employees.
Kiln control	Nippon Steel	Mixes cement.
Microwave oven	Mitsubishi Chemical	Sets lunes power and cooking strategy.
Palmtop computer	Hitachi, Sharp, Sanyo, Toshiba	Recognizes handwritten Kanji characters.
Plasma etching	Mitsubishi Electric	Sets etch time and strategy.

Advantages of Fuzzy Logic System

- The structure of Fuzzy Logic Systems is easy and understandable.

- Fuzzy logic is widely used for commercial and practical purposes.

- It helps you to control machines and consumer products.

- It may not offer accurate reasoning, but the only acceptable reasoning.

- It helps you to deal with the uncertainty in engineering.

- Mostly robust as no precise inputs required.

- It can be programmed to in the situation when feedback sensor stops working.

- It can easily be modified to improve or alter system performance.

- Inexpensive sensors can be used which helps you to keep the overall system cost and complexity low.

- It provides a most effective solution to complex issues.

Disadvantages of Fuzzy Logic Systems

- Fuzzy logic is not always accurate, so the results are perceived based on assumption, so it may not be widely accepted.

- Fuzzy systems don't have the capability of machine learning as-well-as neural network type pattern recognition.

- Validation and Verification of a fuzzy knowledge-based system needs extensive testing with hardware.

- Setting exact, fuzzy rules and, membership functions is a difficult task.

- Some fuzzy time logic is confused with probability theory and the terms.

Fuzzy Logic in Mobile Robot Navigation

An autonomous robot is a programmable and multi-functional machine, able to extract information from its surrounding using different kinds of sensors to plan and execute collision free motions within its environment without human intervention. Navigation is a crucial issue for robots that claim to be mobile. A navigation system can be divided into two layers: High level global planning and Low-level reactive control. In high-level planning, a prior knowledge of environment is available and the robot workspace is completely or partially known. Using the world model, the global planner can determine the robot motion direction and generates minimum-cost paths towards the target in the presence of complex obstacles. However, since it is not capable of changing the motion direction in presence of unforeseen or moving obstacles, it fails to reach target. In contrast, in low-level reactive control, the robot work space is unknown and dynamic. It generates control commands based on perception-action configuration, which the robot uses current sensory information to take appropriate actions without planning process. Thus, it has a quick response in reacting to unforeseen obstacles and uncertainties with changing the motion direction.

Several Artificial intelligence techniques such as reinforcement learning, neural networks, fuzzy logic and genetic algorithms, can be applied for the reactive navigation of mobile robots to improve their performance. Amongst the techniques ability of fuzzy logic to represent linguistic terms and reliable decision making in spite of uncertainty and imprecise information makes it a useful tool in control systems.

Fuzzy control systems are rule-based or knowledge-based systems containing a collection of fuzzy IF-THEN rules based on the domain knowledge or human experts. The simplicity of fuzzy rule-based systems, capability to perform a wide variety tasks without explicit computations and measurements make it extensively popular among the scientists and researcher. This book chapter presents the significance and effectiveness of fuzzy logic in solving the navigation problem.

Robust and reliable navigation in dynamic or unknown environment relies on ability of the robots in moving among unknown obstacles without collision and fast reaction to uncertainties. It is highly desirable to develop these tasks using a technique which utilize human reasoning and decision making. Fuzzy logic provides a means to capture the human mind's expertise. It utilizes this heuristic knowledge for representing and accomplishment of a methodology to develop perception-action based strategies for mobile robots navigation. Furthermore, the methodology of the FLC is very helpful dealing with uncertainties in real world and accurate model of the environment is not absolutely required for navigation. Therefore, based on a simple design, easy implementation and robustness properties of FLC, many approaches were developed to solve mobile robot navigation problem in target tracking, path tracking, obstacle avoidance, behaviour coordination, environment modelling, and layer integration.

Fuzzy Logic for Path Tracking

Path tracking is a crucial function for autonomous mobile robots to navigate along a desired path. This task includes tracking of previously computed paths using a path planner, a defined path by human operator, tracking of walls, road edges, and other natural features in the robot workspace. It involves real-time perception of the environment to determine the position and orientation of the robot with respect to the desired path. For example in figure, if the robot is misplaced, the controller task is to steer it back on course and minimize the orientation error ($\Delta\varphi$) and the position error (Δx). Path tracking difficulties in dealing with imprecise or incomplete perception of environment, representation of inaccuracy in measurements, sensor fusion and compliance with the kinematic limits of the vehicle motivated many researchers to use fuzzy control techniques for path tracking.

Ollero et al. developed a new fuzzy path-tracking method by combining fuzzy logic with the geometric pure-pursuit and the generalized predictive control techniques. Fuzzy logic is applied to supervise path trackers. Input of the fuzzy is the current state of the robot to the path to generate the appropriate steering angle. A new approach proposed by Braunstingl et al. to solve the wall following of mobile robots based on the concept of general perception. To construct a general perception of the surroundings from the measuring data provided by all the sensors and representing, a perception vector is assigned to each ultrasonic sensor. All these vectors adding together then combine into a single vector of general perception. A fuzzy controller then uses the perception information to guide the robot along arbitrary walls and obstacles. Sanchez et al. proposed a fuzzy control system for path tracking of an autonomous vehicle in outdoor environment.

The fuzzy controller is used to generate steering and velocity required to track the path using the data collected from experiments of driving the vehicle by a human. Bento et al. implemented a path-tracking method by means of fuzzy logic for a Wheeled Mobile Robot. Input variables of the fuzzy controller are position and orientation of the robot with respect to the path. Output variables are linear velocity and angular velocity. Hajjaji and Bentalba have designed a fuzzy controller for path tracking control of vehicles using its nonlinear dynamics model. A Takagi–Sugeno (T–S) fuzzy model presents the nonlinear model of the vehicle. Then a model-based fuzzy controller is developed based on the T–S fuzzy model. A wall-following robot presented by Peri & Simon which the robot's motion is controlled by a fuzzy controller to drive it along a predefined path. Antonelli et al. address a path tracking approach based on a fuzzy-logic set of rules which emulates the human driving behavior. The fuzzy system input is represented by approximate information concerning the knowledge of the curvature of the desired path ahead the vehicle and the distance between the next bend and the vehicle. The output is the maximum value of the linear velocity needed to attain by the vehicle in order to safely drive on the path. Yu et al. used Taguchi method to design an optimal fuzzy logic controller for trajectory tracking of a wheeled mobile robot. Recently, Xiong and Qu developed a method for intelligent vehicles' path tracking with two fuzzy controller combinations which controls vehicle direction and a preview fuzzy control method presented by Liao et al. for path tracking of intelligent vehicle. The vehicle speed and direction are adjusted by fuzzy control according to future path information and present path information respectively.

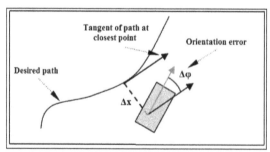

Typical control input variables for path tracking.

Obstacle Avoidance using Fuzzy Logic

Ability of a robot to avoid collision with unforeseen or dynamic obstacles while it is moving towards a target or tracking a path is a vital task in autonomous navigation. Navigation strategies can be classified to global path planning and local path planning. In global path planning, information about the obstacles and a global model of environment is available which mostly Configuration space, Road map, Voronoi diagram and Potential field techniques are used to plan obstacle-free path towards a target. However, in real world a reliable map of obstacle, accurate model of environment and precise sensory data is unavailable due to uncertainties of the environment. While the computed path may remain valid but to response the unforeseen or dynamic obstacles, it is necessary for the robot to alter its path online. In such situations, Fuzzy logic can provide robust and reliable methodologies dealing with the imprecise input with low computational complexity. Different obstacle avoidance approaches were developed during past decades which proposed effective solution to the navigation problems in unknown and dynamic environments.

Chee et al. presented a two-layer fuzzy inference system in which the first layer fuses the sensor readings. The left and right clearances of the robot were found as outputs of the first-layered fuzzy system. The outputs of the first layer together with the goal direction are used as the inputs of the second-layer. Eventually, the final outputs of the controller are the linear velocity and the turning rate of the robot. The second-stage fuzzy inference system employs the collision avoiding, obstacle following and goal tracking behaviours to achieve robust navigation in unknown environments. Dadios and Maravillas proposed and implemented a fuzzy control approach for cooperative soccer micro robots. A planner generates a path to the destination and fuzzy logic control the robot's heading direction to avoid obstacles and other robots while the dynamic position of obstacles, ball and robots are considered. Zavlangas et al. developed a reactive navigation method for omnidirectional mobile robots using fuzzy logic. The fuzzy rule-base generates actuating command to get collision free motions in dynamic environment. The fuzzy logic also provides an adjustable transparent system by a set of learning rules or manually. Seraji and Howard developed a behavior-based navigation method on challenging terrain using fuzzy logic.

The navigation strategy is comprised of three behaviors. Local obstacle avoidance behaviour is consists of a set of fuzzy logic rule statements which generates the robot's speed based on obstacle distance. Parhi described a control system comprises a fuzzy logic controller and a Petri Net for multi robot navigation. The Fuzzy rules steer the robot according to obstacles distribution or targets position. Since the obstacle's position is not known precisely, to avoid obstacles in a cluttered environment fuzzy logic is a proper technique for this task. Combination of the fuzzy logic controller and a set of collision prevention rules implemented as a Petri Net model embedded in the controller of a mobile robot enable it to avoid obstacles that include other mobile robots. A fuzzy controller designed by Lilly for obstacle avoidance of an autonomous vehicle using negative fuzzy rules. The negative fuzzy rules define a set of actions to be avoided to direct the vehicle to a target in presence of obstacles. Chao et al. developed a fuzzy control system for target tracking and obstacle avoidance of a mobile robot. Decision making is handled by the fuzzy control strategy based on the sensed environment using a stereo vision information. A vision- based fuzzy obstacle avoidance proposed for a humanoid robot in. The nearest obstacle to the robot captured by vision system and the difference angle between goal direction and the robot's heading measured by electronic compass are inputs of the fuzzy system to make a decision for appropriate motion of the robot in unknown environment.

Fuzzy Logic for Behavior Coordination

To improve the total performance of a navigation system, complex navigation tasks are broken down into a number of simpler and smaller subsystems (behaviors) which is called behaviorbased system. In a behavior-based system, each behavior receives particular sensory information and transforms them into the predefined response. The behaviors include path tracking, obstacle avoidance, target tracking, goal reaching and etc. Finally, based on command outputs of an active behaviours the robot executes an action.

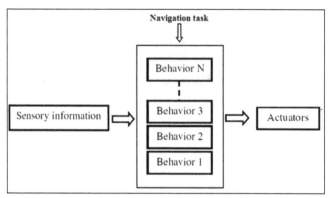

Behavior- based navigation systems overall architecture.

The problems associated with the behavior-based navigation systems is the behavior coordination or action selection. The multiple behaviors may produce several command outputs simultaneously which may cause the robot move in unintended directions or system fail entirely. Reliable and robust operation of the system relies on the decision about how to integrate high level planning and low level execution behaviors, which behavior should be activated (arbitration) and how output commands should be combined into one command to drive the robot (command fusion). Early solutions were developed based on subsumption architecture and motor schemas.

The subsumption architecture is composed of several layers of task-achieving behaviors. Coordination of behaviors is based on Priority arbitration (Competitive architecture). In Priority-based arbitration only a behavior with the highest priority is selected to be active when multiple conflicting behaviors are trigged and the others are ignored. The subsumption approach is based on a static arbitration policy which means that the robot actions are predefined and fixed in dealing with certain situations. Since the behavior coordination is competitive and based on a fixed arbitration, it may leads to erratic operation under certain situations. For example in coordination of goal reaching and obstacle avoidance behaviors with rules like:

Obstacle avoidance rules	Goal reaching rules
IF Obstacle is left THEN turn right	IF goal is right THEN turn right
IF Obstacle is front THEN turn left	IF goal is left THEN turn left

When an obstacle is detected in front of the robot and the goal is at right, the priority is with Obstacle avoidance behavior and the robot turns left while the goal is at right.

The motor schemas architecture proposed by Arkin relies on cooperative coordination (command fusion) of behaviors which the multiple behaviors can produce an output concurrently. In this approach output of each behavior is captured based on their particular influence on overall output. The outputs are blended to vote for or against an action. For example in potential fields the outputs are in the vector form. These outputs are combined and the overall response of the system is achieved by the vector summation. This approach also may lead to conflicting actions or poor performance in certain circumstances. However, fuzzy logic provides a useful mechanism for command fusion coordination and also arbitration fusion coordination. The main fuzzy logic advantages are: i) it can be used for dynamic arbitration which behavior selection is according to the robot's current perceptual state, ii) it allows for easy combination and concurrent execution of various behaviors. A variety of approaches have been developed inspired by the success of fuzzy logic to deal with the behavior coordination limitations.

Leyden designed a fuzzy logic based navigation system to overcome the subsumption control problem. The proposed system is consists of two behaviors. Output of each behavior is a fuzzy set which are combined using a command fusion process to produce a single fuzzy set. Then, the fuzzy set is defuzzified to make a crisp output. Fatmi et al. proposed a two layered behavior coordination approach for behavior design and action coordination using fuzzy logic. The first layer is consists of primitive basic behaviors and the second layer is responsible for decision making based on the context about which behavior(s) should be activated and the selected behaviors are blended. In another work presented by, fuzzy behavior systems proposed for Autonomous navigation of Ground Vehicles in cluttered environment with unknown obstacles. Multivalue reactive fuzzy behaviors are used for arbitrating or fusing of the behaviors which action selection is relied on the available sensor information. In another work by Ramos et al., a hierarchical fuzzy decision-making algorithm introduced for behaviour coordination of a robot based on arbitration mechanisms. In this method behaviors are not combined and just one behavior with maximum resulting value is selected and executed each time. A Fuzzy action selection approach was developed by Jaafar and McKenzie for navigation of a virtual agent. The fuzzy controller is comprised of three behaviors. The objective of this work is to solve the behaviour's conflict. The method uses fuzzy α-levels to compute the behavior's weight and the Huwicz criterion is used to select the final action. Wang and Liu introduced a new behavior-based navigation method called "minimum risk method". This behavior-based method applies the multi-behavior coordination strategy includes the global Goal seeking (GS) and the local Obstacle Avoidance (OA) (or boundary-following) behaviors. The fuzzy logic is applied to design and coordinate the proposed behaviors.

Fuzzy Control System in Mobile Robot Navigation

First we show how to design a Fuzzy Controller and then we present a case study to analyze the performance and operation of the fuzzy logic algorithms in the implementation of different behaviors for mobile robot navigation. Most of the proposed methods have applied fuzzy logic algorithm for velocity control, steering control and command fusion in the design of their behaviors.

Design of a Fuzzy Controller

The schematic diagram of the fuzzy controller is shown in figure. The fuzzy controller design steps include: 1) Initialization, 2) Fuzzification, 3) Inference and 4) Difuzzification.

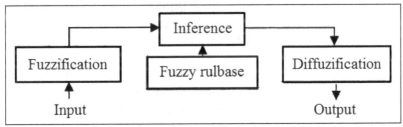

The fuzzy controller structure.

First step is identifying the linguistic input and output variables and definition of fuzzy sets (Initialization). Fuzzification or fuzzy classification is the process of converting a set of crisp data into a set of fuzzy variables using the membership functions (fuzzy sets). For example in figure, the degree of membership for a given crisp is 0.6. Shape of the membership functions depends on the input data can be triangular, piecewise linear, Gaussian, trapezoidal or singleton.

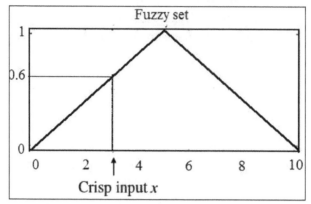

Membership degree of a crisp input x in the fuzzy set.

A rule base is obtained by a set of IF-THEN rules and inference evaluates the rules and combines the results of the rules. The final step is Defuzzification which is the process of converting fuzzy rules into a crisp output. An example of a simple fuzzy control system is shown in figure.

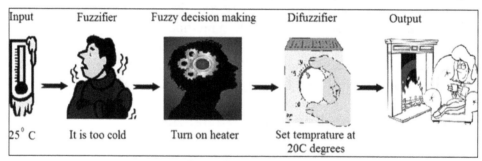

Example of a fuzzy control system.

Fuzzy Logic in Emotional Intelligence Agents

Emotions were proven to lead an important role in human intelligence. Here, we are describing a model called FLAME – Fuzzy Logic Adaptive Model of Emotions. FLAME was modeled to produce motions and to simulate the emotional intelligence process. FLAME was built using fuzzy rules to explore the capability of fuzzy logic in modeling the emotional process. Fuzzy logic helped us in capturing the fuzzy and complex nature of emotions.

"Human beings, viewed as behaving systems, are quite simple. The apparent complexity of our behavior over time is largely a reflection of the complexity of the environment in which we find ourselves." This very famous quote by Simon marked the birth of Artificial Intelligence. Striving towards replicating human intelligence in a machine, Simon tried to build a model for simulating emotions. Even back then, he recognized that emotions play a crucial role in human cognition. We have been conditioned to think that emotions were not a part of human intelligence, but rather hinder humans' thoughts. This idea has been initiated by ancient philosophers such as Plato. Moreover, Descartes reinforced this idea by his famous statement "I think therefore I am".

Today, new evidence has answered the question that Minsky had posed. Minsky, writing on the human mind, said, "The question is not whether intelligent machines can have any emotions, but whether machines can be intelligent without any emotions." A. Demasio presented some neurological evidence to prove that emotions do in fact play an active and important role in the human decision-making process. The interaction between the emotional process and the cognitive process may explain why humans excel at making decisions based on incomplete information – "acting on our gut-feelings".

Following this major breakthrough, many terms emerged, including "emotional intelligence," "social intelligence," "IQ-based social intelligence," and "EQ-based social intelligence." These terms arose from the theory that emphasizes on the existence of many types of intelligence for what we normally call the human intelligence system. Emotional intelligence was defined as a process by which human beings can reason about their emotions and even use them to achieve their goals. This requires self-awareness, self-control and self-perception. Moreover, this also requires understanding of other people's emotions. Thus, EQ-social intelligence was defined as the use of emotional intelligence to develop a more profound communication pattern between groups of people.

Using fuzzy modeling proved to produce a more representative picture of the emotional process, and thus it might produce better believable agents. In the next section, we will discuss the previous models and the problems that can be solved by using fuzzy modeling.

Psychology, Neurology, Philosophy and Cognitive Science have been concerned with modeling the mind and its behavior for many years. Thus, it is not surprising to see many papers/books proposing models of emotions and behaviors. Among the neurological models, LeDoux published his book, The Emotional Brain, to explore the emotional process in the brain.

While in the psychology field, D. Price and J. Barrell developed a mathematical model that described emotions in terms of desires and expectations. Pain was modeled by R. Schumacher and M. Velden and again by S. Tayrer's book. Some hormones sent by the brain sometimes inhibit pain; this idea was adopted by Bolles and Fanselow, who tried to understand the relation between fear and pain.

Inspired by these psychological models and the growing interest in AI, many models that simulate the human mind have been proposed. A description of models of emotions from early 1960's until the 1980's was presented by R. Pfeifer. However, since the psychology of emotions was not yet complete at the time, it was not easy to find a computational model that describes the whole emotional concept.

By the 1990's, the Japanese researchers were interested in a system that can communicate with humans. Emotions were regarded as one of the most important factors in communication. Thus, by 1994, an effort was made by Masuyma to formulate the human emotions into a set of rules. An attempt was made by S. Sugano and T. Ogata to simulate the human mind through an electrically wired robot. A prototype of the decision making process was developed by Inoue, they used neural networks to simulate behavior.

The topic of emotion was regarded as a very challenging topic, since it was hard to fully understand how we feel and why we do feel that way. Part of the reason for the so-called "mystery of emotions" is due to the fact that most of our emotions occur at the subconscious level. Moreover, it is still unclear how emotions transition from the subconscious to the conscious brain.

The Model

Problems with Existing Models

To talk about the problems with the existing models, we need to look at the previous work in more details. Thus, we will take one of these models, namely the OZ project, as an example from which the other models can be understood. In summary, the model first assesses a perceived event as being desirable or undesirable with respect to a goal within the goal structure of the agent. The desirability of the event was measured as a true or false concept.

The model triggered emotions according to the desirability factor. They used Ortony et al.'s model to formulate the rules for the triggering process. Emotions were triggered with different intensities. Intensities are degrees, say a number between 1 and 10, that depicts the strength of an emotion. The intensity degree is then used to map the resulting emotions to a behavior. They followed an interval mapping technique to get an accurate personality.

There are two major problems in the techniques employed. Firstly, desirability is measured as a black or white concept, which then raises questions such as what if an event satisfies a goal to a certain degree? The idea of partial goal successes or failures was not employed. Moreover, the idea of an event satisfying multiple goals or satisfying some goals and not the others was not considered. Secondly, the mapping of the emotional states to a behavior was made according to an interval mapping technique. For instance, a rule in the system states that if the anger level towards subject, g, is greater than 0 and the fear value towards this subject, g, is greater than five, then the aggressive value will be a function of both anger and fear. However, if the anger is greater than 0 and fear is less than 5 then the aggressive value will be a function of the anger. What if the level of fear is 4.9, or 4.7? How does that affect the value of aggressiveness?

A Solution

In order to solve these problems we propose the use of fuzzy logic. Using fuzzy logic, we introduced three concepts:

- Fuzzy Goals: this concept introduces a degree of success and failure associated with achieving goals.

- Fuzzy Membership: the membership of an event to a goal will be a matter of degree, thus an event can be affecting two or more goals with different degrees.

- Fuzzy Mapping: the mixture of emotions is mapped to a behavior through the use of a fuzzy mapping technique.

System Architecture

To understand the emotional process, we will illustrate the whole process through figure. It should be noted that, the figure shows one part of the architecture of FLAME (Fuzzy Logic Adaptive Model of Emotions).

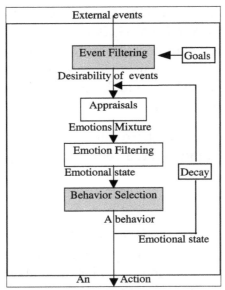

Process of the Emotional Model.

In this figure, boxes represent different processes within the model. Information is passed from one process to the other, as shown in the figure. In the figure above the shaded boxes represent the processes where fuzzy logic was used. In the next couple of paragraphs, we will detail the two fuzzy processes, while summarizing the other processes when they become relevant.

Firstly, we need to set a desirability value for each event perceived by the agent. Thus, we need to identify the degree that an event affects a certain goal, which has a certain priority level. The degree by which a particular event impacts a particular goal is simulated using five fuzzy sets with triangular membership functions. The fuzzy sets are No Impact, High Positive Impact, Low-Positive Impact, Low-Negative Impact and High Negative- Impact. The priority of a goal is dynamically set during the simulation according to the agent's assessment of a particular situation. The priority of each goal is represented using three fuzzy sets of triangular membership functions. The fuzzy sets are termed: No Importance, Some Importance, Extreme Importance.

The event is evaluated by the following rule:

IF   Affect (G_1, E) is A

AND Affect (G_2, E) is B

.....

AND Affect (G_k, E) is H

AND Importance (G_1) is D

AND Importance (G_2) is F

....

AND Importance (G_k) is I

THEN Desirability (E) is C

Where k is the number of goals simulated in the system. This rule reads as follows: if the goal, G_1, is affected by an event, E, to a degree A and goal, G_2, is affected by an event, E, to a degree B, etc., and the importance of the goal, G_1, is D and the importance of goal, G_2, is F, etc., then the desirability of the event, E, will be of degree C. We are using Mamdani's model, with centroid defuzzification to get a desirability degree, which will be sent to the next process. Mamdani's model uses sup-min to get the matching degrees for the n rules.

After calculating the desirability of an event, we employ a variation of Oronty's model to define the emotion triggered by the situation and the event. For example to get the intensity of joy, we employ the following rule:

Joy = the occurrence of a desirable event.

The joy intensity will be a direct function of the level of desirability produced by the fuzzy model after defuzzification. Moreover, other emotions such as hope, fear, relief, etc., need more than just the measure of desirability; expectations and likelihood play an important role in simulating these emotions. The rule we are using to simulate hope is:

Hope = the occurrence of an unconfirmed desirable event.

We use experience to guide the calculation of the likelihood of events to occur. The intensity of hope will be a function of both the desirability and probability of the event to occur.

After firing the rules and getting a mixture of emotions, we will filter the emotion mixture to get an emotional state. The mixture is filtered using some inhibition factors such as the ones employed by Bolles and Fanslow. The emotional state will then pass through a fuzzy mapping phase to determine a behavior.

Fuzzy logic is used once again to determine a behavior given a set of emotions. The behavior depends on the emotions of the agent and the situation or the event that occurred. For example, consider the following rule:

IF   Anger is High

        AND dish-was-taken-away

THEN behavior is Bark-At-user

The behavior barking at user depended on what the user did and the emotional state of the agent. If the user did not take the dish away and the agent was angry for some other reason, he would not be inclined to bark at the user, because the user might not be the cause of his anger. Thus, it is important to identify both the event and the emotion. It is equally important to identify the cause of the event. In this case, we are assuming that non-environmental events such as dish-was-taken-away, throw-ball, ball-was-taken-away, etc. are all caused by the user. To generalize the rule shown above, we used the following fuzzy rules:

IF $emotion_1$ is A

        AND $emotion_2$ is B

.....

AND emotion$_k$ is C

AND Event is E

THEN BEHAVIOR is F

Where k is the number of emotions in the system. A, B and C are fuzzy sets defining the emotional intensity as being High Intensity, Low Intensity or Medium Intensity. Behaviors are simulated as singletons, including Bark-At-User and Play-With-Play. Likewise, events are also simulated as singletons such as dish-was-taken-away, throw-ball, ball-was-taken-away, etc. After selecting a behavior, the emotional state is then decayed and fed back to the system.

References

- What-is-fuzzy-logic: guru99.com, Retrieved 06 April, 2019

- Fuzzy-Logic-System-in-Artificial-Intelligence: theadvancejournalpublications.com, Retrieved 08 January, 2019

- Fuzzy-logic-system-architecture-in-artificial-intelligence, ml-ai: includehelp.com, Retrieved 19 May, 2019

- Artificial-intelligence-fuzzy-logic-systems, artificial-intelligence: tutorialspoint.com, Retrieved 16 June, 2019

- Agents-emotional-intelligence-and-fuzzy-logic- 3766896: researchgate.net, Retrieved 23 July, 2019

Applications of Artificial Intelligence

Artificial intelligence has applications in diverse sectors such as agriculture, robotics, marketing, video games, etc. All these significant applications of artificial intelligence have been carefully analyzed in this chapter.

Application of Artificial Intelligence Techniques in Network Intrusion Detection

Intrusion Detection Systems (IDS) utilizes the different Artificial Intelligence methods for shielding PC and correspondence systems from gatecrashers. Interruption Detection System (IDS) is the way toward observing the occasions happening in system and identifying the indications of interruption.

- Artificial Neural Network in IDS: ANN is a scientific model that comprises of an interconnected gathering of counterfeit neurons which forms the data. In IDS ANN are utilized to display complex connections amongst information sources and yields or to discover designs in information. In this a neuron figures the entirety by increasing contribution by weight and applies an edge. The outcome is transmitted to resulting neurons. Essentially, the ANN has been summed up to: yi = f(σwikxk + μi) (1) k Where wik are weights appended to the sources of info, xk are contributions to the neuron I, μi is a limit, f (•) is an exchange capacity and yi is the yield of the neuron.

- Fuzzy Inference Systems (FIS) in IDS: Sampada et al. proposed two machine learning standards: Artificial Neural Networks and Fuzzy Inference System, for the outline of an Intrusion Detection System. They utilized SNORT to perform ongoing activity examination and parcel signing on IP arrange amid the preparation period of the framework. They built a mark design database utilizing Protocol Analysis and NeuroFuzzy learning technique. They at that point tried and approved the models utilizing the 1998 DARPA Intrusion Detection Evaluation Data and TCP dump crude information. The informational collection contains 24 assault composes. The assaults fall into four principle classes viz. Foreswearing of Service (DOS), Remote to User (R2L), User to Root (U2R), and Probing. From the outcomes, it was demonstrated that the Fuzzy Inference System was quicker in preparing, taking couple of moments, than the Artificial Neural Networks which took couple of minutes to join. For the most part, the two methods ended up being great, however with the Fuzzy Inference System having an edge over Artificial Neural Networks with its higher order exactness's. Their trial additionally demonstrated the significance of variable choice, as the two procedures performed more terrible when every one of the factors were utilized without determination of the factors. Great outcomes were recorded when a subset (around 40%) of the factors were utilized.

Artificial Intelligence in Agriculture

Agriculture is seeing rapid adoption of Artificial Intelligence (AI) and Machine Learning (ML) both in terms of agricultural products and in-field farming techniques. Cognitive computing in particular is all set to become the most disruptive technology in agriculture services as it can understand, learn, and respond to different situations (based on learning) to increase efficiency.

Providing some of these solutions as a service like chatbot or other conversational platform to all the farmers will help them keep pace with technological advancements as well as apply the same in their daily farming to reap the benefits of this service.

Currently, Microsoft is working with 175 farmers to provide advisory services for sowing, land, and fertilizer so on. This initiative has already resulted in 30% higher yield per hectare on an average compared to last year.

Given below are top five areas where the use of cognitive solutions can benefit agriculture.

Growth Driven by IOT

Huge volumes of data get generated every day in both structured and unstructured format. These relate to data on historical weather pattern, soil reports, new research, rainfall, pest infestation, images from Drones and cameras and so on. Cognitive IOT solutions can sense all this data and provide strong insights to improve yield.

Proximity Sensing and Remote Sensing are two technologies which are primarily used for intelligent data fusion. One use case of this high-resolution data is Soil Testing. While remote sensing requires sensors to be built into airborne or satellite systems, proximity sensing requires sensors in contact with soil or at a very close range. This helps in soil characterization based on the soil below the surface in a particular place. Hardware solutions like Rowbot (pertaining to corns) are already pairing data-collecting software with robotics to prepare the best fertilizer for growing f corns in addition to other activities to maximize output.

Image-based Insight Generation

Precision farming is one of the most discussed areas in farming today. Drone-based images can help in in-depth field analysis, crop monitoring, scanning of fields and so on. Computer vision technology, IOT and drone data can be combined to ensure rapid actions by farmers. Feeds from drone image data can generate alerts in real time to accelerate precision farming.

Companies like Aerialtronics have implemented IBM Watson IoT Platform and the Visual Recognition APIs in commercial drones for image analysis in real time. Given below are some areas where computer vision technology can be put to use:

- Disease detection: Preprocessing of image ensure the leaf images are segmented into areas like background, non-diseased part and diseased part. The diseased part is then cropped and send to remote labs for further diagnosis. It also helps in pest identification, nutrient deficiency recognition and more.

Capture of image → Preprocessing → Transmission to remote labs

- Crop readiness identification: Images of different crops under white/UV-A light are captured to determine how ripe the green fruits are. Farmers can create different levels of readiness based on the crop/fruit category and add them into separate stacks before sending them to the market.

- Field management: Using high-definition images from airborne systems (drone or copters), real-time estimates can be made during cultivation period by creating a field map and identifying areas where crops require water, fertilizer or pesticides. This helps in resource optimization to a huge extent.

Identification of Optimal Mix for Agronomic Products

Based on multiple parameters like soil condition, weather forecast, type of seeds, infestation in a certain area and so on, cognitive solutions make recommendations to farmers on the best choice of crops and hybrid seeds. The recommendation can be further personalized based on the farm's requirement, local conditions, and data about successful farming in the past. External factors like marketplace trends, prices or consumer needs may also be factored into enable farmers take a well-informed decision.

Health Monitoring of Crops

Remote sensing techniques along with hyper spectral imaging and 3d laser scanning are essential to build crop metrics across thousands of acres. It has the potential to bring in a revolutionary change in terms of how farmlands are monitored by farmers both from time and effort perspective. This technology will also be used to monitor crops along their entire lifecycle including report generation in case of anomalies.

Automation Techniques in Irrigation and Enabling Farmers

In terms of human intensive processes in farming, irrigation is one such process. Machines trained on historical weather pattern, soil quality and kind of crops to be grown, can automate irrigation and increase overall yield. With close to 70% of the world's fresh water being used in irrigation, automation can help farmers better manage their water problems.

Importance of Drone

As per a recent PWC Study, the total addressable market for Drone-based solutions across the globe is $127.3 billion and for agriculture it is at $32.4 billion.

Drone-based solutions in agriculture have a lot of significance in terms of managing adverse weather conditions, productivity gains, precision farming and yield management.

- Before the crop cycle, drone can be used to produce a 3-D field map of detailed terrain, drainage, soil viability and irrigation. Nitrogen-level management can also be done by drone solutions

- Aerial spraying of pods with seeds and plant nutrients into the soil provides necessary supplements for plants. Apart from that, Drones can be programmed to spray liquids by modulating distance from the ground depending on the terrain

- Crop Monitoring and Health assessment remains one of the most significant areas in agriculture to provide drone-based solutions in collaboration with Artificial Intelligence and computer vision technology. High-resolution cameras in drones collect precision field images which can be passed through convolution neural network to identify areas with weeds, which crops need water, plant stress level in midgrowth stage. In terms of infected plants, by scanning crops in both RGB and near-infra red light, it is possible to generate multispectral images using drone devices. With this, it is possible to specify which plants have been infected including their location in a vast field to apply remedies, instantly. The multi spectral images combine hyper spectral images with 3D scanning techniques to define the spatial information system that is used for acres of land. The temporal component provides the guidance for the entire lifecycle of the plant.

Yield Management using AI

The emergence of new age technologies like Artificial Intelligence (AI), Cloud Machine Learning, Satellite Imagery and advanced analytics are creating an ecosystem for smart farming. Fusion of all this technology is enabling farmers achieves higher average yield and better price control.

Microsoft is currently working with farmers from Andhra Pradesh to provide advisory services using Cortana Intelligence Suite including Machine Learning and Power BI. The pilot project uses an AI sowing app to recommend sowing date, land preparation, soil test-based fertilization, farm yard manure application, seed treatment, optimum sowing depth and more to farmers which has resulted in 30% increase in average crop yield per hectare.

Technology can also be used to identify optimal sowing period, historic climate data, real time Moisture Adequacy Data (MAI) from daily rainfall and soil moisture to build predictability and provide inputs to farmers on ideal sowing time.

To identify potential pest attacks, Microsoft in collaboration with United Phosphorus Limited is building a Pest Risk Prediction API that leverages AI and machine learning to indicate in advance, the risk of pest attack. Based on the weather condition and crop growth stage, pest attacks are predicted as High, Medium or Low.

How Robotics Helping in Digital Farming

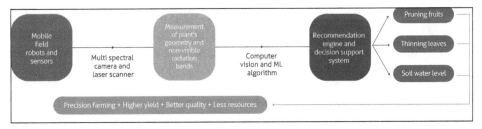

AI Startups in Agriculture

- Prospera, founded in 2014: This Israeli startup has revolutionized the way farming is done. It has developed a cloud-based solution that aggregates all existing data that farmers have like soil/water sensors, aerial images and so on. It then combines it with an in-field device that makes sense of it all. The Prospera device which can be used in green houses or in the field, is powered by a variety of sensors and technologies like computer vision. The inputs from these sensors are used to find a correlation between different data labels and make predictions.

- Blue River technology, founded in 2011: This California-based startup combines artificial intelligence, computer vision and robotics to build next-generation agriculture equipment that reduces chemicals and saves costs. Computer vision identifies each individual plant, ML decides how to treat each individual plant and robotics enables the smart machines to take action.

- FarmBot, founded in 2011: This Company has taken precision farming to a different level by enabling environment conscious people with precision farming technology to grow crops at their own place. The product, FarmBot comes at a price of $4000 and helps the owner to do end-to-end farming all by himself. Ranging from seed plantation to weed detection and soil testing to watering of plants, everything is taken care of by this physical bot using an open source software system.

Challenges in AI Adoption in Agriculture

Though Artificial Intelligence offers vast opportunities for application in agriculture, there still exists a lack of familiarity with high tech machine learning solutions in farms across most parts of the world. Exposure of farming to external factors like weather conditions, soil conditions and presence of pests is quite a lot. So what might look like a good solution while planning during the start of harvesting, may not be an optimal one because of changes in external parameters.

AI systems also need a lot of data to train machines and to make precise predictions. In case of vast agricultural land, though spatial data can be gathered easily, temporal data is hard to get. For example, most of the crop-specific data can be obtained only once in a year when the crops are growing. Since the data infrastructure takes time to mature, it requires a significant amount of time to build a robust machine learning model.

Precision Agriculture

Precision agriculture (PA), satellite farming or site specific crop management (SSCM) is a farming management concept based on observing, measuring and responding to inter and intra-field variability in crops. The goal of precision agriculture research is to define a decision support system (DSS) for whole farm management with the goal of optimizing returns on inputs while preserving resources.

Among these many approaches is a phytogeomorphological approach which ties multi-year crop growth stability/characteristics to topological terrain attributes. The interest in the phytogeomorphological approach stems from the fact that the geomorphology component typically dictates the hydrology of the farm field.

The practice of precision agriculture has been enabled by the advent of GPS and GNSS. The farmer's and/or researcher's ability to locate their precise position in a field allows for the creation of maps of the spatial variability of as many variables as can be measured (e.g. crop yield, terrain features/topography, organic matter content, moisture levels, nitrogen levels, pH, EC, Mg, K, and others). Similar data is collected by sensor arrays mounted on GPS-equipped combine harvesters. These arrays consist of real-time sensors that measure everything from chlorophyll levels to plant water status, along with multispectral imagery. This data is used in conjunction with satellite imagery by variable rate technology (VRT) including seeders, sprayers, etc. to optimally distribute resources. However, recent technological advances have enabled the use of real-time sensors directly in soil, which can wirelessly transmit data without the need of human presence.

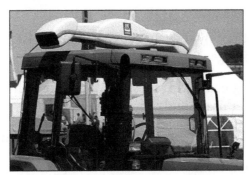

Yara *N-Sensor ALS* mounted on a tractor's canopy – a system that records light reflection of crops, calculates fertilisation recommendations and then varies the amount of fertilizer spread.

Precision agriculture has also been enabled by unmanned aerial vehicles like the DJI Phantom which are relatively inexpensive and can be operated by novice pilots. These agricultural drones can be equipped with hyperspectral or RGB cameras to capture many images of a field that can be processed using photogrammetric methods to create orthophotos and NDVI maps. These drones are capable of capturing imagery for a variety of purposes and with several metrics such as elevation and Vegetative Index (with NDVI as an example). This imagery is then turned into maps which can be used to optimize crop inputs such as water, fertilizer or chemicals such as herbicides and growth regulators through variable rate applications.

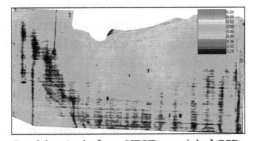

Precision Agriculture NDVI 4 cm/pixel GSD.

Precision agriculture is a key component of the third wave of modern agricultural revolutions. The first agricultural revolution was the increase of mechanized agriculture, from 1900 to 1930. Each farmer produced enough food to feed about 26 people during this time. The 1960s prompted the Green Revolution with new methods of genetic modification, which led to each farmer feeding about 155 people. It is expected that by 2050, the global population will reach about 9.6 billion, and food production must effectively double from current levels in order to feed every mouth. With new technological advancements in the agricultural revolution of precision farming, each farmer will be able to feed 265 people on the same acreage.

The first wave of the precision agricultural revolution came in the forms of satellite and aerial imagery, weather prediction, variable rate fertilizer application, and crop health indicators. The second wave aggregates the machine data for even more precise planting, topographical mapping, and soil data.

Precision agriculture aims to optimize field-level management with regard to:

- Crop science: By matching farming practices more closely to crop needs (e.g. Fertilizer inputs);

- Environmental protection: By reducing environmental risks and footprint of farming (e.g. Limiting leaching of nitrogen);

- Economics: By boosting competitiveness through more efficient practices (e.g. improved management of fertilizer usage and other inputs).

Precision agriculture also provides farmers with a wealth of information to:

- Build up a record of their farm.

- Improve decision-making.

- Foster greater traceability.

- Enhance marketing of farm products.

- Improve lease arrangements and relationship with landlords.

- Enhance the inherent quality of farm products (e.g. Protein level in bread-flour wheat).

Prescriptive Planting

Prescriptive planting is a type of farming system that delivers data-driven planting advice that can determine variable planting rates to accommodate varying conditions across a single field, in order to maximize yield. It has been described as "Big Data on the farm." Monsanto, DuPont and others are launching this technology in the US.

Tools

Precision agriculture is usually done as a four-stage process to observe spatial variability: Precision agriculture uses many tools but here are some of the basics: tractors, combines, sprayers, planters, diggers, which are all considered auto-guidance systems. The small devices on the equipment that uses GIS (geographic information system) are what make precision ag what it is. You can think of the GIS system as the "brain." To be able to use precision agriculture the equipment needs to be wired with the right technology and data systems. More tools include Variable rate technology (VRT), Global positioning system and Geographical information system, Grid sampling, and remote sensors.

Data Collection

Geolocating a field enables the farmer to overlay information gathered from analysis of soils and residual nitrogen, and information on previous crops and soil resistivity. Geolocation is done in two ways:

- The field is delineated using an in-vehicle GPS receiver as the farmer drives a tractor around the field.

- The field is delineated on a basemap derived from aerial or satellite imagery. The base images must have the right level of resolution and geometric quality to ensure that geolocation is sufficiently accurate.

Variables

Intra and inter-field variability may result from a number of factors. These include climatic conditions (hail, drought, rain, etc.), soils (texture, depth, nitrogen levels), cropping practices (no-till farming), weeds and disease. Permanent indicators—chiefly soil indicators—provide farmers with information about the main environmental constants. Point indicators allow them to track a crop's status, i.e., to see whether diseases are developing, if the crop is suffering from water stress, nitrogen stress, or lodging, whether it has been damaged by ice and so on. This information may come from weather stations and other sensors (soil electrical resistivity, detection with the naked eye, satellite imagery, etc.). Soil resistivity measurements combined with soil analysis make it possible to measure moisture content. Soil resistivity is also a relatively simple and cheap measurement.

Strategies

NDVI image taken with small aerial system Stardust II in one flight (299 images mosaic).

Using soil maps, farmers can pursue two strategies to adjust field inputs:

- Predictive approach: based on analysis of static indicators (soil, resistivity, field history, etc.) during the crop cycle.

- Control approach: information from static indicators is regularly updated during the crop cycle by:

  - Sampling: weighing biomass, measuring leaf chlorophyll content, weighing fruit, etc.

  - Remote sensing: measuring parameters like temperature (air/soil), humidity (air/soil/leaf), wind or stem diameter is possible thanks to Wireless Sensor Networks and Internet of things (IoT).

  - Proxy-detection: in-vehicle sensors measure leaf status; this requires the farmer to drive around the entire field.

  - Aerial or satellite remote sensing: multispectral imagery is acquired and processed to derive maps of crop biophysical parameters, including indicators of disease. Airborne instruments are able to measure the amount of plant cover and to distinguish between crops and weeds.

Decisions may be based on decision-support models (crop simulation models and recommendation models) based on big data, but in the final analysis it is up to the farmer to decide in terms of business value and impacts on the environment- a role being takenover by artificial intelligence (AI) systems based on machine learning and artificial neural networks.

It is important to realize why PA technology is or is not adopted, "for PA technology adoption to occur the farmer has to perceive the technology as useful and easy to use. It might be insufficient to have positive outside data on the economic benefits of PA technology as perceptions of farmers have to reflect these economic considerations."

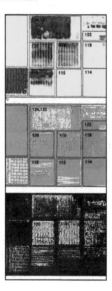

Implementing Practices

New information and communication technologies make field-level crop management more operational and easier to achieve for farmers. Application of crop management decisions calls for agricultural equipment that supports variable-rate technology (VRT), for example varying seed density along with variable-rate application (VRA) of nitrogen and phytosanitary products.

Precision agriculture uses technology on agricultural equipment (e.g. tractors, sprayers, harvesters, etc.):

- Positioning system (e.g. Gps receivers that use satellite signals to precisely determine a position on the globe);

- Geographic information systems (gis), i.e., software that makes sense of all the available data;

- Variable-rate farming equipment (seeder, spreader).

Usage Around the World

The concept of precision agriculture first emerged in the United States in the early 1980s. In 1985, researchers at the University of Minnesota varied lime inputs in crop fields. It was also at this time that the practice of grid sampling appeared (applying a fixed grid of one sample per hectare).

Towards the end of the 1980s, this technique was used to derive the first input recommendation maps for fertilizers and pH corrections. The use of yield sensors developed from new technologies, combined with the advent of GPS receivers, has been gaining ground ever since. Today, such systems cover several million hectares.

In the American Midwest (US), it is associated not with sustainable agriculture but with mainstream farmers who are trying to maximize profits by spending money only in areas that require fertilizer. This practice allows the farmer to vary the rate of fertilizer across the field according to the need identified by GPS guided Grid or Zone Sampling. Fertilizer that would have been spread in areas that don't need it can be placed in areas that do, thereby optimizing its use.

Around the world, precision agriculture developed at a varying pace. Precursor nations were the United States, Canada and Australia. In Europe, the United Kingdom was the first to go down this path, followed closely by France, where it first appeared in 1997-1998. In Latin America the leading country is Argentina, where it was introduced in the middle 1990s with the support of the National Agricultural Technology Institute. Brazil established a state-owned enterprise, Embrapa, to research and develop sustainable agriculture. The development of GPS and variable-rate spreading techniques helped to anchor precision farming management practices. Today, less than 10% of France's farmers are equipped with variable-rate systems. Uptake of GPS is more widespread, but this hasn't stopped them using precision agriculture services, which supplies field-level recommendation maps.

One third of the global population still relies on agriculture for a living. Although more advanced precision farming technologies require large upfront investments, farmers in developing countries are benefitting from mobile technology. This service assists farmers with mobile payments and receipts to improve efficiencies. For example, 30,000 farmers in Tanzania use mobile phones for contracts, payments, loans, and business organization.

The economic and environmental benefits of precision agriculture have also been confirmed in China, but China is lagging behind countries such as Europe and the United States because the Chinese agricultural system is characterized by small-scale family-run farms, which makes the adoption rate of precision agriculture lower than other countries. Therefore, China is trying to better introduce precision agriculture technology into its own country and reduce some risks, paving the way for China's technology to develop precision agriculture in the future.

Pteryx UAV, a civilian UAV for aerial photography and
photo mapping with roll-stabilised camera head.

Economic and Environmental Impacts

Precision agriculture, as the name implies, means application of precise and correct amount of inputs like water, fertilizer, pesticides etc. at the correct time to the crop for increasing its productivity and maximizing its yields. Precision agriculture management practices can significantly reduce the amount of nutrient and other crop inputs used while boosting yields. Farmers thus obtain a return on their investment by saving on water, pesticide, and fertilizer costs.

The second, larger-scale benefit of targeting inputs concerns environmental impacts. Applying the right amount of chemicals in the right place and at the right time benefits crops, soils and groundwater, and thus the entire crop cycle. Consequently, precision agriculture has become a cornerstone of sustainable agriculture, since it respects crops, soils and farmers. Sustainable agriculture seeks to assure a continued supply of food within the ecological, economic and social limits required to sustain production in the long term.

Precision agriculture reduces the pressure on agriculture for the environment by increasing the efficiency of machinery and putting it into use. For example, the use of remote management devices such as GPS reduces fuel consumption for agriculture, while variable rate application of nutrients or pesticides can potentially reduce the use of these inputs, thereby saving costs and reducing harmful runoff into the waterways.

Emerging Technologies

Precision agriculture is an application of breakthrough digital farming technologies. Over $4.6 billion has been invested in agriculture tech companies—sometimes called agtech.

Robots

Self-steering tractors have existed for some time now, as John Deere equipment works like a plane on autopilot. The tractor does most of the work, with the farmer stepping in for emergencies. Technology is advancing towards driverless machinery programmed by GPS to spread fertilizer or plow land. Other innovations include a solar powered machine that identifies weeds and precisely kills them with a dose of herbicide or lasers. Agricultural robots, also known as AgBots, already exist, but advanced harvesting robots are being developed to identify ripe fruits, adjust to their shape and size, and carefully pluck them from branches.

Drones and Satellite Imagery

Advances in drone and satellite technology benefits precision farming because drones take high quality images, while satellites capture the bigger picture. Light aircraft pilots can combine aerial photography with data from satellite records to predict future yields based on the current level of field biomass. Aggregated images can create contour maps to track where water flows, determine variable-rate seeding, and create yield maps of areas that were more or less productive.

The Internet of Things

The Internet of things is the network of physical objects outfitted with electronics that enable data collection and aggregation. IoT comes into play with the development of sensors and farm-management software. For example, farmers can spectroscopically measure nitrogen, phosphorus, and potassium in liquid manure, which is notoriously inconsistent. They can then scan the ground to see where cows have already urinated and apply fertilizer to only the spots that need it. This cuts fertilizer use by up to 30%. Moisture sensors in the soil determine the best times to remotely water plants. The irrigation systems can be programmed to switch which side of tree trunk they water based on the plant's need and rainfall.

Innovations are not just limited to plants—they can be used for the welfare of animals. Cattle can be outfitted with internal sensors to keep track of stomach acidity and digestive problems. External sensors track movement patterns to determine the cow's health and fitness, sense physical injuries, and identify the optimal times for breeding. All this data from sensors can be aggregated and analyzed to detect trends and patterns.

As another example, monitoring technology can be used to make beekeeping more efficient. Honeybees are of significant economic value and provide a vital service to agriculture by pollinating a variety of crops. Monitoring of a honeybee colony's health via wireless temperature, humidity and CO_2 sensors helps to improve the productivity of bees, and to read early warnings in the data that might threaten the very survival of an entire hive.

Smartphone Applications

Smartphone and tablet applications are becoming increasingly popular in precision agriculture. Smartphones come with many useful applications already installed, including the camera, microphone, GPS, and accelerometer. There are also applications made dedicated to various agriculture applications such as field mapping, tracking animals, obtaining weather and crop information, and more. They are easily portable, affordable, and have a high computing power.

Machine Learning

Machine learning is commonly used in conjunction with drones, robots, and internet of things devices. It allows for the input of data from each of these sources. The computer then processes this information and sends the appropriate actions back to these devices. This allows for robots to deliver the perfect amount of fertilizer or for IoT devices to provide the perfect quantity of water directly to the soil. The future of agriculture moves more toward a machine learning architecture every year. It has allowed for more efficient and precise farming with less human manpower.

Automation in Agriculture

Agriculture is the oldest and most important economic activity of humanity, because it provides the food, fiber and the fuel necessary for our survival. With the world population expected to reach 9 billion by 2050, agricultural production must double to meet the growing demand for food and bioenergy. Taking into account the limited resources of land, water and manpower, it is estimated that the efficiency of agricultural productivity should increase by 25% to achieve this goal by limiting the growing pressure exerted by agriculture on the environment. With population growth and rising food demand, the agricultural industry knows how important it is to move quickly to ensure that supply meets demand. The agricultural industry uses robots for a wide range of tasks to meet these needs. Automation is an illumination of the human resources of the labor camp. From last two decades, the concept of industrial automation in agriculture has not developed much.

Automation to agriculture helps create the various advances in the industry and helps farmers to save time and money. Some of the Scientific contributions towards the mobile robot, the flying robot and the forest robot are exclusively for agriculture. Even in developing countries, farmers are interested in using robots to take care of the fields pick the fruit or even maintain the animal, agricultural robots must have human interaction to compensate for the problems of programming complexity. The technological challenges will soon be largely resolved and the industry will be in the process of creating and testing a corporate case, both as a team and as a service.

New developed robots will be able to monitor crops and animals. This would include the control of growth and disease models. Using Wi-Fi technology, the machine can navigate crops without damaging them, even on rough terrain. The device is designed to collect information on soil composition, temperature, humidity and the general conditions of the plants to be sent to the farmer. The mechanical design consists of the end effector, the manipulator and the clamp, the manipulator design includes the task, the economic efficiency and the required movements, the final effectors in the agricultural robot is the device located at the end of the robotic arm and use for various agricultural operations.

Robots and drones have already quietly begun to transform many aspects of agriculture. Thousands of robotic milking parlors have already been installed around the world, creating a $ 1.9 billion sector that is estimated to increase to $ 8 billion by 2023. Mobile robots are also penetrating dairy farms, helping to automate tasks such as pushing or cleaning manure. Also the automatic driving and tractor driving technologies are generalized thanks to the improvements and the cost reduction of the RTK GPS technology. In fact, more than 300k of tractors with automatic transmission or tractor was sold in 2016, reaching over 660k units a year in 2027.

The use of robotics can replace many of the ordinary and often arduous work in various sectors of farming and animal husbandry. Robot platforms can carry workers to pick fruit, and some automation can pick the fruit itself. There are also autonomous robots that can harvest crops in field. They can automate crop spraying and spread fertilizer through driverless tractor. They can even sheer sheep and milk cows. However, these farming tasks are not the only way things are automated in the agricultural field. There are also industrial applications that make life easier for those involved in agriculture.

Agricultural robotics is also quickly developing on the earth. Vision enabled robotics implements have been in viable use for some years in organic farming. These implements follow the crop rows, identify the weeds, and aid with mechanical hoeing. The next generation of these innovative robotic implements is also in its early phase of commercial deployment.

To make a selective collection effectively two criteria are required; the ability to detect the quality factor before harvest and the ability to collect the product of interest without damaging the rest of the crop. Most agricultural equipment is becoming larger and therefore is not suitable for this approach. Smaller and more versatile selective collection equipment is needed. Either the crop can be inspected before harvesting so that the necessary information about where the crop of interest is located, or that the harvester can have mounted sensors that can determine crop conditions. He selective harvester can harvest that ready crop, allowing the rest to mature, dry or ripen, etc. Alternatively, small harvesters of stand-alone crops could be used to selectively harvest the entire crop from a selected area and transport it to a stationary processing system that could clean, cut and perhaps pack the product. This is not a new idea, but the updating of a system that used stationary threshers from many years ago. Alternatively, a separator header could be used to collect the heads of the cereals and send them to threshing.

Agricultural automation is a continuous development. The existing research technologies give rise to the possibility of developing a completely new mechanization system to support the cultivation system based on small intelligent machines. This system replaces the complete energy on the application with intelligently targeted inputs thus reducing the cost of inputs while increasing the level of care. This can improve the economics of crop production and harvest less environmental impact.

Artificial Intelligence in Government

The potential applications of AI in government are massive, and many new ones are still to be discovered and developed.

There are benefits for all aspects and departments of government.

For example, in past health department restaurant testing, restaurants were inspected on a rotating basis but selected mostly at random. AI can mine and develop useful insights from the millions of social media posts that occur every day about restaurants. Using this information, tweets in this example, the Las Vegas health department fine-tuned their selection of restaurants to inspect, based on the content of the unstructured data of social media. The result was an increase in citations, 9,000 fewer cases of food poisoning, and over 500 less food poisoning related hospital admissions over that period.

Many local municipalities or government departments are already investing in and using AI in call centers or customer service. The vast majority of calls coming in are fairly basic, repeat questions or routine reports.

By making use of intelligent chatbots, this process can be automated. This automation will improve service and user experience, as it will be faster and more accurate. The chatbots can answer questions, provide information, receive, and report information, and guide citizens with applications.

For example, the United States Army uses an interactive virtual assistant to check qualifications, answer questions, and refer potential recruits to human recruiters. It does the work of 55 recruiters, and at a 94% accuracy rate that is improving as the machine learns.

The Department of Energy's self-learning weather forecasting technology uses machine learning, sensor information, cloud-motion physics derived from sky cameras, and satellite observations to improve solar forecasting accuracy by 30%.

Law enforcement, public safety, and criminal justice can all benefit from the power of AI. Facial and image recognition software can quickly and more accurately analyze thousands of hours of video footage in crime or terrorist-related issues, narrowing the search down and showing where people should focus their attention.

Again, instead of replacing the human element, it is merely enhancing the process and freeing them up for urgent, feet on the ground tasks, not behind a computer screen for days on end. The United States has already successfully developed a form of 'Predictive Policing' using AI.

Historical crime data is analyzed in seconds helping to narrow the suspect search down with great accuracy. Overall, government work, perhaps more than the private sector, is content transfer intensive. The content from one piece of paper is transferred manually to another, to another system, or between systems. There's a set of technologies called robotic process automation that automatically transfers information. This technology means that a child welfare worker can now spend time with families and children, and the parole officer can spend time with parolees.

These are just a few examples, but there are huge possibilities for all sectors of government, from social welfare, finance, education, to public transport, and many others.

Uses of AI in Government

The potential uses of AI in government are wide and varied, with Deloitte considering that "Cognitive technologies could eventually revolutionize every facet of government operations". Mehr suggests that six types of government problems are appropriate for AI applications:

- Resource allocation such as where administrative support is required to complete tasks more quickly.

- Large datasets where these are too large for employees to work efficiently and multiple datasets could be combined to provide greater insights.

- Expert's shortage including where basic questions could be answered and niche issues can be learned.

- Predictable scenario: Historical data makes the situation predictable.

- Procedural: Repetitive tasks where inputs or outputs have a binary answer.

- Diverse data where data takes a variety of forms (such as visual and linguistic) and needs to be summarised regularly.

Meher states that "While applications of AI in government work have not kept pace with the rapid expansion of AI in the private sector, the potential use cases in the public sector mirror common applications in the private sector."

Potential and actual uses of AI in government can be divided into three broad categories: those that contribute to public policy objectives; those that assist public interactions with the government; and other uses.

Contributing to Public Policy Objectives

There are a range of examples of where AI can contribute to public policy objectives. These include:

- Receiving benefits at job loss, retirement, bereavement and child birth almost immediately, in an automated way (thus without requiring any actions from citizens at all).

- Classifying emergency calls based on their urgency (like the system used by the Cincinnati Fire Department in the United States).

- Detecting and preventing the spread of diseases.

- Assisting public servants in making welfare payments and immigration decisions.

- Adjudicating bail hearings.

- Triaging health care cases.

- Monitoring social media for public feedback on policies.

- Monitoring social media to identify emergency situations.

- Identifying fraudulent benefits claims.

- Predicting a crime and recommending optimal police presence.

- Predicting traffic congestion and car accidents.

- Anticipating road maintenance requirements.

- Identifying breaches of health regulations.

- Providing personalised education to students.

- Marking exam papers.

- Assisting with defence and national security.

- Making symptom based health Chatbot AI Vaid for diagnosis.

Assisting Public Interactions with Government

AI can be used to assist members of the public to interact with government and access government services, for example by:

- Answering questions using virtual assistants or chatbots.

- Directing requests to the appropriate area within government.

- Filling out forms.

- Assisting with searching documents (e.g. IP Australia's trade mark search).

- Scheduling appointments.

Examples of virtual assistants or chatbots being used by government include the following:

- Launched in February 2016, the Australian Taxation Office has a virtual assistant on its website called "Alex". As at 30 June 2017, Alex could respond to more than 500 questions, had engaged in 1.5 million conversations and resolved over 81% of enquiries at first contact.

- Australia's National Disability Insurance Scheme (NDIS) is developing a virtual assistant called "Nadia" which takes the form of an avatar using the voice of actor Cate Blanchett. Nadia is intended to assist users of the NDIS to navigate the service. Costing some $4.5 million, the project has been postponed following a number of issues. Nadia was developed using IBM Watson, however, the Australian Government is considering other platforms such as Microsoft Cortana for its further development.

- The Australian Government's Department of Human Services uses virtual assistants on parts of its website to answer questions and encourage users to stay in the digital channel. As at December 2018, a virtual assistant called "Sam" could answer general questions about family, job seeker and student payments and related information. The Department also introduced an internally-facing virtual assistant called "MelissHR" to make it easier for departmental staff to access human resources information.

Other Uses

Other uses of AI in government include:

- Translation,

- Drafting documents.

Potential Benefits

AI offers potential efficiencies and costs savings for the government. For example, Deloitte has estimated that automation could save US Government employees between 96.7 million to 1.2 billion hours a year, resulting in potential savings of between $3.3 billion to $41.1 billion a year. The Harvard Business Review has stated that while this may lead a government to reduce employee numbers, "Governments could instead choose to invest in the quality of its services. They can re-employ workers' time towards more rewarding work that requires lateral thinking, empathy, and creativity — all things at which humans continue to outperform even the most sophisticated AI program."

5 Challenges for Government Adoption of AI

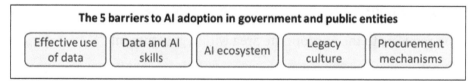

The 5 barriers to AI adoption in government and public entities

| Effective use of data | Data and AI skills | AI ecosystem | Legacy culture | Procurement mechanisms |

Through extensive stakeholder consultation we have identified five key barriers to AI adoption in government:

Effective use of Data

We live in a digital world, and every day we leave behind a trail of digital data, from step counts to internet browsing patterns. IBM estimated in 2017 that 90% of the world's data had been created in the past two years. The problem is, our organizations, both public and private, were not created to handle and take advantage of this volume and variety of data. Most organizations have a very rudimentary understanding of their data assets (i.e. the data they hold and the infrastructure that holds that data) and trying to answer even basic questions such as how many databases exist within the organization, which database contains what information, or how data is collected in the first place, can be challenging. This is a significant problem given data is the fuel that powers modern AI solutions.

A parallel roadblock is that most organizations do not have data governance processes in place, such as established data owners, an enterprise data champion, such as a Chief Data Officer; tools for their employees to safely and efficiently access and take advantage of enterprise data, or practices to manage and ensure data privacy and integrity. Organizations that do not possess the capabilities to understand and manage their data cannot take advantage of AI.

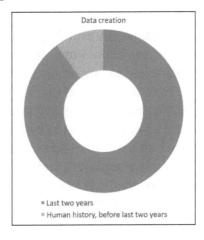

Data and AI Skills

AI and data management skills are in short supply. While the learning curve for data management is relatively surmountable, obtaining the required skills to develop AI solutions is much harder. Organizations place a premium on attracting high-calibre AI talent, raising compensation and making it difficult for organizations with smaller hiring budgets, like government, to attract top candidates. Public agencies find themselves without core AI skills, which hinders their ability to deploy and operate AI solutions.

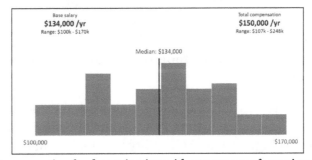

Compensation for data scientists with 1 to 5 years of experience.

In addition, government personnel in non-technical roles, such as department directors, policy-makers, and procurement officials do not always have enough understanding about data and AI. This includes technical knowledge and most importantly knowledge of the legal and ethical implications of using vast amounts of data, where the main concern is privacy. This makes it difficult for them to feel comfortable investing in the technology, or be aware of existing laws that have a direct effect on AI projects, such as data and privacy legislation.

Embarking on AI projects without having a full understanding of applicable local laws threatens constituents' rights, such as privacy, and the government's long-term ability to deploy AI with full public support. This can have as large an effect on AI procurement as a lack of technical AI skills.

Government agencies that do have AI in-house knowledge face an added complexity: lack of communication. Silos between functions make it hard for AI resources and their colleagues, such as policy-makers, to have frequent touch points and take full advantage of each other's knowledge.

The AI Environment

The AI landscape is very complex and continuously evolving. In more established technology sectors there are a few well-known players so buyers know where to go. For example, the cloud landscape is dominated by Alibaba, Amazon, Google and Microsoft, which together account for approximately 84% of the global public cloud market. In contrast, the AI market, which also has significant presence from tech heavy weights, is more fragmented and has many small players continuously appearing. Consider the Canadian AI environment: a study conducted by Deloitte Canada identified more than 800 AI companies. Of these, a majority had fewer than 50 employees and more than 50% had been established in the last five years. The number of players and the speed of change in the AI markets are large enough to potentially hinder a buyer who is new to the AI market. Many buyers might not even be aware of the complete landscape in the first place.

This diversity of players in this system stems from the numerous AI start-ups that have appeared across multiple geographies. This represents a second challenge for government: there is a considerable amount of AI know-how inside small, newer organizations that have limited experience working with government and difficulty scaling for large projects. Governments need to find ways to involve these newer players, both to utilize their considerable expertise, and to foster the growth of AI industry hubs that can contribute significantly to the local economy.

Legacy Culture

All organizations face challenges in adopting new technologies. However, public entities tend to be less agile than their private sector counterparts, owing in part to their established practices and processes. In parts of the private sector a strong culture for experimentation encourages employees to innovate, and positive performance is rewarded. In government there can be less encouragement for employees to take risks.

While many government employees derive much of their work satisfaction from having the opportunity to positively impact society rather than from financial compensation, it can be difficult to adopt a transformative technology such as AI if agility is not inherent to the organization's culture.

Procurement Mechanisms

AI presents challenges that current procurement mechanisms do not address, for example, the private sector treats algorithms as IP. Governments who purchase off-the-shelf algorithms may want to be able to understand and edit them as required throughout the lifecycle of the tool – customization is very common in software procurement – yet AI providers are likely to object to this.

A parallel discussion is the inability of government to avoid vendor lock-in where algorithms are treated like IP, given the original provider would most likely not consent to other AI developers accessing their algorithm. For most technologies this affects maintenance, but for AI it also impacts the ability of government to continuously update the algorithm with new data in order to keep it relevant, significantly affecting its lifespan.

In addition, public procurement mechanisms are well known for being slow and complicated. Common impediments include extensive terms and conditions, long wait times from tender response submission to final decision and proposals that ask for specific solutions as opposed to focusing on the challenge or opportunity at hand. These factors make it problematic for providers to respond, especially small enterprises. For example, long wait times make it very difficult for small enterprises to commit to future staffing requirements, since they usually need to staff resources on projects as soon as one becomes available, in order to manage a positive cash flow.

Government faces significant challenges for widespread AI adoption. Contrary to the popular belief that technology is the main roadblock, technical challenges form just part of the task at hand and this is the most straightforward part to address. Culture and processes, both ingrained in organizations, also need adjustment before AI can be fully exploited.

Artificial Intelligence in Robotics

Artificial intelligence (AI) is arguably the most exciting field in robotics. It's certainly the most controversial: Everybody agrees that a robot can work in an assembly line, but there's no consensus on whether a robot can ever be intelligent.

Like the term "robot" itself, artificial intelligence is hard to define. Ultimate AI would be a recreation of the human thought process -- a man-made machine with our intellectual abilities. This would include the ability to learn just about anything, the ability to reason, the ability to use language and the ability to formulate original ideas. Roboticists are nowhere near achieving this level of artificial intelligence, but they have made a lot of progress with more limited AI. Today's AI machines can replicate some specific elements of intellectual ability.

Computers can already solve problems in limited realms. The basic idea of AI problem-solving is very simple, though its execution is complicated. First, the AI robot or computer gathers facts about a situation through sensors or human input. The computer compares this information to stored data and decides what the information signifies. The computer runs through various possible actions and predicts which action will be most successful based on the collected information. Of course, the computer can only solve problems it's programmed to solve -- it doesn't have any generalized analytical ability.

Artificial intelligence in robots gives companies new opportunities to increase productivity, make work safer, and save people valuable time. Substantial research is being devoted to using AI to expand robot functionality. Commercially available applications include the use of AI to:

- Enable robots to sense and respond to their environment: This vastly increases the range of functions robots can perform.

- Optimise robot and process performance, saving companies money.

- Enable robots to function as mobile, interactive information systems in numerous settings from public spaces to hospitals to retail outlets, saving individuals time.

Examples of Artificial Intelligence in Robotics

Sense-and-Respond

- Identifying, picking, and passing objects: Traditionally, robots have been able to pick up objects in a pre-programmed trajectory in which the object must be known and in the expected place. Robots equipped with sensors can now be programmed using artificial intelligence to identify specific objects regardless of their spatial location. 3D vision software allows the robot to detect objects that are hidden by other objects. Through machine learning, one of the technologies classed as AI, the robot can teach itself in a very short time how to pick up an object it has not encountered before, applying the appropriate level of force. The machine learning algorithm continues to improve as it picks. Picking technology is advancing rapidly but it is currently very difficult for robots to pick objects that are not rigid – for example, goods in plastic wrapping or floppy materials, or have irregular and variable shapes – such as fruit and vegetables – with an accuracy and speed that is commercially viable.

- Inspection: Artificial intelligence enables robots to inspect a wide variety of objects to detect faults – from fruit and vegetables to underwater pipelines.

- Mobility: AI technologies are enabling advanced mobility in robots. Whilst robots have been mobile for over 60 years (the first Automated Guided Vehicle was introduced in 1953), AI enables robot mobility in unpredictable environments. Mobile robots have traditionally been programmed to execute a specific set of manoeuvres in a linear fashion, guided by signals (magnetic, laser, lidar) from devices installed for this purpose in their environment. They have not traditionally been programmed to deal with unexpected events – for example, if they encounter an obstacle, they can stop to avoid collision, but they will not be able to find an alternative route to their goal. In contrast, an AI-enabled mobile robot gets from A to B by building a real-time map (or updating a preprogrammed map in real-time) of its environment and of its location within that environment, planning a path to the programmed goal, sensing obstacles and re-planning a path in-situ. Mobile robots using AI are in commercial use in a number of industries and applications such as:

  - Fetching and carrying goods in factories, warehouses, hospitals.

  - Performing inventory management (mobile robots using RFID scanners or vision technologies).

  - Cleaning – from offices to large pieces of equipment such as ship hulls

  - Exploration of environments dangerous for humans – e.g deep-sea, space, contaminated environments.

Process Optimisation

AI is used to optimise robot accuracy and reliability. Most large industrial robot manufacturers offer customers services using AI to analyse data from robots in real time to predict whether and when a robot is likely to require maintenance, enabling manufacturers to avoid costly machine downtime. Robot performance can also be optimised through analysis of data from sensors - tracking, for example, its movement and power consumption. The robot programme can be adjusted automatically based on the output of the AI algorithm.

Predictive maintenance and process optimisation do not require AI. However, AI technologies improve the speed and accuracy of both activities, resulting in cost savings. In large-scale manufacturing automation projects robots are typically connected to other machinery – including other robots – and AI is used to optimise the whole process, analysing data from all machines.

Mobile Information Robots

Mobile robots are being used as information booths to assist customers in environments such as hotels, hospitals, airports and shops. They can answer questions, lead customers to requested products or locations and can video-link the customer to a human service agent.

Use of AI in Robots Affected Workers and Jobs

Intelligent robots can make work safer and more satisfying. Robots are assuming an increasing range of jobs that are dangerous for humans, such as cleaning toxic or infected environments.

AI expands the potential for robots to share tasks or processes with workers, taking on those parts of the task or process that are unergonomic and repetitive, such as lifting, fetching and carrying. These applications do not depend on AI, but AI technologies enable the robot to work effectively in unpredictable or rapidly-changing environments.

Focus of AI Research in Robots

The main areas of focus of AI research in robots are:

- Expanding picking capabilities to deal with objects that are not rigid or are not in static locations.

- Expanding robot mobility to work effectively in non-standard environments (such as rough terrain).

- Enabling control of robots through verbal commands and gestures.

- Making robots easier to programme: Robots can already be programmed by physical demonstration (the robot is guided through the required motion path and force/torque measurements are translated into code). Research is ongoing in applying AI to enable robots to learn by watching video demonstrations, and by independent trial and error. Reducing robot programming time and costs will increase robot adoption by small-to-medium sized companies, making them more productive. Connected robots will also be able to learn together, running effectively as parallel computers.

It is important to note that it will be some time before these technologies are commercially viable, let alone ubiquitous - it typically takes several years or even decades for new technologies to be adopted at scale.

How do Robots and Artificial Intelligence Work Together?

The answer is simple. Artificial Intelligence or AI gives robots a computer vision to navigate sense and calculate their reaction accordingly. Robots learn to perform their tasks from humans through machine learning which again is a part of computer programming and AI.

Since the time John McCarthy has coined the term Artificial Intelligence in 1956, it has created a lot of sensation. This is because AI has the power to give life to robots and empower them to take their decisions on their own. Depending on the use and the tasks that the robot has to perform different types of AI is used. They are as follows:

- Weak Artificial Intelligence: This type of AI is used to create a simulation of human thought and interaction. The robots have predefined commands and responses. However, the robots do not understand the commands they do only the work of retrieving the appropriate response when the suitable command is given. The most suitable example of this is Siri and Alexa. The AI in these devices only executes the tasks as demanded by the owner.

- Strong Artificial Intelligence: This type of AI is used in those robots who perform their tasks on their own. They do not need any kind of supervision once they are programmed to do the task correctly. This type of AI is widely used nowadays as many of the things are becoming automated and one of the most interesting examples is self-driving cars and internet cars. This type of AI is also used in humanoid robots which can sense their environment quite well and interact with their surroundings. Also, robotic surgeons are becoming popular day by day as there is no human intervention required at all.

- Specialized Artificial Intelligence: This type of AI is used when the robot needs to perform only specified special tasks. It is restricted only to limited tasks. This includes mainly industrial robots which perform specified and repetitive tasks like painting, tightening, etc.

Artificial Intelligence in Heavy Industry

For a large group of industries such as gaming, banking, retail, commercial, and government, etc. AI is extensively used and is slowly impending in the manufacturing sector, facilitating the industrial Automation. AI-driven machines are laying an easier path to the future by yielding a bunch of benefits – offering new opportunities, enhancing production efficiencies, and bringing machine interaction closer to human interaction. The Fourth Industrial Revolution is knowledge-based work, carried out by the automation; by creating new ways to automate tasks, we can rebuild the way people and machines live, interact & collaborate, to make a superior, stronger digital economy.

AI facilitates to conquer many internal challenges that have been around in the industry: from expertise shortage to complexity in decision making, issues related to integration, and overloaded information.

Potential Benefits

AI-driven machines ensure an easier manufacturing process, along with many other benefits, at each new stage of advancement. Technology creates new potential for task automation while increasing the intelligence of human and machine interaction. Some benefits of AI include directed automation, 24/7 production, safer operational environments, and reduced operating costs.

Directed Automation

AI and robots can execute actions repeatedly without any error, and design more competent production models by building automation solutions. They are also capable of eliminating human errors and delivering superior levels of quality assurance on their own.

24/7 Production

While humans must work in shifts to accommodate sleep and mealtimes, robots can keep a production line running continuously. Businesses can expand their production capabilities and meet higher demands for products from global customers due to boosted production from this round-the-clock work performance.

Safer Operational Environment

More AI means fewer human laborers performing dangerous and strenuous work. Logically speaking, with fewer humans and more robots performing activities associated with risk, the number of workplace accidents should dramatically decrease. It also offers a great opportunity for exploration because companies do not have to risk human life.

Condensed Operating Costs

With AI taking over day-to-day activities, a business will have considerably lower operating costs. Rather than employing humans to work in shifts, they could simply invest in AI. The only cost incurred would be from maintenance after the machinery is purchased and commissioned.

Environmental Impacts

Self-driving cars are potentially beneficial to the environment. They can be programmed to navigate the most efficient route and reduce idle time, which could result in less fossil fuel consumption and greenhouse gas (GHG) emissions. The same could be said for heavy machinery used in heavy industry. AI can accurately follow a sequence of procedures repeatedly, whereas humans are prone to occasional errors.

Additional Benefits of AI

AI and industrial automation have advanced considerably over the years. There has been an evolution of many new techniques and innovations, such as advances in sensors and the increase of computing capabilities. AI helps machines gather and extract data, identify patterns, adapt to new trends through machine intelligence, learning, and speech recognition make quick data-driven decisions, advance process effectiveness, minimize operational costs, facilitate product development, and enable extensive scalability.

Potential Negatives

High cost

Though the cost has been decreasing in the past few years, individual development expenditures can still be as high as $300,000 for basic AI. Small businesses with a low capital investment may have difficulty generating the funds necessary to leverage AI. For larger companies, the price of AI may be higher, depending on how much AI is involved in the process. Because of higher costs, the feasibility of leveraging AI becomes a challenge for many companies. However, with the availability of open-source, artificial intelligence software can assist with minimizing cost.

Reduced Employment Opportunities

Job opportunities will grow with the advent of AI; however, some jobs might be lost because AI would replace them. Any job that involves repetitive tasks is at risk of being replaced. In 2017, Gartner predicted 500,000 jobs would be created because of AI, but also predicted that up to 900,000 jobs could be lost because of it. These figures stand true for jobs only within the United States. In 2014, Google, valued at $370 billion, had only 55,000 employees, which is just one-tenth of the size of AT&T's workforce back in the 1960s. This is one effect of AI in the workplace. As AI machines execute jobs that humans perform, they can be more cost-effective than humans themselves.

AI Decision-making

AI is only as intelligent as the individuals responsible for its initial programming. In 2014, an active shooter situation led to people calling Uber to escape the prone area. Instead of recognizing the dangerous situation, the algorithm Uber used saw a rise in demand and increased its prices. This type of situation can be dangerous in the heavy industry, where one mistake can cost lives or cause injury.

Environmental Impacts

Only 20 percent of electronic waste was recycled in 2016, despite 67 nations having enacted e-waste legislation. Electronic waste is expected to reach 52.2 million tons in the year 2021. The manufacture of digital devices and other electronics goes hand-in-hand with AI development which is poised to damage the environment. In September 2015, the German car company Volkswagen witnessed an international scandal. The software in the cars falsely activated emission controls of nitrogen oxide gases (NOx gases) when they were undergoing a sample test. Once the cars were on the road, the emission controls deactivated and the NOx emissions increased up to 40 times. NOx gases are harmful because they cause significant health problems, including respiratory problems and asthma. Further studies have shown that additional emissions could cause over 1,200 premature deaths in Europe and result in $2.4 million worth of lost productivity.

AI trained to act on environmental variables might have erroneous algorithms, which can lead to potentially negative effects on the environment. Algorithms trained on biased data will produce biased results. The COMPAS judicial decision support system is one such example of biased data producing unfair outcomes. When machines develop learning and decision-making ability that is not coded by a programmer, the mistakes can be hard to trace and see. As such, the management and scrutiny of AI-based processes are essential.

Effects of AI in the Manufacturing Industry

The number of industrial robots has increased significantly since the 2000s. The low operating costs of robots make them competitive with human workers. In the finance sector, computer algorithms can execute stock trades much faster than a human, needing only a fraction of a second. As these technologies become cheaper and more accessible, they will be implemented more widely, and humans might be increasingly replaced by AI.

Experts disagree on what impact automation technologies will have on the workforce. Some warn of staggering unemployment, but others point out that technology may create new job categories that will employ these displaced workers. A third group argues that computers will have little effect on employment.

Decreased Workforce

In 2014, Google, valued at $370 billion, had only 55,000 employees which are just a tenth of the size of AT&T's workforce in the 1960s.

Current Use

Landing.ai, a startup formed by Andrew Ng, developed machine-vision tools that detect microscopic defects in products at resolutions well beyond the human vision. The machine-vision tools use a machine-learning algorithm tested on small volumes of sample images. The computer not only 'sees' the errors but processes the information and learns from what it observes.

In 2014, China, Japan, the United States, the Republic of Korea and Germany together contributed to 70 percent of the total sales volume of robots. In the automotive industry, a sector with a particularly high degree of automation, Japan had the highest density of industrial robots in the world at 1,414 per 10,000 employees.

Generative design is a new process born from artificial intelligence. Designers or engineers specify design goals (as well as material parameters, manufacturing methods, and cost constraints) into the generative design software. The software explores all potential permutations for a feasible solution and generates design alternatives. The software also uses machine learning to test and learn from each iteration to test which iterations work and which iterations fail. It is said to effectively rent 50,000 computers [in the cloud] for an hour.

Artificial intelligence has gradually become widely adopted in the modern world. AI personal assistants, like Siri or Alexa, have been around for military purposes since 2003.

The Future of Artificial Intelligence in Manufacturing Industries

Making use of AI in manufacturing plants enables businesses to completely transform their proceedings. Let's have a glance at how AI is helping the manufacturing sector to accomplish:

- Directed Automation: The utilisation of AI and robots is particularly observed in industrial manufacturing as they revolutionize mass-production. Robots are capable of doing recurring activities, designing the production model, rising competence, building automation solutions, eradicating human error and delivering superior levels of quality assurance.

- 24 x 7 Production: While humans are forced to work in 3 shifts for ensuring continuous production, while robots are capable to work for 24/7 in the production line. Businesses can be witnessed to expand in terms of production capabilities and meet the high demand of customers worldwide.

- Safer Operational Environment: With several errors taking place on the manufacturing plant, a step towards AI means less human resource have to carry out dangerous and overly laborious work. As robots replace humans and perform normal and risky activities, the number of workplace accidents will decrease all across.

- Novel Opportunities for Humans: As AI takes over the manufacturing plant and automates boring and ordinary human tasks, workers will get to focus on complex and innovative tasks. While AI takes care of unskilled labor, humans can focus on driving innovation and routing their business to advanced levels.

- Condensed Operating Costs: Although, bringing AI onto the manufacturing industry would necessitate a huge capital investment, the ROI is significantly high. As intelligent machines start taking care of day-to-day-activities, businesses can enjoy considerably lower operating cost.

Artificial Intelligence used in Video Games

Artificial intelligence in video games is largely used to determine the behavior of non-player characters (NPCs) in games. The application of the term "artificial intelligence" might be a misnomer, as many games don't use true AI techniques. Game developers are usually not AI researchers, and many games use simple predetermined patterns.

A lot of AI in game development goes toward defining the way a computer opponent behaves. Behavior can range from relatively simple patterns in action games all the way to chess programs that can beat champion human players.

Many early video games like Pong only allowed human opponents to face each other. Though computer-controlled opponents existed from the very beginning in Computer Space. While human opponents can obviously still be a lot of fun to play against, the video game industry really took off when microprocessors allowed players to square off against more sophisticated and challenging computer opponents.

Space Invaders provided an early example of the challenge that computer-controlled opponents could bring to a game. As the player shot down the aliens, the game sped up considerably with fewer opponents. This was a side effect of the limitations of the hardware at the time, but Tomohiro Nishikado, the inventor of the game for Taito, left it in because it made the gameplay so exciting.

Even while AI researchers debate whether AI in games is the real thing, game developers have used techniques from AI research to create more challenging opponents. They can examine player behavior and change their responses to make the games more challenging using emergent behavior.

Techniques used in AI game programming include decision trees and pathfinding.

Some AI opponents in first-person shooter games can listen for player movements, look for footprints or even take cover when a human opponent fires on them.

Artificial intelligence has long been used to simulate human players in board games. Computer chess players are the best-known example. Modern chess programs are able to easily beat the best human players. IBM's Deep Blue computer famously beat Garry Kasparov in 1997.

The term "game AI" is used to refer to a broad set of algorithms that also include techniques from control theory, robotics, computer graphics and computer science in general, and so video game AI may often not constitute "true AI" in that such techniques do not necessarily facilitate computer learning or other standard criteria, only constituting "automated computation" or a predetermined and limited set of responses to a predetermined and limited set of inputs.

Many industry and corporate voices claim that so-called video game AI has come a long way in the sense that it has revolutionized the way humans interact with all forms of technology, although many expert researchers are skeptical of such claims, and particularly of the notion that such technologies fit the definition of "intelligence" standardly used in the cognitive sciences. Industry voices make the argument that AI has become more versatile in the way we use all technological devices for more than their intended purpose because the AI allows the technology to operate in multiple ways, allegedly developing their own personalities and carrying out complex instructions of the user.

However, many in the field of AI have argued that video game AI is not true intelligence, but an advertising buzzword used to describe computer programs that use simple sorting and matching algorithms to create the illusion of intelligent behavior while bestowing software with a misleading aura of scientific or technological complexity and advancement. Since game AI for NPCs is centered on appearance of intelligence and good gameplay within environment restrictions, its approach is very different from that of traditional AI.

Theories and Algorithms

Practical AI for video game development involves applying algorithms, such as the Minimax algorithm, into machine learning in order to provide the technology with all of the information it needs to outsmart a human. After applying game theories and formula information into AI technology, scientists found that they could program a computer with enough information to beat professionals at no-limit Texas hold'em.

According to Author and Engineer, George Epstein, "The AI researchers used game theory — the mathematics of strategic decision making — to find the best strategy for each hand, while faced with a variety of uncertainties.

AI is able to do this because the information it holds brings each decision down to a science. All of the information used by machine learning came from humans, but with enough information from enough resources, the machine has more strategic knowledge than is possible for a human to have in mind at all times.

Views

Many experts complain that the "AI" in the term "game AI" overstates its worth, as game AI is not about intelligence, and shares few of the objectives of the academic field of AI. Whereas "real AI" addresses fields of machine learning, decision making based on arbitrary data input, and even the ultimate goal of strong AI that can reason, "game AI" often consists of a half-dozen rules of thumb, or heuristics, that are just enough to give a good gameplay experience. Historically, academic game-AI projects have been relatively separate from commercial products because the academic approaches tended to be simple and non-scalable. Commercial game AI has developed its own set of tools, which have been sufficient to give good performance in many cases.

Game developers' increasing awareness of academic AI and a growing interest in computer games by the academic community is causing the definition of what counts as AI in a game to become less idiosyncratic. Nevertheless, significant differences between different application domains of AI mean that game AI can still be viewed as a distinct subfield of AI. In particular, the ability to legitimately solve some AI problems in games by cheating creates an important distinction. For example, inferring the position of an unseen object from past observations can be a difficult problem when AI is applied to robotics, but in a computer game a NPC can simply look up the position in the game's scene graph. Such cheating can lead to unrealistic behavior and so is not always desirable. But its possibility serves to distinguish game AI and leads to new problems to solve, such as when and how to use cheating.

The major limitation to strong AI is the inherent depth of thinking and the extreme complexity of the decision making process. This means that although it would be then theoretically possible to make "smart" AI the problem would take considerable processing power.

Usage

In Computer Simulations of Board Games

- Computer chess,
- Computer Go,
- Computer checkers,
- Computer poker players,
- Computer bridge,
- Computer shogi,
- Computer Arimaa,
- Logistello, which plays Reversi,
- Rog-O-Matic, which plays Rogue,
- Computer players of Scrabble,

- A variety of board games in the Computer Olympiad,

- General game playing,

- Solved games have a computer strategy which is guaranteed to be optimal, and in some cases force a win or draw.

In Modern Video Games

Game AI/heuristic algorithms are used in a wide variety of quite disparate fields inside a game. The most obvious is in the control of any NPCs in the game, although "scripting" (decision tree) is currently the most common means of control. These handwritten decision trees often result in "artificial stupidity" such as repetitive behavior, loss of immersion, or abnormal behavior in situations the developers did not plan for.

Pathfinding, another common use for AI, is widely seen in real-time strategy games. Pathfinding is the method for determining how to get a NPC from one point on a map to another, taking into consideration the terrain, obstacles and possibly "fog of war". Commercial videogames often use fast and simple "grid-based pathfinding", wherein the terrain is mapped onto a rigid grid of uniform squares and a pathfinding algorithm such as A* or IDA* is applied to the grid. Instead of just a rigid grid, some games use irregular polygons and assemble a navigation mesh out of the areas of the map that NPCs can walk to. As a third method, it is sometimes convenient for developers to manually select "waypoints" that NPCs should use to navigate; the cost is that such waypoints can create unnatural-looking movement. In addition, waypoints tend to perform worse than navigation meshes in complex environments. Beyond static pathfinding, navigation is a sub-field of Game AI focusing on giving NPCs the capability to navigate in a dynamic environment, finding a path to a target while avoiding collisions with other entities (other NPC, players...) or collaborating with them (group navigation). Navigation in dynamic strategy games with large numbers of units, such as Age of Empires or Civilization V, often performs poorly; units often get in the way of other units.

Rather than improve the Game AI to properly solve a difficult problem in the virtual environment, it is often more cost-effective to just modify the scenario to be more tractable. If path finding gets bogged down over a specific obstacle, a developer may just end up moving or deleting the obstacle. In Half-Life, the path finding algorithm sometimes failed to find a reasonable way for all the NPCs to evade a thrown grenade; rather than allow the NPCs to attempt to bumble out of the way and risk appearing stupid, the developers instead scripted the NPCs to crouch down and cover in place in that situation.

The concept of emergent AI has recently been explored in games such as *Creatures*, *Black & White* and *Nintendogs* and toys such as Tamagotchi. The "pets" in these games are able to "learn" from actions taken by the player and their behavior is modified accordingly. While these choices are taken from a limited pool, it does often give the desired illusion of an intelligence on the other side of the screen.

Video Game Combat AI

Many contemporary video games fall under the category of action, first person shooter, or adventure. In most of these types of games there is some level of combat that takes place. The AI's ability to be efficient in combat is important in these genres. A common goal today is to make the AI more human, or at least appear so.

One of the more positive and efficient features found in modern-day video game AI is the ability to hunt. AI originally reacted in a very black and white manner. If the player were in a specific area then the AI would react in either a complete offensive manner or be entirely defensive. In recent years, the idea of "hunting" has been introduced; in this 'hunting' state the AI will look for realistic markers, such as sounds made by the character or footprints they may have left behind. These developments ultimately allow for a more complex form of play. With this feature, the player can actually consider how to approach or avoid an enemy. This is a feature that is particularly prevalent in the stealth genre.

Another development in recent game AI has been the development of "survival instinct". In-game computers can recognize different objects in an environment and determine whether it is beneficial or detrimental to its survival. Like a user, the AI can look for cover in a firefight before taking actions that would leave it otherwise vulnerable, such as reloading a weapon or throwing a grenade. There can be set markers that tell it when to react in a certain way. For example, if the AI is given a command to check its health throughout a game then further commands can be set so that it reacts a specific way at a certain percentage of health. If the health is below a certain threshold then the AI can be set to run away from the player and avoid it until another function is triggered. Another example could be if the AI notices it is out of bullets, it will find a cover object and hide behind it until it has reloaded. Actions like these make the AI seem more human. However, there is still a need for improvement in this area.

Another side-effect of combat AI occurs when two AI-controlled characters encounter each other; first popularized in the id Software game *Doom*, so-called 'monster infighting' can break out in certain situations. Specifically, AI agents that are programmed to respond to hostile attacks will sometimes attack *each other* if their cohort's attacks land too close to them. In the case of *Doom*, published gameplay manuals even suggest taking advantage of monster infighting in order to survive certain levels and difficulty settings.

Uses in Games Beyond NPCs

Georgios N. Yannakakis suggests that academic AI developments may play roles in game AI beyond the traditional paradigm of AI controlling NPC behavior. He highlights four other potential application areas:

- Player-experience modeling: Discerning the ability and emotional state of the player, so as to tailor the game appropriately. This can include dynamic game difficulty balancing, which consists in adjusting the difficulty in a video game in real-time based on the player's ability. Game AI may also help deduce player intent (such as gesture recognition).

- Procedural-content generation: Creating elements of the game environment like environmental conditions, levels, and even music in an automated way. AI methods can generate new content or interactive stories.

- Data mining on user behavior: This allows game designers to explore how people use the game, what parts they play most, and what causes them to stop playing, allowing developers to tune gameplay or improve monetization.

- Alternate approaches to NPCs: These include changing the game set-up to enhance NPC believability and exploring social rather than individual NPC behavior.

Rather than procedural generation, some researchers have used generative adversarial networks (GANs) to create new content. In 2018 researchers at Cornwall University trained a GAN on a thousand human-created levels for DOOM; following training, the neural net prototype was able to design new playable levels on its own. Similarly, researchers at the University of California prototyped a GAN to generate levels for Super Mario.

Cheating AI

> Dani Bunten was once asked how to play-balance a game. Her one word answer was "Cheat." Asked what to do if gamers complained, she said, "Lie!"
>
> —Johnny L. Wilson

> Gamers always ask if the AI cheats (presumably so they can complain if they lose).
>
> —Terry Lee Coleman

In the context of artificial intelligence in video games, cheating refers to the programmer giving agents actions and access to information that would be unavailable to the player in the same situation. Believing that the Atari 8-bit could not compete against a human player, Chris Crawford did not fix a bug in Eastern Front that benefited the computer-controlled Russian side.

For example, if the agents want to know if the player is nearby they can either be given complex, human-like sensors (seeing, hearing, etc.), or they can cheat by simply asking the game engine for the player's position. Common variations include giving AIs higher speeds in racing games to catch up to the player or spawning them in advantageous positions in first person shooters. The use of cheating in AI shows the limitations of the "intelligence" achievable artificially; generally speaking, in games where strategic creativity is important, humans could easily beat the AI after a minimum of trial and error if it were not for this advantage. Cheating is often implemented for performance reasons where in many cases it may be considered acceptable as long as the effect is not obvious to the player. While cheating refers only to privileges given specifically to the AI—it does not include the inhuman swiftness and precision natural to a computer—a player might call the computer's inherent advantages "cheating" if they result in the agent acting unlike a human player. Sid Meier stated that he omitted multiplayer alliances in Civilization because he found that the computer was almost as good as humans in using them, which caused players to think that the computer was cheating. Developers say that most are honest but they dislike players erroneously complaining about "cheating" AI. In addition, humans use tactics against computers that they would not against other people.

Examples:

- Creatures

Creatures is an artificial life program where the user "hatches" small furry animals and teaches them how to behave. These "Norns" can talk, feed themselves, and protect themselves against vicious creatures. It was the first popular application of machine learning in an interactive simulation. Neural networks are used by the creatures to learn what to do. The game is regarded as a breakthrough in artificial life research, which aims to model the behavior of creatures interacting with their environment.

- Sid Meier's Alpha Centauri

- Halo: Combat Evolved

A first-person shooter where the player assumes the role of the Master Chief, battling various aliens on foot or in vehicles. Enemies use cover very wisely, and employ suppressing fire and grenades. The squad situation affects the individuals, so certain enemies flee when their leader dies. A lot of attention is paid to the little details, with enemies notably throwing back grenades or team-members responding to you bothering them. The underlying "behavior tree" technology has become very popular in the games industry (especially since Halo 2).

- F.E.A.R.

A first-person shooter where the player helps contain supernatural phenomenon and armies of cloned soldiers. The AI uses a planner to generate context-sensitive behaviors, the first time in a mainstream game. This technology is still used as a reference for many studios. The enemies are capable of using the environment very cleverly, finding cover behind tables, tipping bookshelves, opening doors, crashing through windows, and so on. Squad tactics are used to great effect. The enemies perform flanking maneuvers, use suppressing fire, etc.

- S.T.A.L.K.E.R. series

A first-person shooter survival horror game where the player must face man-made experiments, military soldiers, and mercenaries known as Stalkers. The various encountered enemies (if the difficulty level is set to its highest) use combat tactics and behaviours such as healing wounded allies, giving orders, out-flanking the player or using weapons with pinpoint accuracy.

- Far Cry 2

A first-person shooter where the player fights off numerous mercenaries and assassinates faction leaders. The AI is behavior based and uses action selection, essential if an AI is to multitask or react to a situation. The AI can react in an unpredictable fashion in many situations. The enemies respond to sounds and visual distractions such as fire or nearby explosions and can be made to investigate, the player utilising these distractions to their advantage. Certain AI non-playable characters will react negatively to being bumped into, for example by shoving away, swearing at, or aiming at the player with their weapon. Injured enemies can call for help while on the ground, or display distress, etc.

- StarCraft II

A real-time strategy game where a player takes control of one of three factions in a 1v1, 2v2, or 3v3 battle arena. The player must defeat their opponents by destroying all their units and bases. This is accomplished by creating units that are effective at countering your opponents' units. Players can play against multiple different levels of AI difficulty ranging from very easy to Cheater 3 (insane).

The AI is able to cheat at the difficulty Cheater 1 (vision), where it can see units and bases when a player in the same situation could not. Cheater 2 gives the AI extra resources, while Cheater 3 give an extensive advantage over its opponent.

A.I. in Alien: Isolation

One of the more popular forms of advanced A.I. in video games recently is the Alien from Creative Assembly's Alien: Isolation. There are some misunderstandings about how the A.I. works behind the scenes. However, it is a remarkable display of the ways in which A.I. can be used to create an engaging and unpredictable environment for the player.

The alien in Alien: Isolation has two driving A.I. forces controlling its movements and behavior: Director A.I. and Alien A.I. The Director A.I. is a passive controller that is in charge of creating an enjoyable player experience. In order to achieve this, the Director A.I. knows where both the player and alien are at all times. However, it does not share this knowledge with the alien. The Director A.I. keeps an eye on what is referred to as the Menace Gauge, which is essentially just a measure of expected player stress levels determined by a multitude of factors such as the alien's proximity to the player, the amount of time the alien spends near the player, the amount of time spent in sight of the player, the amount of time spent visible on the motion tracker device, etc. This Menace Gauge informs the alien's Job Systems, which is essentially just a task tracker for the alien. If the Menace Gauge reaches a certain level, the priority of the task "search new location zone" will grow until the alien moves away from the player into a separate area.

Behavioral Decision Trees

Before diving into how the Alien A.I. works in action, it is important to first highlight the structure that informs the decision-making process. The Alien A.I. uses an extensive behavioral decision tree with over 100 nodes and 30 selector nodes. Imagine the simple example below:

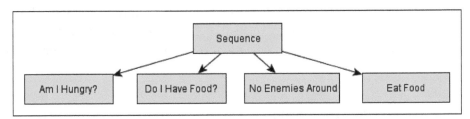

The way a behavior tree works is by asking questions from left to right. A success allows progression along the tree, while a fail would revert back to the sequence node. Here is the process: Sequence -> Am I Hungry?(success) -> Sequence(running) -> Do I Have Food?(success) -> Sequence(running) -> No Enemies Around(success) -> Sequence(running) -> Eat Food(success) -> Sequence(success) -> Parent Node. If, at any point, one of the nodes returns a (fail), the entire sequence would fail. For example, if it turned out that "Do I Have Food?" failed, it would not check to see if there were any enemies around and it would not eat the food. Instead, the sequence would fail and that would be the end of that sequence.

Sequences can obviously get much more complex, and become multilayered in depth. Here is a deeper example:

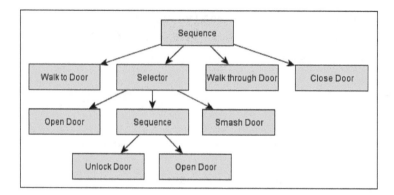

Remember, when a sequence either succeeds or fails it returns the result to its Parent node. In the example above, let's assume that we have succeeded in approaching the door, but failed to open the door as it was locked and we had no key. The sequence node was marked as a fail. As a result, the behavior tree path reverted to the parent node of that sequence. Here is what this parent node might look like:

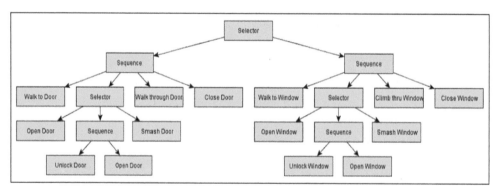

So, we have failed at opening the door, but we haven't given up yet. Our parent node has another sequence for us to try. This time it involves entering through a window instead. The Alien A.I. has 30 different selector nodes and 100 total nodes, so it is exponentially more complicated than this example, but I hope this gives you an idea about how the Alien A.I. works under the hood.

Back to Alien A.I.

The Alien A.I. is the system that controls the alien's actions. It is never provided information about the player's location. The only information it receives from the Director A.I. is which general area it should search. Beyond that, it must find the player on its own. It does have some tools to use that help it in hunting down the player. The first is the Sensor System which allows the alien to pick up on audio and visual cues in the environment. Noises such as footsteps, gunshots, the opening of doors, even the beeping of the motion tracker, all of these help the alien to track down the player. The audio range depends on the type of noise that was created. In addition to audio sensors, the alien can also pick up on visual sensors such as glimpsing Ripley running past, or seeing a door open in view, etc.

Another tool the alien has to hunt down the player is the Searching System. There are specific areas that the developers have determined to be good hiding spots that the alien is pre-programmed to search. However, it does not search them in any particular order, and will even double check areas that have already been visited. Of course, if the alien hears a noise or sees a visual cue, it will search an area that the developers have not specifically outlined.

The most commonly discussed topic about Alien: Isolation is how the alien seems to learn more about the player as the game progresses. The actions it makes seem to become more complex as it learns certain traits about a player's play style. Surprisingly to some, the way the developers achieved this was not by building in a complex neural network into the alien's A.I. system. To show how the game accomplishes this sense of alien learning we need to refer back to the Alien A.I.'s behavioral decision tree.

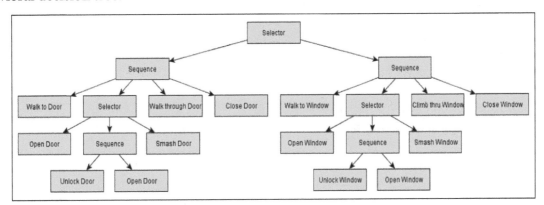

At the start of the game, there are sections of this behavioral tree that are blocked out to the alien. The areas that are blocked out are inaccessible to the alien, meaning it cannot access certain behaviors and actions. For example, at the start of the game the section of the tree that responds to the sound of a door opening in the distance may not be active. If a player opens a door in the alien's view it could unlock that section of the behavioral tree so that, in the future, the sound of a door opening will trigger a response. As the player progresses through the game, more and more of the alien's behavioral tree is unlocked. This gives the illusion that the alien is learning and adapting to the player's gaming style.

Marketing and Artificial Intelligence

Artificial intelligence (AI) in marketing is the process of utilizing data models, mathematics and algorithms to generate insights that can be used by marketers. Marketers will use AI-derived insights to guide future decisions about campaign spending, strategy and content topics. AI in marketing can be used in planning, production personalization, promotion, and performance stages of marketing. In addition, AI can be used in an unattended manner, to directly instrument and optimize campaigns without human intervention.

Marketers leverage artificial intelligence in one of two ways: first, by purchasing or licensing marketing technology software that has artificial intelligence capabilities; second, by using computer programming to implement artificial intelligence algorithms and techniques.

AI in marketing utilizes machine learning and neural networks to derive analysis and pattern matching insights from large sets of customer and user data (e.g., purchases, web visits, clicks, product usage, etc.). The insights are delivered to marketers via dashboards, reports and recommendations.

For example, predictive marketing solutions apply artificial intelligence to lead scoring and qualification. Attributes of existing customers are analyzed to qualify the likelihood of sales leads become future customers. AI-powered features are now a part of numerous marketing technology systems, such as email marketing, marketing automation and predictive analytics.

In addition to assisting with marketing campaigns, artificial intelligence can be applied to content creation. For example, the Associated Press uses an AI solution called Automated Insights to produce 4,400 quarterly earnings stories. This software solution uses AI techniques to generate stories (i.e., based on data) that read just like a human wrote them.

Another avenue available to marketers is to use programming languages such as Python and R to code AI methodologies and algorithms (e.g., text mining, time-series forecasting and driver analysis). To accomplish this, the marketer (or, a programmer or data scientist hired by the marketer) needs to be proficient in mathematics, data science, statistics and programming.

Artificial Neural Networks

An artificial neural network is a form of computer program modeled on the brain and nervous system of humans. Neural networks are composed of a series of interconnected processing neurons functioning in unison to achieve certain outcomes. Using "human-like trial and error learning methods neural networks detect patterns existing within a data set ignoring data that is not significant, while emphasizing the data which is most influential".

From a marketing perspective, neural networks are a form of software tool used to assist in decision making. Neural networks are effective in gathering and extracting information from large data sources and have the ability to identify the cause and effect within data. These neural nets through the process of learning, identify relationships and connections between databases. Once knowledge has been accumulated, neural networks can be relied on to provide generalizations and can apply past knowledge and learning to a variety of situations.

Neural networks help fulfill the role of marketing companies through effectively aiding in market segmentation and measurement of performance while reducing costs and improving accuracy. Due to their learning ability, flexibility, adaption and knowledge discovery, neural networks offer many advantages over traditional models. Neural networks can be used to assist in pattern classification, forecasting and marketing analysis.

Pattern Classification

Classification of customers can be facilitated through the neural network approach allowing companies to make informed marketing decisions. An example of this was employed by Spiegel Inc., a firm dealing in direct-mail operations who used neural networks to improve efficiencies. Using software developed by NeuralWare Inc., Spiegel identified the demographics of customers who had made a single purchase and those customers who had made repeat purchases. Neural networks where then able to identify the key patterns and consequently identify the customers that were most likely to repeat purchase. Understanding this information allowed Speigel to streamline marketing efforts, and reduced costs.

Forecasting

Sales forecasting "is the process of estimating future events with the goal of providing benchmarks for monitoring actual performance and reducing uncertainty". Artificial intelligence techniques have emerged to facilitate the process of forecasting through increasing accuracy in the areas of demand for products, distribution, employee turnover, performance measurement and inventory control. An example of forecasting using neural networks is the Airline Marketing Assistant/Tactician; an application developed by BehabHeuristics which allows for the forecasting of passenger demand and consequent seat allocation through neural networks. This system has been used by Nationalair Canada and USAir.

Marketing Analysis

Neural networks provide a useful alternative to traditional statistical models due to their reliability, time-saving characteristics and ability to recognize patterns from incomplete or noisy data. Examples of marketing analysis systems include the Target Marketing System developed by Churchull Systems for Veratex Corporation. This support system scans a market database to identify dormant customers allowing management to make decisions regarding which key customers to target.

When performing marketing analysis, neural networks can assist in the gathering and processing of information ranging from consumer demographics and credit history to the purchase patterns of consumers.

AI is allowing organizations to "deliver an ad experience that is more personalized for each user, shapes the customer journey, influences purchasing decisions, and builds brand loyalty" ("How"). AI technology allows marketers to separate their consumers into distinct personas and understand what motivates their consumers. Here they can then focus on the specific needs of their audience and create a long-lasting relationship with the brand (Kushmaro). Ultimately brands want to create that loyalty with a consumer, and AI will allow them to better achieve this. "Pini Yakuel, founder and CEO of Optimove. "By analyzing customers based on their movement among segments over time, we can achieve dynamic micro-segmentation, and predict future behavior in a very accurate fashion'" (Kushmaro). Being able to predict the future behaviors of consumers is very important. This way marketers can specifically market to consumers based on their current behaviors and the predictions of their future behaviors. This will allow for a loyal relationship between the consumer and the brand and will ultimately help businesses.

Application of Artificial Intelligence to Marketing Decision Making

Marketing is a complex field of decision making which involves a large degree of both judgment and intuition on behalf of the marketer. The enormous increase in complexity that the individual decision maker faces renders the decision making process almost an impossible task. Marketing decision engine can help distill the noise. The generation of more efficient management procedures have been recognized as a necessity. The application of Artificial intelligence to decision making through a Decision Support System has the ability to aid the decision maker in dealing with uncertainty in decision problems. Artificial intelligence techniques are increasingly extending decision support through analyzing trends; providing forecasts; reducing information overload; enabling communication required for collaborative decisions, and allowing for up-to-date information.

The Structure of Marketing Decisions

Organizations' strive to satisfy the needs of the customers, paying specific attention to their desires. A consumer-orientated approach requires the production of goods and services that align with these needs. Understanding consumer behavior aids the marketer in making appropriate decisions. Thus, the decision making is dependent on the marketing problem, the decision maker, and the decision environment.

Expert System

An expert system is a software program that combines the knowledge of experts in an attempt to solve problems through emulating the knowledge and reasoning procedures of the experts. Each expert system has the ability to process data, and then through reasoning, transform it into evaluations, judgments and opinions, thus providing advises to specialized problems.

The use of an expert system that applies to the field of marketing is MARKEX (Market Expert). These Intelligent decision support systems act as consultants for marketers, supporting the decision maker in different stages, specifically in the new product development process. The software provides a systematic analysis that uses various methods of forecasting, data analysis and multi-criteria decision making to select the most appropriate penetration strategy. BRAND-FRAME is another example of a system developed to assist marketers in the decision-making process. The system supports a brand manager in terms of identifying the brand's attributes, retail channels, competing brands, targets and budgets. New marketing input is fed into the system where BRANDFRAME analyses the data. Recommendations are made by the system in regard to marketing mix instruments, such as lowering the price or starting a sales promotional campaign.

Artificial Intelligence and Automation Efficiency

Application to Marketing Automation

In terms of marketing, automation uses software to computerize marketing processes that would have otherwise been performed manually. It assists in effectively allowing processes such as customer segmentation, campaign management and products promotion, to be undertaken at a more efficient rate. Marketing automation is a key component of Customer Relationship Management (CRM). Companies are using systems that employ data-mining algorithms that analyses the customer database, giving further insight into the customer. This information may refer to socio-economic characteristics, earlier interactions with the customer, and information about the purchase history of the customer. Various systems have been designed to give organizations control over their data. Automation tools allow the system to monitor the performance of campaigns, making regular adjustments to the campaigns to improve response rates and to provide campaign performance tracking.

Automation of Distribution

Distribution of products requires companies to access accurate data so they are able to respond to fluctuating trends in product demand. Automation processes are able to provide a comprehensive system that improves real-time monitoring and intelligent control. Amazon acquired Kiva Systems, the makers of the warehouse robot for $775 million in 2012. Prior to the purchase of the automated system, human employees would have to walk the enormous warehouse, tracking and retrieving books. The Kiva robots are able to undertake order fulfillment, product replenishment, as well as heavy lifting, thus increasing efficiency for the company.

Use of Artificial Intelligence to Analyze Social Networks on the Web

A social network is a social arrangement of actors who make up a group, within a network; there can be an array of ties and nodes that exemplifies common occurrences within a network and common relationships. Lui, describes a social network as, "the study of social entities (people in organization, called actors), and their interactions and relationships. The interactions and relationships can be represented with a network or graph, where each vertex (or node) represents an actor and each link represents a relationship." At the present time there is a growth in virtual social networking with the common emergence of social networks being replicated online, for example social networking sites such as Twitter, Facebook and LinkedIn. From a marketing perspective, analysis and simulation of these networks can help to understand consumer behavior and opinion. The use of Agent-based social simulation techniques and data/opinion mining to collect social knowledge of networks can help a marketer to understand their market and segments within it.

Social Computing

Social computing is the branch of technology that can be used by marketers to analyze social behaviors within networks and also allows for creation of artificial social agents. Social computing provides the platform to create social based software; some earlier examples of social computing are such systems that allow a user to extract social information such as contact information from email accounts e.g. addresses and companies titles from ones email using Conditional Random Field (CRFs) technology.

Data Mining

Data mining involves searching the Web for existing information namely opinions and feelings that are posted online among social networks. "This area of study is called opinion mining or sentiment analysis. It analyzes people's opinions, appraisals, attitudes, and emotions toward entities, individuals, issues, events, topics, and their attributes". However searching for this information and analysis of it can be a sizeable task, manually analyzing this information also presents the potential for researcher bias. Therefore, objective opinion analysis systems are suggested as a solution to this in the form of automated opinion mining and summarization systems. Marketers using this type of intelligence to make inferences about consumer opinion should be wary of what is called opinion spam, where fake opinions or reviews are posted in the web in order to influence potential consumers for or against a product or service.

Search engines are a common type of intelligence that seeks to learn what the user is interested in to present appropriate information. PageRank and HITS are examples of algorithms that search for information via hyperlinks; Google uses PageRank to control its search engine. Hyperlink based intelligence can be used to seek out web communities, which is described as 'a cluster of densely linked pages representing a group of people with a common interest'.

Centrality and prestige are types of measurement terms used to describe the level of common occurrences among a group of actors; the terms help to describe the level of influence and actor holds within a social network. Someone who has many ties within a network would be described as a 'central' or 'prestige' actor. Identifying these nodes within a social network is helpful for marketers to find out who are the trendsetters within social networks.

Social Media AI-based Tools

Ellott looked at the AI based tools that are transforming social media markets. There are six areas of social media marketing that are being impacted by AI: content creation, consumer intelligence, customer service, influencer marketing, content optimization, and competitive intelligence. One tool, Twizoo, uses AI to gather reviews from social networking sites about restaurants to help users find a place to eat. Twizoo had much success from the feedback of their users and expanded by launching "a widget where travel and hospitality websites could instantly bring those social media reviews to their own audiences".

Influencer marketing is huge on social media. Many brands collaborate and sponsor popular social media users and try to promote their products to that social media user's followers. This has been a huge tactic for Sugar Bear Hair and Fab Fit Fun. One company, InsightPool, uses AI to search through over 600 million influencers on social media to find the influencers who fit the brand's personality and target audience. This can be an effective tool when searching for new influencers or a specific audience. It could also be cost effective to find someone who is not famous (like Kardashians/Bachelorette cast) but could also influence a large audience and bring in sales.

Examples of AI in Marketing

Recommendations/Content Curation

Predictive analytics allows Netflix to surface and finesse recommendations. This kind of clustering algorithm is continually improving suggestions, allowing users to make the most of their subscription.

Under Armour is one of the many companies to have worked with IBM's Watson. The sports apparel company combines user data from its Record app with third-party data and research on fitness, nutrition etc.

The result is the ability for the brand to offer up relevant (personalized) training and lifecycle advice based on aggregated wisdom.

IBM explained: A 32-year-old woman who is training for a 5km race could use the app to create a personalized training and meal plan based on her size, goals, lifestyle.

The app could map routes near her home/office, taking into account the weather and time of day. It can watch what she eats and offer suggestions on how to improve her diet to improve performance.

Search Engines

In late October 2015, Google announced it was using RankBrain, an AI system, to interpret a 'very large fraction' of search queries.

RankBrain should mean better natural language processing (NLP) to help find relevance in content and queries, as well as better interpretation of voice search and user context.

Preventing Fraud and Data Breaches

Analysing credit/debit card usage patterns and device access allows security specialists to identify points of compromise.

The relevance of AI is not just for card issuers, though. Retailers, for example, have been subject to high profile data breaches (e.g. Neiman Marcus) as a result of a system based solely on user-names and passwords (without any stronger type of authentication).

This area of security analytics has been around for years but is becoming more sophisticated. Solutions have to react quickly to new fraudster tactics and analyse unstructured data, too. And this is where AI can help.

Natural language processing (NLP) can be used to look at text within transactions, for example, transforming it into structured data.

Newer AI implementations, such as that used by the United Services Automobile Association (USAA, which provides financial services for ex-military), will identify anomalies in behaviour even on the first instance.

Social Semantics

Deep learning has plenty to get its teeth into on social.

Sentiment analysis, product recommendations, image and voice recognition – there are many areas where AI has the potential to allow social networks to improve at scale.

Website Design

The Grid is an 'AI' website design platform.

Intelligent image recognition and cropping, algorithmic pallette and typography selection – The Grid is using AI in certain areas to effectively automate web design.

Product Pricing

With thousands of products and many factors that impact sales, an estimate of the price to sales ratio or price elasticity is difficult.

Dynamic price optimisation using machine learning can help in this regard – correlating pricing trends with sales trends by using an algorithm, then aligning with other factors such as category management and inventory levels.

Predictive Customer Service

Knowing how a customer might get in touch and for what reason is valuable information.

Not only does it allow for planning of resource (e.g. do we have enough people on the phones?) but also allows personalisation of communications.

Another project being tested at USAA uses this technique. It involves an AI technology built by Saffron, now a division of Intel. Analysing thousands of factors allows the matching of broad patterns of customer behavior to those of individual members. The AI has so far helped USAA improve its guess rate from 50% to 88%, increasingly knowing how users will next contact and for what products.

Ad Targeting

As Andrew Ng, Chief Scientist at Baidu Research says: "Deep learning [is] able to handle more signal for better detection of trends in user behavior. Serving ads is basically running a recommendation engine, which deep learning does well."

Optimising bids for advertisers, algorithms will achieve the best cost per acquisition (CPA) from the available inventory.

When it comes to targeting of programmatic ads, machine learning helps to increase the likelihood a user will click. This might be optimising what product mix to display when retargeting, or what ad copy to use for what demographics.

Speech Recognition

Skype Translator now supports Arabic, English, French, German, Italian, Mandarin, Brazilian Portuguese, and Spanish.

Translation of speech has come so far due to progress in neural networks over the past five years.

Siri and Cortana and other personal assistants also use speech recognition of course, so many consumers are aware of how accurate they are. Speech recognition is particularly important in the Chinese market, where using a keyboard to type small and intricate characters can be laborious. Baidu is making big strides on this front with voice search.

Language Recognition

Behind speech recognition sits the challenge of language recognition: what language means in relation to other things and concepts.

However, language recognition may be increasingly used by brands to digest unstructured information from customers and prospects.

WayBlazer is a so-called 'cognitive travel platform', a B2B service using IBM's Watson AI to power consumer applications from third parties such as hotel chains and airlines.

So, for example, images, recommendations and travel insight are personalised depending on customer data, which might be unstructured text, e.g. 'We want a family beach holiday with plenty of kids activities but also culture'.

Customer Segmentation

Plugging first- and third-party data into a clustering algorithm, then using the results in a CRM or custom experience system is a burgeoning use of machine learning.

Companies such as AgilOne are allowing marketers to optimise email and website comms, continually learning from user behaviour.

Sales Forecasting

Conversion management again, but this time using inbound communication.

Much like predictive customer service, inbound emails can be analysed and appropriate action taken based on past behaviours and conversions. Should a response be sent, a meeting invite, an alert created, or the lead disqualified altogether? Machine learning can help with this filtering process.

Image Recognition

Google Photos allows you to search your photos for 'cats'. Facebook recognises faces, as does Snapchat Face Swap.

Baidu have also designed DuLight for the visually impaired. The early prototype recognises what is in front of the wearer and then describes it back to them. Of course, for marketers the uses could be manyfold, from content searching to innovative customer experiences.

Content Generation

At the moment, content generation is chiefly done using structured data. Wordsmith is a platform created by Automated Insights that allows the automatic generation of news articles – for example, from financial reports.

This relies on the reports being fed into a CSV in the right way – it's essentially automation.

However, in the not-too-distant future, the plan is to do this sort of content generation with unstructured data using AI.

Bots, PAs and Messengers

Chatbots are thought by many to be the future of user input on mobile, replacing apps.

Simply talking or typing to a chatbot will allow a service to be delivered through the analysis of natural language combined with understanding of a brand's datasets.

Facebook's platform, previewed at F8, could conservatively soon lead to chatbots replacing '1-800 numbers, offering more comfortable customer support experiences without the hassle of synchronous phone conversations, hold times and annoying phone trees.'

Artificial Intelligence in Healthcare

Artificial Intelligence (AI) is commonly known for its ability to have machines perform tasks that are associated with the human mind – like problem solving. However, what's less understood is how AI is being used within specific industries, such as healthcare.

The healthcare industry continues to evolve as machine learning and AI in technology become more popular in the digital age. Spending on AI in healthcare is projected to grow at an annualized 48% between 2017 and 2023.

Machine learning has the potential to provide data-driven clinical decision support (CDS) to physicians and hospital staff – paving the way for an increased revenue potential. Machine learning, a subset of AI designed to identify patterns, uses algorithms and data to give automated insights to healthcare providers.

Artificial Intelligence in Medicine

AI in medicine refers to the use of artificial intelligence technology/automated processes in the diagnosis and treatment of patients who require care. Whilst diagnosis and treatment may seem like simple steps, there are many other background processes that must take place in order for a patient to be properly taken care of, for example:

- Gathering of data through patient interviews and tests.

- Processing and analysing results.

- Using multiple sources of data to come to an accurate diagnosis.

- Determining an appropriate treatment method (often presenting options).

- Preparing and administering the chosen treatment method.

- Patient monitoring.

- Aftercare, follow-up appointments etc.

The argument for increased use of AI in medicine is that quite a lot of the above could be automated - automation often means tasks are completed more quickly, and it also frees up a medical professional's time when they could be performing other duties, ones that cannot be automated, and so are seen as a more valuable use of human resources.

According to a study from 2016, physicians spend much more time on data entry and desk work than they do actually talking to and engaging with patients. This revealed, said AMA Immediate Past President Steven Stack, "what many physicians are feeling—data entry and administrative tasks are cutting into the doctor-patient time that is central to medicine and a primary reason many of us became physicians."

The push, therefore, is not to excessively over-automate the medical and health care fields, but to deliberately and sensibly identify those areas where automation could free up time and effort. The goal is a balance between the effective use of technology and AI and the human strengths and judgement of trained medical professionals. Various specialties in medicine have shown an increase in research regarding AI.

Radiology

The ability to interpret imaging results with radiology may aid clinicians in detecting a minute change in an image that a clinician might accidentally miss. A study at Stanford created an algorithm that could detect pneumonia at that specific site, in those patients involved, with a better average F1 metric (a statistical metric based on accuracy and recall), than the radiologists involved in that trial. The radiology conference Radiological Society of North America has implemented presentations on AI in imaging during its annual meeting. The emergence of AI technology in radiology is perceived as a threat by some specialists, as the technology can achieve improvements in certain statistical metrics in isolated cases, as opposed to specialists.

Imaging

Recent advances have suggested the use of AI to describe and evaluate the outcome of maxillo-facial surgery or the assessment of cleft palate therapy in regard to facial attractiveness or age appearance.

In 2018, a paper published in the journal Annals of Oncology mentioned that skin cancer could be detected more accurately by an artificial intelligence system (which used a deep learning convolutional neural network) than by dermatologists. On average, the human dermatologists accurately detected 86.6% of skin cancers from the images, compared to 95% for the CNN machine.

Telehealth

The increase of Telemedicine, has shown the rise of possible AI applications. The ability to monitor patients using AI may allow for the communication of information to physicians if possible disease activity may have occurred. A wearable device may allow for constant monitoring of a patient and also allow for the ability to notice changes that may be less distinguishable by humans.

Electronic Health Records

Electronic health records are crucial to the digitailization and information spread of the healthcare industry. However logging all of this data comes with its own problems like cognitive overload and burnout for users. EHR developers are now automating much of the process and even starting to use natural language processing (NLP) tools to improve this process. One study conducted by the Centerstone research insititute found that predictive modeling of EHR data has achieved 70–72% accuracy in predicting individualized treatment response at baseline. Meaning using an AI tool that scans EHR data it can pretty accurately predict the course of disease in a person.

Industry

The subsequent motive of large based health companies merging with other health companies, allow for greater health data accessibility. Greater health data may allow for more implementation of AI algorithms.

A large part of industry focus of implementation of AI in the healthcare sector is in the clinical decision support systems. As the amount of data increases, AI decision support systems become more efficient. Numerous companies are exploring the possibilities of the incorporation of big data in the health care industry.

The following are examples of large companies that have contributed to AI algorithms for use in healthcare.

IBM

IBM's Watson Oncology is in development at Memorial Sloan Kettering Cancer Center and Cleveland Clinic. IBM is also working with CVS Health on AI applications in chronic disease treatment and with Johnson & Johnson on analysis of scientific papers to find new connections for drug development. In May 2017, IBM and Rensselaer Polytechnic Institute began a joint project entitled Health Empowerment by Analytics, Learning and Semantics (HEALS), to explore using AI technology to enhance healthcare.

Microsoft

Microsoft's Hanover project, in partnership with Oregon Health & Science University's Knight Cancer Institute, analyzes medical research to predict the most effective cancer drug treatment options for patients. Other projects include medical image analysis of tumor progression and the development of programmable cells.

Google

Google's DeepMind platform is being used by the UK National Health Service to detect certain health risks through data collected via a mobile app. A second project with the NHS involves analysis of medical images collected from NHS patients to develop computer vision algorithms to detect cancerous tissues.

Intel

Intel's venture capital arm Intel Capital recently invested in startup Lumiata which uses AI to identify at-risk patients and develop care options.

Startups

Kheiron Medical developed deep learning software to detect breast cancers in mammograms.

Medvice provides real time medical advice to clients, who can access and store their Electronic Health Records (EHRs) over a decentralized blockchain. Medvice uses machine learning aided decision making to help physicians predict medical red flags (i.e. medical emergencies which require clinical assistance) before serving them. Predictive Medical Technologies uses intensive care unit data to identify patients likely to suffer cardiac incidents. Modernizing Medicine uses knowledge gathered from healthcare professionals as well as patient outcome data to recommend treatments. "Compassionate AI Lab" uses grid cell, place cell and path integration with machine learning for the navigation of blind people. Nimblr.ai uses an A.I. Chatbot to connect scheduling EHR systems and automate the confirmation and scheduling of patients.

Infermedica's free mobile application Symptomate is the top-rated symptom checker in Google Play. The company also released the first AI-based voice assistant symptom checker for three major voice platforms: Amazon Alexa, Microsoft Cortana, and Google Assistant.

A team associated with the University of Arizona and backed by BPU Holdings began collaborating on a practical tool to monitor anxiety and delirium in hospital patients, particularly those with Dementia. The AI utilized in the new technology – Senior's Virtual Assistant – goes a step beyond and is programmed to simulate and understand human emotions (artificial emotional intelligence). Doctors working on the project have suggested that in addition to judging emotional states, the application can be used to provide companionship to patients in the form of small talk, soothing music, and even lighting adjustments to control anxiety.

Other

Digital consultant apps like Babylon Health's GP at Hand, Ada Health, and Your.MD use AI to give medical consultation based on personal medical history and common medical knowledge. Users report their symptoms into the app, which uses speech recognition to compare against a database of illnesses. Babylon then offers a recommended action, taking into account the user's medical history. Entrepreneurs in healthcare have been effectively using seven business model archetypes to take AI solution to the marketplace. These archetypes depend on the value generated for the target user (e.g. patient focus vs. healthcare provider and payer focus) and value capturing mechanisms (e.g. providing information or connecting stakeholders).

Implications

The use of AI is predicted to decrease medical costs as there will be more accuracy in diagnosis and better predictions in the treatment plan as well as more prevention of disease. Already, there is evidence that the use of chatbots leads to positive outcomes in the field of mental health.

Other future uses for AI include Brain-computer Interfaces (BCI) which are predicted to help those with trouble moving, speaking or with a spinal cord injury. The BCIs will use AI to help these patients move and communicate by decoding neural activates.

Virtual nursing assistants are predicted to become more common and these will use AI to answer patient's questions and help reduce unnecessary hospital visits. They will be useful as they are available 24/7 and may eventually be able to give wellness checks with the use of AI and voice.

As technology evolves and is implemented in more workplaces, many fear that their jobs will be replaced by robots or machines. The U.S. News Staff writes that in the near future, doctors who utilize AI will "win out" over the doctors who don't. AI will not replace healthcare workers but instead allow them more time for bed side cares. AI may avert healthcare worker burn out and cognitive overload. Overall, as Quan-Haase says, technology "extends to the accomplishment of societal goals, including higher levels of security, better means of communication over time and space, improved health care, and increased autonomy". As we adapt and utilize AI into our practice we can enhance our care to our patients resulting in greater outcomes for all.

Examples of AI in Healthcare and Medicine

AI can improve healthcare by fostering preventative medicine and new drug discovery. Two examples of how AI is impacting healthcare include.

IBM Watson's ability to pinpoint treatments for cancer patients, and Google Cloud's Healthcare app that makes it easier for health organizations to collect, store and access data.

Business Insider Intelligence reported that researchers at the University of North Carolina Lineberger Comprehensive Cancer Center used IBM Watson's Genomic product to identify specific treatments for over 1,000 patients. The product performed big data analysis to determine treatment options for people with tumors who were showing genetic abnormalities.

Comparatively, Google's Cloud Healthcare application programming interface (API) includes CDS offerings and other AI solutions that help doctors make more informed clinical decisions regarding patients. AI used in Google Cloud takes data from users' electronic health records through machine learning – creating insights for healthcare providers to make better clinical decisions.

Google worked with the University of California, Stanford University, and the University of Chicago to generate an AI system that predicts the outcomes of hospital visits. This act as a way to prevent readmissions and shorten the amount of time patients are kept in hospitals.

Benefits, Problems, Risks and Ethics of AI in Healthcare

Integrating AI into the healthcare ecosystem allows for a multitude of benefits, including automating tasks and analyzing big patient data sets to deliver better healthcare faster, and at a lower cost.

30% of healthcare costs are associated with administrative tasks. AI can automate some of these tasks, like pre-authorizing insurance, following-up on unpaid bills, and maintaining records, to ease the workload of healthcare professionals and ultimately save them money.

AI has the ability to analyze big data sets – pulling together patient insights and leading to predictive analysis. Quickly obtaining patient insights helps the healthcare ecosystem discover key areas of patient care that require improvement.

Wearable healthcare technology also uses AI to better serve patients. Software that uses AI, like FitBits and smartwatches, can analyze data to alert users and their healthcare professionals on potential health issues and risks. Being able to assess one's own health through technology eases the workload of professionals and prevents unnecessary hospital visits or remissions.

As with all things AI, these healthcare technology advancements are based on data humans provide – meaning, there is a risk of data sets containing unconscious bias. There is potential for coder bias and bias in machine learning to affect AI findings. In the sensitive healthcare market, especially, it will be critical to establish new ethics rules to address - and prevent - bias around AI.

Future of Artificial Intelligence in Healthcare

The use of AI in the healthcare market is growing due to the continued demand for wearable technology, digital medicine, and the industry's overall transformation into the modern, digital age.

Hospitals and healthcare professionals are seeing the benefits in using AI in technology and storing patients' data on private clouds, like the Google Cloud Platform. AI allows doctors and patients to more easily access health records and assess patient's health data that is recorded over a period of time via AI-infused technology.

Health tech companies, startups, and healthcare professionals are discovering new ways to incorporate AI into the healthcare market; and, the speed at which we improve the healthcare system through AI will only continue to accelerate as the industry dives deeper into digital health.

References

- Automation-new-horizon-in-agricultural-machinery: longdom.org, Retrieved 14 February, 2019

- Artificial-Intelligence-in-Government-1361: witi.com, Retrieved 16 April, 2019

- Artificial-intelligence-government-public-sector: weforum.org, Retrieved 04 February, 2019

- Artificial-intelligence-in-robotics: geeksforgeeks.org, Retrieved 15 August, 2019

- The-future-of-artificial-intelligence-in-manufacturing-industries: plantautomation-technology.com, Retrieved 23 January, 2019

- How-is-artificial-intelligence-used-in-video-games- 33419: techopedia.com, Retrieved 16 June, 2019

- Artificial-intelligence-in-marketing: searchcustomerexperience.techtarget.com, Retrieved 25 July, 2019

- Examples-of-artificial-intelligence-in-marketing: aibusiness.com, Retrieved 23 March, 2019

Permissions

All chapters in this book are published with permission under the Creative Commons Attribution Share Alike License or equivalent. Every chapter published in this book has been scrutinized by our experts. Their significance has been extensively debated. The topics covered herein carry significant information for a comprehensive understanding. They may even be implemented as practical applications or may be referred to as a beginning point for further studies.

We would like to thank the editorial team for lending their expertise to make the book truly unique. They have played a crucial role in the development of this book. Without their invaluable contributions this book wouldn't have been possible. They have made vital efforts to compile up to date information on the varied aspects of this subject to make this book a valuable addition to the collection of many professionals and students.

This book was conceptualized with the vision of imparting up-to-date and integrated information in this field. To ensure the same, a matchless editorial board was set up. Every individual on the board went through rigorous rounds of assessment to prove their worth. After which they invested a large part of their time researching and compiling the most relevant data for our readers.

The editorial board has been involved in producing this book since its inception. They have spent rigorous hours researching and exploring the diverse topics which have resulted in the successful publishing of this book. They have passed on their knowledge of decades through this book. To expedite this challenging task, the publisher supported the team at every step. A small team of assistant editors was also appointed to further simplify the editing procedure and attain best results for the readers.

Apart from the editorial board, the designing team has also invested a significant amount of their time in understanding the subject and creating the most relevant covers. They scrutinized every image to scout for the most suitable representation of the subject and create an appropriate cover for the book.

The publishing team has been an ardent support to the editorial, designing and production team. Their endless efforts to recruit the best for this project, has resulted in the accomplishment of this book. They are a veteran in the field of academics and their pool of knowledge is as vast as their experience in printing. Their expertise and guidance has proved useful at every step. Their uncompromising quality standards have made this book an exceptional effort. Their encouragement from time to time has been an inspiration for everyone.

The publisher and the editorial board hope that this book will prove to be a valuable piece of knowledge for students, practitioners and scholars across the globe.

Index